EXIM
MANAGEMENT

EXIM
MANAGEMENT

S. Soundaian

Associate Professor
Department of Business Administration
VHNSN College
Virudhunagar
Tamil Nadu

MJP Publishers

MJP PUBLISHERS

© Publishers, 2011   47, Nallathambi Street
All rights reserved   Triplicane
                       Chennai 600 005

To

My dear Parents

Soundaiah & Ponnammal

PREFACE

International trade in today's world has become imperative as well as the need of the hour. Importing and exporting for a country are like two eyes of a living being. A country with even reasonable aspirations must embark upon international trade. No country can sufficiently manufacture all its requirements on its own soil. Only the Gandhian ideal of rural economy can make it possible. But the so-called Gandhian ideals cannot be put to practice in today's dynamic world.

Importing is very necessary due to reasons well known. To match the growing needs of the masses, imports are essential. To maintain price stability of essential commodities in countries like India, imports are vital. Also, the modern human community likes to enjoy the benefits of modern technology. This is the basic right of every human being. Democracy has to prevail in this sphere also. Today's average Indian finds in his/her home all the comforts created by modern technology.

Exporting has become inevitable to organisations due to various reasons. Expansion is one reason. Another is that customers are available across the borders for their products. Areva is one such company which is engaged in the manufacture of atomic reactors and uranium. Even a small country like Bangladesh is able to export large quantities of garments at very low rates. These facts have made international trade essential for not only large manufacturers but also small and medium-sized industries.

Indian companies are rapidly gaining confidence and are now major players in globalized business through international expansion. From the steel industry to the film industry, from the automobile industry to the IT industry, Indian companies are setting themselves up as powerhouses of tomorrow's global economy. Exporting can help businesses to utilise their capacity more efficiently, gain economies of scale, and even out seasonal fluctuations in demand for their products. Exporting can also enable businesses to exploit unique or niche advantages in technology and other areas such as pricing, packaging, delivery and after-sales service.

Another possible advantage of tapping the international market is the lower cost of production. With the increase of supplies needed for a wider target market, the cost of production per unit of product should decrease. China is a good example. The next significant foreign trade benefit for small businesses is the potential gain of knowledge. By entering the international market, a company can gain various experiences which can be used to improve both its domestic and foreign businesses.

A small business can also benefit from selling its excess products internationally. If the company exports its goods, it does not have to give huge discounts to its domestic market or throw away excess products. Excess products can be sold to other markets that are not so important to the long-term future. And lastly, exporting can lengthen the life of a product. A typical product has a life cycle of *launch–growth–maturity–decline*. An exporting business is able to extend these stages and significantly extend the lifetime of its products by launching them in the export markets while the domestic market is still in maturity. Product development to replace that product in the home market can then be financed by export sales and hey presto! Your entire product cycle becomes self-sufficient and one financial strain on your business has been eradicated.

With these benefits that come with importing and exporting, businesses should consider tapping the international market. The size of the business is irrelevant: what matters is the will to succeed in the world market. All it needs is high quality and useful products, and a good entrepreneur who is a risk taker in order to succeed.

This book contains all the necessary information and guidelines to all those concerned with importing and exporting in a simple and comprehensive style. The topics covered in this book will be interesting and useful to its readers, both students and businessmen.

S. Soundaian

CONTENTS

3. BASIC EXPORT PRACTICES 49

| 7. | **INTERNATIONAL BUSINESS CONTRACTS** | **151** |

10. FOREIGN EXCHANGE MANAGEMENT IN INDIA217

18. SHIPPING AND CUSTOMS PROCEDURES   425

19. INTERNATIONAL AIR CARGO TRANSPORT 441

20. ARBITRATION IN INDIA   473

APPENDICES   487

ABBREVIATIONS

ACI	Airports Council International
AD/CVD	Anti dumping/countervailing duties
ADR	The European Agreement Concerning the International Carriage of Dangerous Goods by Road
ADR/GDR	American Global Depository Receipts
AEA	The Association of European Airlines
AEPC	Apparel Export Promotion Council
AFTA	ASEAN Free Trade Area
AIAI	All India Association of Industries
AIR	All Industry Rate
ANF	Aayaat Niryaat Form
APEDA	Agricultural and Processed Food Products Export Development Authority
APTA	Asia-Pacific Trade Agreement
ARO	Advance Release Order
ASI	Archaeological Survey of India
ATIFTAP	Foreign Trade in Asia and the Pacific
BIMSTEC	Bay of Bengal Initiative for Multi-Sectoral Technical and Economic Cooperation
BIN	Business Identification Number
BoP	Balance of Payment
BP	Biotechnology Park
BPLR	Benchmark Prime Lending Rate
BSEC	Black Sea Economic Cooperation
C & F	Carriage and Freight
C.I.F/c.i.f	Cost, Insurance and Freight
CAD	Cash Against Delivery
CCP	Customs Clearance Permit
CEI	Central European Initiative
CEPA	Comprehensive Economic Partnership Agreement
CEPC	Carpet Export Promotion Council of India

CHA	Clearing House Agent, Customs House Agent
CII	Confederation of Indian Industries
CISG	Contracts for the International Sale of Goods
CKD	Completely Knocked Down
CoO	Certificate of Origin
CPT	Carriage Paid To
CSP	Common Service Provider
CTC	Chennai Trade Centre
D/A	Documents against acceptance
D/P	Documents against payment
DBK	Duty Drawback Scheme
DBOD	Department of Banking Operations and Development
DDU	Delivered Duty Unpaid
DEPB	Duty Entitlement Pass Book
DFIA	Duty Free Import Authorisation
DoC	Department of Commerce
DoR	Department of Revenue
DTRM	Directorate of Trade Remedy Measures
EATCHIP	European Air Traffic Control Harmonisation and Integration Programme
ECB	External Commercial Borrowings
ECGC	The Export Credit and Guarantee Corporation of India
ECR	Export Credit Refinance
ECSI	Export Cargo Shipping Instruction/Export Shipping Cargo Instruction
EDI	Electronic Data Interchange
EEPC	Engineering Export Promotion Council
EEZ	Exclusive Economic Zone
EGM	Export General Manifest
EHS	Early Harvest Scheme
EHTP	Electronic Hardware Technology Park
EIC	Export Inspection Council
EMC	Export Management Company
EO	Export Obligation
EOU	Export-Oriented Unit
EPB	Export Promotion Board
EPC	Export Promotion Council
EPCG	Export Promotion Capital Goods
ERIC	Export Risks Insurance Corporation

ERs	Essential Requirements
ESCAP	Economic and Social Commission for Asia and the Pacific
ESEs	Emerging and Small Exporters
ETC	Export Trading Company
EU	European Union
EuroGAP	European Good Agricultural Practices
EXW	Ex Works
F & FP	Fish and Fishery Products
F.O.B/f.o.b.	Free on Board
FCL	Full Container Loads
FDI	The Foreign Direct Investment
FEDAI	Foreign Exchange Dealers Association of India
FEMA	Foreign Exchange Management Act
FERA	Foreign Exchange Regulations Act
FIATA	International Federation of Freight Forwarders' Associations
FIEO	Federation of Indian Exporters' Organisations
FIRC	Foreign Inward Remittance Certificate
FOB	Free on Board
FPA	Free of Particular Average
FPS	Focus Product Scheme
FTA	Free Trade Agreement
FTP	Foreign Trade Policy
FVCIs	Foreign Venture Capital Investors
GCES	General Conditions of Export Sales
GCR	General Cargo Rates
GR	Guaranteed Receipt
GSP	Generalised System of Preferences
GSTP	Global System of Trade Preferences
HACCP	Hazard Analysis Critical Control Point
HAWB	House Air Waybill
HBP	Handbook of Procedures
HEPC	Handloom Export Promotion Council
HS	Harmonised System
HWB	House Waybill
IATA	International Air Transport Association
IATTO	International Association of Trade Training Organisations
IBA	Indian Banks' Association

ICAO	International Civil Aviation Organisation
ICC	International Chamber of Commerce, Institute Cargo Clause
ICEGATE	Indian Customs and Central Excise Electronic Commerce/Electronic Data Interchange (EC/EDI) Gateway
ICES	The International Council for the Exploration of the Sea
IEC	Importer Exporter Code
IECN	Import Export Code Number
IGM	Import General Manifest
IMO	International Maritime Organisation
IPRs	Intellectual Property Rights
IQF	Individual Quick Freezing
IRDA	The Insurance Regulatory and Development Authority
ISA	International Seabed Authority
ISLFTA	India–Sri Lanka Free Trade Agreement
ISPS Code	The International Ship and Port Facility Security Code
ITC(HS)	Indian Trade Classification (Harmonised System)
ITC	Indian Trade Classification, International Trade Centre
ITF	International Task Force
ITPO	Indian Trade Promotion Organisation
IVCUs	India Venture Capital Undertakings
JBC	Joint Business Council
L/C	Letter of Credit
LCIA	London Court of International Arbitration
LCL	Less-than-container loads
LUT	Legal Undertaking
MARPOL	The International Convention for the Prevention of Pollution from Ships
MAWB	Master Air Waybill
MOU	Memorandum of Understanding
MPD	Monetary Policy Department
MPEDA	Marine Products Export Development Authority
NCTS	New Computerised Transit System
NES	New Export System
NHB	National Housing Bank
NIC	National Informatics Centre
NOC	No Objection Certificate
NTBs	Non-tariff barriers
OECD	Organisation of Economic Cooperation and Development

PAN	Permanent Account Number
PCFC	Packing Credit in Foreign Currency, Pre-shipment Credit in Foreign Currency
PMOs	Produce Marketing Organisations
PRO	Producer Responsibility Obligations
PUC	Pollution under Control
QR	Quantitative Restrictions
RA	Regional Authority/Regional Licensing Authority
RBI	Reserve Bank of India
RCMC	Registration-cum-Membership Certificate
RES	Remote EDI System
RID	Reglement concernant le transport International ferroviare des merchandises Dangereuses par chemin de fer
RLA	Regional Licensing Authority
S/O	Shipping Order
SAFE	Framework of Standards to Secure and Facilitate Global Trade
SAFTA	South Asian Free Trade Area
SAPTA	SAARC Preferential Trading Agreement
SDF	Statutory Declaration Form
SDRs	Special Drawing Rights
SEZ	Special Economic Zone
SFIS	Served from India Scheme
SIDBI	Small Industries Development Bank of India
SION	Standard Input Output Norms
SKD	Semi Knocked Down
SLBC	State Level Bankers' Committee
SLEPC	State Level Export Promotion Committee
SOFTEX	Software Export
SOLAS	International Convention for the Safety of Life at Sea
SSA	Sub Saharan Africa
STE	State Trading Enterprise
STPI	Software Technology Parks of India
STP	Software Technology Park
TACT	The Air Cargo Tariff
TIDCO	Tamil Nadu Industrial Development Corporation
TNTPO	Tamil Nadu Trade Promotion Organisation
TRACECA	Transport Corridor Europe Caucasus Asia
TRA	Telegraphic Release Advice

TT	Telegraphic Transfer
UJN	Unique Job Number
ULDs	Unit Load Devices
UNCITRAL	United Nations Commission on International Trade Law
UNCLOS	The United Nations Convention on the Law of the Sea
UNCTAD	The UN Conference on Trade and Development
UNIDROIT	International Institute for the Unification of Private Law
UPU	Universal Postal Union
URL	Uniform Resource Locator
VEU	Validated End User
VICS BoL	Voluntary Interindustry Commerce Solutions Bill of Lading
WA	With Average
WCO	World Customs Organisation
WSC	World Shipping Council
WTO	World Trade Organisation

FOREIGN TRADE POLICY

1

LEARNING OBJECTIVES

After reading this chapter, you will be able to know the

* objectives and the highlights of the new Foreign Trade Policy (FTP) of India

* achievements of the previous FTP

* action plan of the government for accomplishing the objectives of the new FTP

* special focus initiatives of the government

KEY TERMS

* Fiscal incentives
* Market diversification
* Special focus initiatives
* Project exports
* EPCG schemes
* Advance authorisation schemes
* Status-holders
* Towns of export excellence
* Transaction costs
* Directorate of trade remedy measures

INTRODUCTION

The world trade, in recent times, has been witnessing one of the most severe global recessions of the post-World War II period. Countries across the world have been affected in varying degrees. All major economic indicators of industrial production, trade, capital flows, unemployment, per capita investment and consumption have taken a hit. The 12% drop in the volume of world trade in 2009 was larger than most economists had predicted. This contraction also exceeded the WTO's earlier forecast of a 10% decline. World trade volumes fell on three other occasions after 1965 (– 0.2% in 2001, – 2% in 1982, and –7% in 1975), but none of these episodes approached the magnitude of the latest economic slide which the developed world witnessed during 2008–09. However, the global economy has already begun to pull out of a recession unprecedented in the post–World War II era, but stabilisation has been highly uneven and the recovery is expected to be sluggish. Economic growth during 2009–10 was projected to be about only ½ percentage points higher than projected in the April 2009 World Economic Outlook (WEO), reaching 2.5% in 2010.

Though India has not been affected to the same extent as other economies of the world, the country's exports have suffered a decline in the last ten months of the fiscal year 2008–09 due to a contraction in demand in the traditional markets of our exports. The protectionist measures being adopted by some of these countries have aggravated the problem. After four clear quarters of recession there is some sign of a turnaround and the emergence of 'green shoots'. India's exports increased to a 15-month high in December 2009 as recovery in the global economy boosted demand for South Asian nations' products. Overseas shipments surged to US$ 14.6 billion after rising 18.2% from a year earlier in the previous month the first increase in 14 months. Exports have been rebounding after an average 17.4% decline in the previous year.

ACHIEVEMENTS OF THE FOREIGN TRADE POLICY OF 2004–09

The new Foreign Trade Policy (FTP) states that before defining the objectives of the new policy, it would be useful to take stock of achievements in the foreign trade over the previous five years (2004–09). The policy announced by the United Progressive Alliance (UPA) Government in 2004 had set two objectives, namely,

   i. to double percentage share of global merchandise trade within five years and

   ii. use trade expansion as an effective instrument of economic growth and employment generation.

Agriculture and industry has shown remarkable resilience and dynamism in contributing to a healthy growth in exports.

In the previous FTP period, exports witnessed a robust growth of US$ 168 billion in 2008–09 from US$ 63 billion in 2003–04. The country's share of global merchandise trade was 0.83% in 2003; it rose to 1.45% in 2008 as per WTO estimates. India's share of global commercial services export was 1.4% in 2003; it rose to 2.8% in 2008. India's total share in goods and services trade was 0.92% in 2003; it increased to 1.64% in 2008. On the employment front, studies have suggested that nearly 14 million jobs were created directly or indirectly as a result of augmented exports in the last five years.

OBJECTIVES OF THE NEW FOREIGN TRADE POLICY

The new FTP was unveiled by the Union Minister for Commerce and Industry, Anand Sharma, on August 27, 2009. According to this policy, the short term objective is to arrest and reverse the declining trend of exports and to provide additional support especially to those sectors which have been hit badly by recession in the developed world. The government has laid down a policy objective of achieving an annual export growth of 15% with an annual export target of US$ 200 billion by March 2011. In the remaining three years of this FTP, that is up to 2014, the country is expected to come back on the high export growth path of around 25% per annum. By 2014, the government expects to double India's exports of goods and services. The long term policy objective for the government is to double India's share in global trade by 2020.

THE ACTION PLAN

In order to meet these objectives, the Government is determined to follow a mix of policy measures such as:

* fiscal incentives
* institutional changes
* procedural rationalisation
* enhanced market access across the world
* diversification of export markets

Improving infrastructure related to exports, bringing down transaction costs, and providing full refund of all indirect taxes and levies, would be the three pillars, which will support the government in its efforts to achieve this target. Endeavour will be made by it to see that the Goods and Services Tax rebates replace all indirect taxes and levies on exports.

At this juncture, the government is also determined to provide adequate confidence to the exporters to maintain their market presence even in a period of stress. A special thrust needs to be provided to employment intensive sectors which have witnessed job losses in the wake of the recession, especially in the fields of textile, leather, handicrafts, and the like. The government has introduced several new proposals and concessions to promote foreign trade.

SPECIAL FOCUS INITIATIVES

With a view to continuously increasing the country's percentage share of global trade and expanding employment opportunities, certain special focus initiatives have been identified/ continued by the government for market diversification, technological upgradation, support to status holders, agriculture, handlooms, handicraft, gems and jewellery, leather, marine, electronics and IT hardware manufacturing industries, green products, exports of products from North-East, sports goods and toys sectors. Government of India promises in its new FTP, concerted efforts to promote exports in these sectors by specific sectoral strategies that shall be notified from time to time. Further sectoral initiatives in other sectors will also be announced from time to time by the government.

MARKET DIVERSIFICATION

Weaker demand in developed economies, triggered by falling asset prices and increased economic uncertainty has pulled down the growth rate of India's exports to developed countries. There are no clear signals as to when the markets in developed countries would revivefully. To insulate Indian exports from the decline in demand from developed countries, the focus in this policy has been on diversification of Indian exports to other markets, specially those located in Latin America, Africa, parts of Asia and Oceania. To achieve diversification of Indian exports, the following initiatives have been taken under this policy.

1. Twenty six new countries have been included within the ambit of Focus Market Scheme (FMS).

2. The incentives provided under Focus Market Scheme have been increased from 2.5% to 3%.

3. There has been a significant increase in the outlay under Market Linked Focus Product Scheme (MLFPS) by inclusion of more markets and products. This ensures support for exports to all countries in Africa and Latin America.

TECHNOLOGICAL UPGRADATION

To usher in the next phase of export growth, India needs to move up in the value chain of export goods. This objective is sought to be achieved by encouraging technological upgradation of our export sector. A number of initiatives have been taken in this Policy to focus on technological upgradation, such initiatives include:

1. The EPCG Scheme at zero duty has been introduced for certain engineering products, electronic products, basic chemicals and pharmaceuticals, apparel and textiles, plastics, handicrafts, chemicals and allied products and leather and leather products.

2. The existing 3% EPCG scheme has been considerably simplified to ease its usage by the exporters.

3. To encourage value added manufacture export, a minimum of 15% value addition on imported inputs under Advance Authorisation Scheme has been stipulated.

4. A number of products including automobiles and other engineering products have been included for incentives under Focus Product, and MLFP schemes.

5. Steps to encourage project exports shall be taken.

SUPPORT TO STATUS-HOLDERS

The Government recognised that "status-holders" contribute approximately 60% of India's goods exports. To inspire and encourage the status holders, as well as to encourage technological upgradation of export production, additional duty credit scrip at 1% of the FOB of past export shall be granted for specified product groups including leather, specific sub-sectors in engineering, textiles, plastics, handicrafts and jute. This duty credit scrip can be used for import of capital goods by these status holders. The imported capital goods shall be subject to actual user condition.

Initiatives in other sectors are as follows:

Agriculture and village industry

1. Vidhesh Krishi and Gram Udyog Yojana (VKGUY)

2. Capital goods imported under EPCG will be permitted to be installed anywhere in AEZ.

3. Import of restricted items, such as panels, are allowed under various export promotion schemes.

4. Imports of inputs, such as pesticides, are permitted under advance authorisation for agro exports.

5. New towns of export excellence with a threshold limit of Rs. 150 crore shall be notified.

6. Certain specified flowers, fruits and vegetables are entitled to a special duty credit scrip, in addition to the normal benefit under VKGUY.

Handlooms

1. Specific funds have been earmarked under Market Access Initiative (MAI)/Market Development Assistance (MDA) schemes for promoting handloom exports.

2. Duty free import entitlement of specified trimmings and embellishments is 5% of FOB value of exports during previous financial year.

3. Duty free import entitlement of hand knotted carpet samples is 1% of FOB value of exports during previous financial year.

4. Duty free import of old pieces of hand knotted carpets on consignment basis for re-export after repair is permitted.

5. New towns of export excellence with a threshold limit of Rs. 150 crore shall be notified for handlooms also.

6. Machinery and equipment for effluent treatment plants is exempt from customs duty.

Handicrafts

1. Duty free import entitlement of tools, trimmings and embellishments is 5% of FOB value of exports during previous financial year. Entitlement is broad banded, and shall extend also to merchant exporters tied up with supporting manufacturers.

2. Handicraft EPC has been authorised to import trimmings, embellishments and consumables on behalf of those exporters for whom directly importing may not be viable.

3. Specific funds are earmarked under MAI and MDA Schemes for promoting Handicraft exports.

4. CVD is exempted on duty free import of trimmings, embellishments and consumables.

5. New towns of export excellence with a reduced threshold limit of Rs. 150 crore shall be notified.

6. Machinery and equipment for effluent treatment plants are exempt from customs duty.

7. All handicraft exports would be treated as special focus products and entitled to higher incentives.

Gems and jewellery

1. Import of gold of 8 kg and above is allowed under replenishment scheme, subject to import being accompanied by an Assay Certificate specifying purity, weight and alloy content.

2. Duty free import entitlement (based on FOB value of exports during previous financial year) of consumables and tools, for (a) jewellery made out of: (i) precious metals (other than gold and platinum)—2%; (ii) gold and platinum—1%; (iii) rhodium-finished silver—3% and (b) cut and polished diamonds—1%.

3. Duty free import entitlement of commercial samples shall be Rs. 300,000.

4. Duty free re-import entitlement for rejected jewellery shall be 2% of FOB value of exports.

5. Import of diamonds on consignment basis for Certification/Grading and re-export by the authorised offices/agencies of Gemological Institute of America (GIA) in India or other approved agencies will be permitted.

6. Personal carriage of gems and jewellery products in case of holding/participating in overseas exhibitions increased to US$ 5 million and to US$ 1 million in case of export promotion tours.

7. Extension in number of days for re-import of unsold items in case of participation in an exhibition in USA increased to ninety days.

8. In an endeavour to make India an international diamond trading hub, it is planned to establish "Diamond Bourse(s)".

Leather and footwear

1. Duty-free import entitlement of specified items is 3% of FOB value of exports of leather garments during preceding financial year.

2. Duty-free entitlement for import of trimmings, embellishments and footwear components for footwear (leather as well as synthetic), gloves, travel bags and handbags is 3% of FOB value of exports of previous financial year. Such entitlement shall also cover packing material, such as printed and non-printed shoeboxes, small cartons made of wood, tin or plastic materials for packing footwear.

3. Machinery and equipment for effluent treatment plants shall be exempted from basic customs duty.

4. Re-export of unsuitable imported materials such as raw hides and skins and wet blue leathers is permitted.

5. CVD is exempted on lining and interlining material notified at S.No. 168 of Customs Notification No. 21/2002 dated 01.03.2002. CVD is exempted on raw, tanned and dressed fur skins falling under Chapter 43 of ITC (HS).

6. Re-export of unsold hides, skins and semi-finished leather shall be allowed from public bonded warehouse at 50% of the applicable export duty.

Marine sector

1. Imports for technological upgradation under EPCG in fisheries sector (except fishing trawlers, ships, boats and other similar items) exempted from maintaining average export obligation.

2. Duty free import of specified specialised inputs/chemicals and flavouring oils is allowed to the extent of 1% of FOB value of preceding financial year's export.

3. To allow import of monofilament longline system for tuna fishing at a concessional rate of duty and bait fish for tuna fishing at nil duty.

4. A self-removal procedure for clearance of seafood waste is applicable, subject to prescribed wastage norms.

5. Marine products are considered for VKGUY scheme.

Electronics and IT hardware manufacturing industries

1. Expeditious clearance of approvals required from DGFT shall be ensured.

2. Exporters/associations would be entitled to utilise MAI and MDA schemes for promoting electronics and IT hardware manufacturing industry exports.

Sports goods and toys

1. Duty-free import of specified specialised inputs allowed to the extent of 3% of FOB value of preceding financial year's export.

2. Sports goods and toys shall be treated as a priority sector under MDA/MAI Scheme. Specific funds would be earmarked under MAI/MDA scheme for promoting exports from this sector.

3. Applications relating to sports goods and toys shall be considered for fast track clearance by DGFT.

4. Sports goods and toys are treated as special focus products and entitled to higher incentives.

Green products and technologies

India aims to become a hub for production and export of green products and technologies. To achieve this objective, special initiative will be taken to promote development and manufacture of such products and technologies for exports. To begin with, focus would be on items relating to transportation, solar and wind power generation and other products as may be notified which will be incentivized under Reward Schemes of Chapter 3 of FTP.

INCENTIVES FOR EXPORTS FROM THE NORTH-EASTERN REGION

In order to give a fillip to exports of products from the north-eastern states, notified products of this region would be incentivized under Reward Schemes of Chapter 3 of FTP.

HIGHLIGHTS OF THE NEW FOREIGN TRADE POLICY

Let us now discuss highlights of the new FTP briefly.

STABLE POLICY ENVIRONMENT

The government wants to provide a stable policy environment conducive for foreign trade and has decided to continue with the DEPB Scheme upto December 2010 and income tax benefits under Section 10(A) for IT industry and under Section 10(B) for 100% export oriented units for one additional year till 31st March 2011. Enhanced insurance coverage and exposure for exports through ECGC schemes was ensured till 31st March 2010. It has also taken a view to continue with the interest subvention scheme for this purpose. The Government has also stipulated a minimum 15% value addition on imported inputs under advance authorisation scheme.

DIVERSIFICATION OF EXPORT MARKETS

The Government has recognised the need to take an initiative to diversify the country's export markets and offset the inherent disadvantage for the exporters in emerging markets of Africa, Latin America, Oceania and CIS countries such as credit risks, higher trade costs, and the like, through appropriate policy instruments. It has endeavoured to diversify products and markets through rationalisation of incentive schemes including the enhancement of incentive rates which have been based on the perceived long term competitive advantage of India in a particular product group and market. New emerging markets have been given a special focus to enable competitive exports. This would of course be contingent upon availability of adequate exportable surplus for a particular product. Additional resources have been made available under the MDA Scheme and the MAI Scheme. Incentive schemes are being rationalised to identify leading products which would catalyse the next phase of export growth.

As part of its policy of market expansion, the government has signed a Comprehensive Economic Partnership Agreement with South Korea which will give enhanced market access to Indian exports. It has also signed a Trade in Goods Agreement with ASEAN which came into force on May 17, 2010, giving enhanced market access to several items of Indian exports. These trade agreements are in-line with India's *Look East* Policy. The government has also concluded the Mercosur Preferential Trade Agreement. The government seeks to promote Brand India through six or more "Made in India" shows to be organised across the world every year.

TECHNOLOGY UPGRADATION

In the era of global competitiveness, there is an imperative need for Indian exporters to upgrade their technology and reduce their costs. Accordingly, an important element of the Foreign Trade Policy is to help exporters in technological upgradation. Technological upgradation of exports is sought to be achieved by promoting imports of capital goods for certain sectors under EPCG at 0% duty.

TOWNS OF EXPORT EXCELLENCE

For upgradation of export sector infrastructure, "Towns of Export Excellence" and units located therein would be granted additional focussed support and incentives. Jaipur, Srinagar and Anantnag have been recognised as "Towns of Export Excellence" for handicrafts; Kanpur, Dewas and Ambur have been recognised as "Towns of Export Excellence" for leather products; and Malihabad for horticultural products.

The Foreign Trade Policy is committed to support the growth of project exports. A high level coordination committee is being established in the Department of Commerce to facilitate the export of manufactured goods/project exports creating synergies in the line of credit extended through EXIM Bank for new and emerging markets. This committee would have representation from the Ministry of External Affairs, Department of Economic Affairs, EXIM Bank and the Reserve Bank of India. The government would like to encourage production and export of "green products" through measures such as phased manufacturing programme for green vehicles, zero duty EPCG scheme and incentives for exports.

EPCG Scheme Relaxations

To increase the life of existing plant and machinery, export obligation on import of spares, moulds and the like under EPCG Scheme has been reduced to 50% of the normal specific export obligation. Taking into account the decline in exports, the facility of Re-fixation of Annual Average Export Obligation for a particular financial year in which there is decline in exports from the country, has been extended for the 5-year Policy period 2009–14.

Gems and Jewellery Sector

To neutralise duty incidence on gold jewellery exports, it has now been decided to allow Duty Drawback on such exports. In an endeavour to make India an international diamond trading hub, it is planned to establish "Diamond Bourse(s)". A new facility to allow import on consignment basis of cut and polished diamonds for the purpose of grading/certification, has been introduced. To promote export of gems and jewellery products, the value limits of personal carriage have been increased from US$ 2 million to US$ 5 million in case of participation in overseas exhibitions. The limit in case of personal carriage, as samples, for export promotion tours, has also been increased from US$ 0.1 million to US$ 1 million.

Agriculture Sector

To reduce transaction and handling costs, a single window system to facilitate export of perishable agricultural produce has been introduced. The system will involve creation of multifunctional nodal agencies to be accredited by Agricultural and Processed Food Products Export Development Authority (APEDA).

Leather Sector

Leather sector shall be allowed re-export of unsold imported raw hides and skins and semi-finished leather from public bonded ware houses, subject to payment of 50% of the applicable export duty. Enhancement of FPS rate to 2%, would also significantly benefit the leather sector.

Tea

Minimum value addition under Advance Authorisation Scheme for export of tea has been reduced from the existing 100% to 50%. DTA sale limit of instant tea by EOU units has been increased from the existing 30% to 50%. Export of tea has been covered under VKGUY scheme benefits.

Pharmaceutical sector

Export Obligation Period for advance authorisations issued with 6-APA as input has been increased from the existing 6 months to 36 months, as is available for other products. Pharma sector has been extensively covered under MLFPS for countries in Africa and Latin America; some countries in Oceania and Far East.

Handloom sector

To simplify claims under FPS, requirement of "Handloom Mark" for availing benefits under the scheme has been removed.

EOUs

EOUs have been allowed to sell products manufactured by them in DTA up to a limit of 90% instead of existing 75%, without changing the criteria of 'similar goods', within the overall entitlement of 50% for DTA sale. To provide clarity to the customs field formations, DOR shall issue a clarification to enable procurement of spares beyond 5% by granite sector EOUs. EOUs will now be allowed to procure finished goods for consolidation along with their manufactured goods, subject to certain safeguards. During this period of downturn, Board of Approvals (BOA) will consider extension of block period by one year for calculation of Net Foreign Exchange earning of EOUs. They will now be allowed CENVAT credit facility for the component of SAD and education cess on DTA sale.

Thrust to Value-added Manufacturing

To encourage value-added manufactured export, a minimum of 15% value addition on imported inputs under Advance Authorisation Scheme has now been prescribed. It includes coverage of Project Exports and a large number of manufactured goods under FPS and MLFPS.

DEPB

DEPB rate shall also include factoring of custom duty component on fuel where fuel is allowed as a consumable in standard input-output norms (SION).

Flexibility Provided to Exporters

Payment of customs duty for Export Obligation (EO) shortfall under Advance Authorisation/ DFIA/EPCG Authorisation has been allowed by way of debit of Duty Credit scrips. Earlier the payment was allowed in cash only. Import of restricted items as replenishment shall now be allowed against transferred DFIAs, in line with the erstwhile DFRC scheme. Time limit of 60 days for re-import of exported gems and jewellery items for participation in exhibitions has been extended to 90 days in case of USA. Transit loss claims received from private approved insurance companies in India will now be allowed for the purpose of EO fulfillment under

Export Promotion schemes. At present, the facility has been limited to public sector general insurance companies only.

WAIVER OF INCENTIVES RECOVERY ON RBI-SPECIFIC WRITE-OFF

In cases, where RBI specifically writes off the export proceeds realisation, the incentives under the FTP shall now not be recovered from the exporters, subject to certain conditions.

SIMPLIFICATION OF PROCEDURES

Procedures have been simplified for processing the applications quickly. The following are the proposals of the new FTP:

1. To facilitate duty free import of samples by exporters, number of samples/pieces has been increased from the existing 15 to 50. Customs clearance of such samples shall be based on declarations given by the importers with regard to the limit of value and quantity of samples.

2. To allow exemption for up to two stages from payment of excise duty in lieu of refund, in case of supply to an advance authorisation holder (against invalidation letter) by the domestic intermediate manufacturer. It would allow exemption for supplies made to a manufacturer, if such manufacturer in turn supplies the products to an ultimate exporter. At present, exemption is allowed up to one stage only.

3. Greater flexibility has been permitted to allow conversion of shipping bills from one export promotion scheme to another. Customs shall now permit this conversion within three months, instead of the present limited period of only one month.

4. To reduce transaction costs, dispatch of imported goods directly from the Port to the site has been allowed under advance authorisation scheme for deemed supplies. At present, the duty free imported goods could be taken only to the manufacturing unit of the authorisation holder or its supporting manufacturer.

5. Disposal of manufacturing wastes/scrap will now be allowed after payment of applicable excise duty, even before fulfillment of export obligation under Advance Authorisation and EPCG Scheme. Regional authorities have now been authorised to issue licences for import of sports weapons by "renowned shooters", on the basis of NOC from the Ministry of Sports and Youth Affairs. Now there will be no need to approach DGFT head quarters in such cases.

6. The procedure for issue of Free Sale Certificate has been simplified and the validity of the Certificate has been increased from 1 year to 2 years. This will solve the problems faced by the medical devices industry.

7. Automobile industry having their own Research and Development establishment would be allowed free import of reference fuels (petrol and diesel), up to a maximum of 5 kl per annum, which are not manufactured in India. Acceding to the demand of trade and industry, the application and redemption forms under EPCG scheme have been simplified.

REDUCTION OF TRANSACTION COSTS

No fee shall now be charged for grant of incentives under the schemes in Chapter 3 of FTP. Further, for all other Authorisations/licence applications, maximum applicable fee is being reduced to ₹100,000 from the existing ₹1,50,000 (for manual applications) and ₹50,000 from the existing ₹75,000 (for EDI applications). To further Electronic Data Interchange (EDI) initiatives, Export Promotion Councils/Commodity Boards have been advised to issue RCMC through a web based online system. It is expected that issuance of RCMC would become EDI enabled before the end of 2009. Electronic Message Exchange between Customs and the DGFT in respect of incentive schemes under Chapter 3 will become operational by 31.12.2009. This will obviate the need for verification of scrips by Customs facilitating faster clearances. However, this has not become operational till July, 2010.

For EDI ports, with effect from December '09, double verification of shipping bills by customs for any of the DGFT schemes shall be dispensed with. In cases, where the earlier authorisation has been cancelled and a new authorisation has been issued in lieu of the earlier authorisation, application fee paid already for the cancelled authorisation will now be adjusted against the application fee for the new one, subject to payment of a minimum fee of ₹200. An Inter-Ministerial Committee will be formed to redress/resolve problems/issues of exporters. An updated compilation of Standard Input Output Norms (SION) and ITC (HS) Classification of Export and Import Items has also been published.

DIRECTORATE OF TRADE REMEDY MEASURES

To enable support to Indian industry and exporters, especially the micro, small, and medium enterprises (MSMEs), in availing their rights through trade remedy instruments under the WTO framework, the government has proposed to set up a Directorate of Trade Remedy Measures (DTRM).

The new FTP also states that the e-trade project would be implemented in a time bound manner to bring all stake holders on a common platform in order to reduce the transaction cost and institutional bottlenecks. Additional ports/locations would be enabled on the EDI in future. An Inter-Ministerial Committee has been established to serve as a single window mechanism for resolution of trade related grievances.

SUMMARY

* Exports are the major focus of India's trade policy with the thrust area being the exports involving higher value additions.

* Most items can be freely exported from India. A few items are subject to export control in order to avoid shortages in the domestic market, to conserve national resources and to protect the environment.

* Five years ago the Government of India announced India's first ever integrated Foreign Trade Policy for the period 2004–09. At that time the government indicated two major objectives, namely

  1. to double the percentage of global merchandise trade within 5 years, and

  2. to use trade expansion as an effective instrument of economic growth and employment generation. The government, through various steps, not only achieved but also exceeded the targets.

* At present, the government has announced its new FTP for the period 2009–2014 and this new FTP contains many sops to foreign trade to help them fight the global recessionary trend successfully.

* In this chapter we discussed the various aspects of the Indian government's new Foreign Trade Policy related to Gems and jewellery sector, Agriculture sector, Leather, Tea, Pharmaceutical sector, Handloom sector, EOUs, and so on.

* While the policy has already been in action, the government has assured to revisit it after a 2-year period to make necessary adjustments in it taking into account the global economic trend prevailing then.

REVIEW QUESTIONS (SHORT)

1. State briefly the achievements of the 2004–09 Foreign Trade Policy.
2. What are the objectives of the new Foreign Trade Policy?
3. State briefly the action plan proposed by the government to promote foreign trade.
4. State briefly the government's move on technological upgradation.
5. State briefly the government's move to promote gem and jewellery sector.
6. State briefly the government's move to promote handicrafts sector.
7. What do you mean by stable policy environment?
8. What do you mean by diversification of export markets?
9. What are 'towns of export excellence'?
10. Explain the need for a Directorate of Trade Remedy Measures.

REVIEW QUESTIONS (DETAILED)

1. Write an essay on special focus initiatives of the new Foreign Trade Policy.
2. Write an essay the on the highlights of the new foreign trade policy.
3. Discuss the proposals of the government in connection with simplication of procedures in foreign trade.

REFERENCE

1. Government of India's New Foreign Trade Policy Statement 2009–2014.

2

TRENDS IN INDIA'S FOREIGN TRADE

LEARNING OBJECTIVES

After reading this chapter, you will be able to know

* the main parameters of India's foreign trade
* India's external trade scenario
* India's principal commodities of export and import
* the status of external trade with the US, Japan, China, European Union, Africa, and ASEAN
* the extent of impact of recession in developed countries on India's exports
* India's Balance of Payments position

INTRODUCTION

India's foreign trade has undergone a sea change since the time of liberalisation of the economy and government's new economic policy which was announced in 1991. In recent years India's intra-country and global trade growth and contribution cannot be ignored. India's trade and investment success have helped in changing its image from an "agriculture-based country" to an "industry-based country". Further, the stupendous success of India's efforts in boosting international trade has projected the country as a worthy global trade destination and a high potential market of one billion plus consumers. Technological advancements of the country offer a dynamic window to reach out to large Indian and international consumers, with the spectrum of high-technology-based services at one end and traditional wares on the other adding to a befitting display of India's versatility covering a broad industrial portfolio.

Indian foreign trade has particularly flourished from the contribution of the following sectors:

- Engineering
- Automobiles
- Electronics
- Chemicals
- Drugs and pharmaceutical
- Jute
- Rubber
- Handicrafts
- Jewellery
- Consumer goods

PARAMETERS OF INDIAN FOREIGN TRADE

The main parameters of Indian foreign trade are:

- *Exports* Exports during May, 2010 were valued at US$ 16,145 million which is 35.1% higher in dollar terms than the level of US$ 11,952 million during May, 2009.

- *Imports* Imports during May, 2010 were valued at US$ 27,437 million representing an increase of 38.5% over the level of imports valued at US$ 19,806 million in May, 2009.

- *Crude oil and non-oil imports* Oil imports during May, 2010 were valued at US$ 18,593 million which is 66.7% higher than oil imports valued at US$ 5,306 million in the corresponding period previous year. Non-oil imports during April–May 2010 are estimated at US$ 37,822 million which is 31.3% higher than the level of such imports valued at US$ 28,813 million in April–May, 2009.

⊙ *Trade balance* The trade deficit for April–May, 2010 was estimated at US$ 21,712 million which is higher than the deficit at US$ 14,509 million during April–May, 2009.

"Opening up of doors" policies undertaken by the countries over the world has given a boost to the Indian exports sector. In the same direction, the Government of India has come up with many friendly steps for developing the exports sector of the country. Even imports of goods and services have become easier recently.

For the first time, the government terminated the five-year Exim Policy 2002–07 and replaced it with Foreign Trade Policy (FTP) for a term of five years starting from the fiscal year on the 31st August 2004. It takes an integrated view of the overall development of the country's foreign trade.

FOREIGN TRADE STRATEGY

The short-term objectives of the new FTP are as follows:

1. to arrest and reverse the declining trend of exports and to provide additional support especially to those sectors which have been hit badly by recession in the developed world.

2. to achieve an annual export growth of 15% with an annual export target of US$ 200 billion by March 2011.

The long-term objectives of the government are as follows:

1. to make a come back on the high export growth path of around 25% per annum in order to double India's exports of goods and services by 2014.

2. to double India's share in global trade by 2020.

In order to meet these objectives, the Government is determined to follow a mix of policy measures including fiscal incentives, institutional changes, procedural rationalisation, enhanced market access across the world and diversification of export markets. Improvement in infrastructure related to exports, bringing down transaction costs, and providing full refund of all indirect taxes and levies, would be the three pillars, which will support the nation to achieve this target. Efforts would be made to see that the Goods and Services Tax rebates replace all indirect taxes and levies on exports.

TRADE SCENARIO

India's total external trade (exports plus imports including re-exports) in the year 1950–51 stood at ₹1,214 crore. Since then, this has witnessed continuous increase with occasional downturns. During 2007–08, the value of India's external trade reached ₹16,05,022 crore. A statement indicating India's total export, import, total value of foreign trade and balance of trade from the year 1989–90 to 2009–10(November–December), in rupee terms, is given in Table 2.1.

Table 2.1 India's International Trade Performance (₹ in crores)

Year	Exports	Growth Rate	Imports	Growth Rate	Trade Deficit
1989–90	27,658	36.7	35,328	25.1	–7670
1990–91	32,558	17.7	43,193	22.3	–10,635
1991–92	44,042	35.3	47,851	10.8	–3809
1992–93	53,688	21.9	63,375	32.4	–9687
1993–94	69,751	29.9	73,101	15.3	–3350
1994–95	82,674	18.5	89,971	23.1	–7297
1995–96	1,06,353	28.6	1,22,678	36.4	–16,325
1996–97	1,18,817	11.7	1,38,920	13.2	–20,103
1997–98	1,30,101	9.5	1,54,176	11.0	–24,075
1998–99	1,39,753	7.4	1,78,332	15.7	–38,579
1999–2000	1,59,561	14.2	2,15,236	20.7	–55,675
2000–01	2,03,571	27.6	2,30,873	7.3	–27,302
2001–02	2,09,018	2.7	2,45,200	6.2	–36,182
2002–03	2,55,137	22.1	2,97,206	21.2	–42,069
2003–04	2,93,367	15.0	3,59,108	20.8	–65,741
2004–05	3,75,340	27.9	5,01,065	39.5	–1,25,725
2005–06	4,56,418	21.6	6,60,409	31.8	–2,03,991
2006–07	5,71,779	25.3	8,40,506	27.3	–2,68,727
2007–08	6,55,863	14.7	1012311	20.4	–3,56,448
2008–09	8,40,755	28.2	13,74,436	35.8	–5,33,681
2009–10 (Apr.–Dec.)	5,99,244		9,55,166		

Source: Export-Import Data Bank, Department of Commerce, Government of India.

India's exports of merchandise goods touched the target of US$159 billion in 2007–08 recording a growth of around 26% in dollar terms. In rupee terms, the exports of merchandise goods during 2008–09 was valued at ₹8,40,755 crore compared to ₹6,55,869 crore in 2007–08 with a growth rate of 28.2%. India's growth of exports is much higher than that of the world economy as well as many major economies of the world.

At the same time, imports increased from ₹10,12,311 crore in 2007–2008 to ₹13,74,436 crore during 2008–2009 thereby registering a growth of 35.8% in rupee terms. The trade deficit in 2008–09 increased to ₹(–) 5,33,681 crore as against ₹(–) 3,56,448 crore during 2007–08.

India has trading relations with all the major trading blocks and all the geographical regions of the world (see Table 2.2). During 2008–09, Asia and ASEAN accounted for 52.12% of India's total exports, followed by Europe (21.24%) and America (15.48%). India's imports were highest from Asia and ASEAN (61.99%) followed by Europe (18.85%) and America (10.25%), during the same period.

Table 2.2 External Trade with Regions During 2007–08 and 2009–10

Region	Exports (₹ in crores)			Imports (₹ in crores)		
	2007–08	2008–09	2009–10 (Apr.–Dec.)	2007–08	2008–09	2009–10 (Apr.–Dec.)
Europe:						
EU countries	1,38,860	1,79,214	1,23,930	1,54,656	1,94,434	1,29,899
Other WE countries	10,638	11,694	7846	52,946	64,485	54,034
East Europe	427	538	425	144	143	184
Africa	46,462	51,668	36,420	60,056	85,389	67,475
America (North and Latin)	1,11,260	1,30,573	89,429	1,18,967	1,40,961	92,635
Asia and ASEAN	3,33,307	4,19,493	3,18,236	6,02,974	8,52,060	6,34,054
Unspecified Region	22,306	20,802	17,261	7255	66,903	3931

Source: Export-Import Data Bank, Department of Commerce, Government of India.

IMPORT OF PRINCIPAL COMMODITIES

India's total imports increased from ₹10,12,311 crore during 2007–08 to ₹13,74,435 crore during 2008–09 registering an increase of 35.77% during the year (Table 2.3). India's imports during 2009–10 (November–December) were ₹9,55,165 crore.

India's imports of principal commodities are broadly categorised in five major groups namely

1. Bulk imports include Cereals and preparations, fertilisers, edible oil, sugar, pulp and waste paper, paper board and newsprint manufactures, crude rubber, non-ferrous metals, metalliferrous ores and metal scrap, iron and steel, petroleum crude and products,

2. Machinery,

3. Pearls, precious and semi-precious stones,

4. Project goods, and

5. Others.

Disaggregated data on imports by principal commodities are available for the period 2008–09 (April–February). As compared to the corresponding period of the previous year, the imports during the period 2008–09 (April–February) was mainly driven by commodities such as petroleum crude and products, fertilisers manufactured, pearls, precious and semi-precious stones, coal, coke and briquettes, inorganic chemicals, vegetable oils, manufactures of metals, project goods, and so on.

The share of top five principal commodities in India's total imports during 2008–09 (April–February) include petroleum products (32.8%), electronic goods (7.4%), machinery except electronic (7.3%), gold (6.1%), pearls, and precious and semi-precious stones (4.9%).

Table 2.3   The details of Indian Imports of Principal Commodities

Commodities	2007–08 (Apr.–Feb.)	2008–09 (P) (Apr.–Feb.)	Percentage change
1. Bulk Imports	404,458	5,73,170	41,71
Cereals and preparations	2,829	195	–93.09
Fertilisers	20,512	60,522	195.06
Edible Oil	9,623	14,446	50.12
Sugar	5	423	7672.31
Pulp and waste paper	2,864	3,451	20.51
Paper board and mfrs.	5,760	5,835	1.30
Newsprint	1,997	3,608	80.67
Crude rubber	2,856	3,799	33.02
Non-ferrous Metals	12,651	13,446	6.28
Metalliferous ores and products	28,983	34,244	18.15
Iron and Steel	32,348	40,123	24.03
Petroleum crude and products	2,84,029	3,93,076	38.39

(Contd.)

Table 2.3   (Continued)

Commodities	2007–08 (Apr.–Feb.)	2008–09 (P) (Apr.–Feb.)	Percentage change
2. Pearls, Precious and Semi-Precious Stones	29,181	58,237	99.57
3. Machinery	1,20,920	1,43,949	19.04
Machine Tools	8,062	9,696	20.27
Machinery other than electrical	71,789	86,926	21.08
Electrical Machinery	10,521	13,411	27.46
Transport equipment	30,547	33,916	11.03
4. Project Goods	4,489	12,885	187.01
5. Others	3,11,350	4,10,119	31.72
Electronic goods	73,804	88,828	20.36
Gold and Silver	65,926	82,060	24.47
Organic and Inorganic chemicals.	36,467	51,705	41.78
Coal, coke and briquettes	23,549	42,691	81.29
Artificial resins, etc.	13,529	15,736	16.32
Professional instruments, etc.	14,031	16,852	20.11
Manufactures of metals	9,706	13,458	38.65
Medicinal and Pharma, products.	6,183	7,588	22.72
Chemical products	5,822	8,215	41.1
Wood and wood products	4,910	5,590	13.84
Total	8,70,399	1,198,360	37.68

(P) Provisional Figures

Source: National Portal Content Management Team.

TOP TEN COMMODITIES OF IMPORT

Top ten commodities imported by India during April–September 2007 in decreasing order are:

- petroleum crude and products,
- gold and silver,
- electronic goods,
- machinery other than electrical,
- organic and inorganic chemicals,
- pearls
- precious and semi-precious stones

- iron and steel
- metalliferrous ores and products
- coal, coke and briquettes
- transport equipment

These commodities alone accounted for about 78.8% of the total imports made by India during April–September 2007.

Regionwise Imports

Imports were made mainly from the five regions viz.

1. Asia and ASEAN,
2. Europe,
3. America,
4. Africa, and
5. CIS and Baltics.

Of India's total imports during April–September 2007 from these regions, Asia and ASEAN occupies the top rank with a share of (61.13%), followed by Europe (21.20%), America (9.05%), Africa (6.68%) and CIS and Baltics (1.58%). Europe, Asia and ASEAN, America, Africa, CIS and Baltics and have positive growth rates of 23.65%, 11.80%, 11.56%, 8.22%, and 1.11% respectively.

Import from Top Ten Countries

Among the ten most favourite trade partners in India's imports during April–September 2007 are China PRP (11.2%), followed by Saudi Arabia (7.2%), USA (5.8%), Switzerland (5.6%), the United Arab Emirates (5.5%), Iran (4.2%), Australia (4.0%), FRG (3.8%), Nigeria (3.3%), and Singapore (3.1%). Imports from these ten countries alone accounted for as high as 53.6% of total imports (₹4,56,103.47 crores).

Import of Sensitive Items

The total import of sensitive items (food grains, automobiles, alcoholic beverages, plantation products like, tea, coffee, rubber, spices and fruits and vegetables, besides small scale industry (SSI) items, etc.) for the period April–December 07 has been ₹20,589 crores as compared to ₹18,532 crores during the corresponding period of last year, thereby showing an increase of 11.1%. The gross import of all commodities during same period of current year is ₹6,82,088 crore as compared to ₹6,11,522 crore during the same period of last year. Thus import of sensitive items constituted 3.0% of the gross imports during last year as well as current year. Imports of spices, marble and granite, and milk and milk products have shown a decline at broad group level during the period.

EXPORTS OF INDIA

Foreign trade is important to the economy because of the country's need to import a variety of products. India exports a huge number of products and imports equally a good number of required products. Exports are the major focus of India's trade policy. Many items are freely exported from India.

India's trade data released by the Ministry of Commerce and Industry came in line with market expectations. While exports declined by 33% in March 2009 to $ 11.5 billion compared to $ 17.2 billion in the same month of the previous year, imports dipped 34% to $15.5 billion from $ 23.6 billion. As a result, the trade deficit in March at $ 4 billion was substantially smaller than the $6.3 billion in March the previous year.

While this is so, focus should also be made to not only increasing the foreign exchange reserves but also generation of employment and creation of newer markets. Even the government has understood these vital facts and is now focussing on strengthening the employment intensive export sectors. The export sector accounts for not less than 16 million jobs and has the potential to double in the next couple of years. The export sector is largely run by an unorganised, informal workforce. This has been a concern to many owing to the fact that the labour laws in the country are outdated and need reforms. The government needs to carefully study and take immediate action.

Top Export Markets for India

The US, the UAE, China, Singapore, the UK, Hong Kong, Netherlands, Germany, Belgium, and Italy are the top markets for Indian goods. The US accounted for US$ 20.7 billion, the UAE for US$ 15.6 billion, China for US$ 10.8 billion, Singapore for US$ 7.4 billion, the UK for US$ 6.7 billion, Hong Kong for US$ 6.3 billion, the Netherlands US$ 5.2 billion, Germany for US$ 5.1 billion, Belgium for US$ 4.2 billion, and Italy for US$ 3.9 billion. Figure 2.1 explains these statistics.

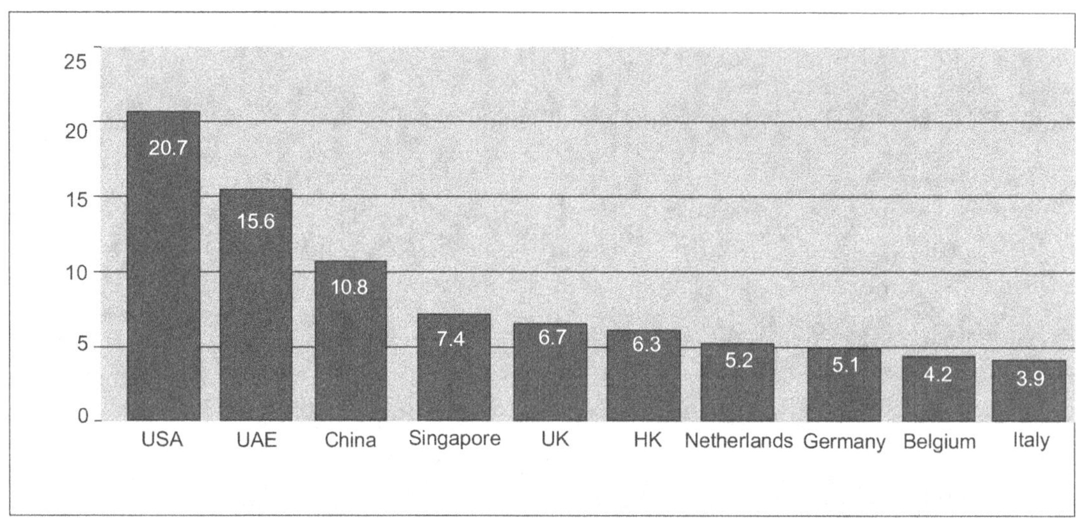

Figure 2.1 Top Export Markets for India (FY 2008, US$ in billion)

India's Software Exports

India's software exports for the financial years 2002–2008 have been as follows (in US$ billion): 2002:7.7; 2003:9.9; 2004:12.9; 2005:17.7; 2006:23.6; 2007:31.3; and 2008:40.3. It has recorded an average growth rate of 32.1%. This is depicted in Figure 2.2.

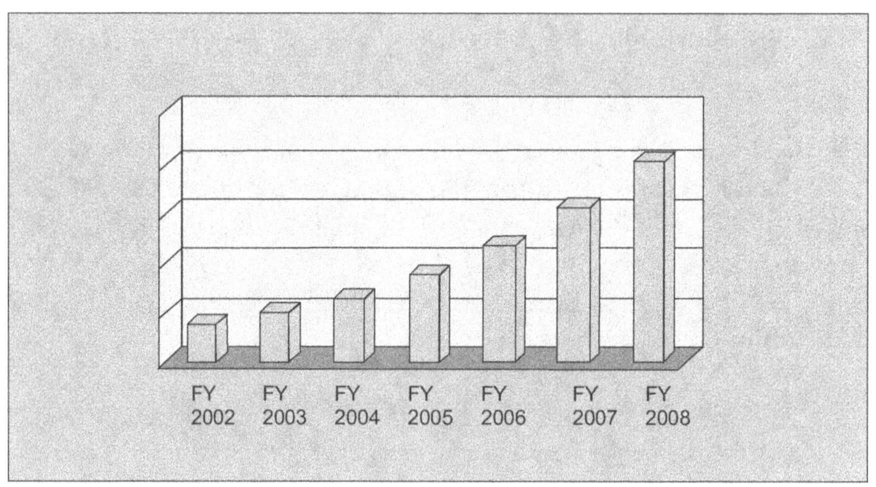

Figure 2.2 India: software exports FY 2002–2008 (US$ billion)

India's Exports: Shifting Southwards

When we look at the export trend, it is evident the Indian exports have been steadily increasing to the Asian countries. This is clearly inferred from the figures (See Table 2.4). In the year

2001, exports to Asia were only 38.7% of total exports. It has gone up to 51.7% during the year 2008, a remarkable growth of 33.6%. At the same time, we can notice a downward trend in the case of Europe, North America, CIS and Baltics, and others. Export to North America fell down to 39.7% in the year 2008 from the level of 22.4% to 13.4%. European region and CIS and Baltics have also seen similar trend in exports from India. Exports to Africa have also shown a remarkable upward trend from 4.1% to 7.1% of total Indian exports. Other regions of the world have shown a decline from 4.3% to just 0.3% during the same period. Table 2.4 and Figure 2.3 show this trend clearly.

Table 2.4 India's Export Market FY 2001 (US$ 44 bn.) and FY 2008 (US$ 163 bn.): A Comparison

Region	FY 2001	FY 2008	Growth %
Europe	25.9	22.9	–11.5
North America	22.4	13.5	–39.7
Asia and ASEAN	38.7	51.7	+33.6
Africa	4.1	7.1	+73.2
CIS and Baltics	2.3	1.1	–52.2
LAC	2.2	3.5	+59.1
Others	4.3	0.3	–93.0

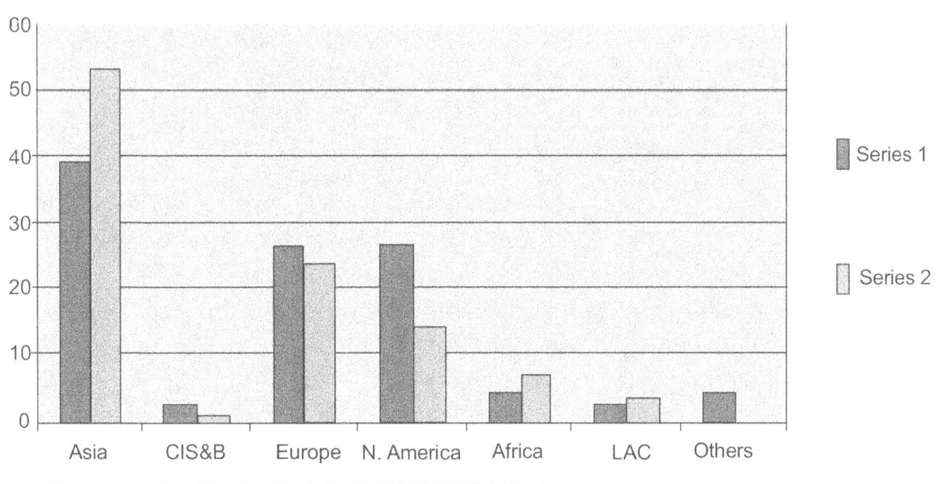

Series 1: India's Foreign Trade in FY 2001 (US$ 44 bn.)
Series 2: India's Foreign Trade in FY 2008 (US$ 163 bn.)

Figure 2.3 Direction of India's Foreign trade Shifting towards South: A Comparison between 2001 and 2008

Reasons for the shift   Even though quantity-wise export is the highest to the US, the rate of growth has declined considerably due to several reasons, whereas rate of growth of exports to ASEAN and China have sharply increased. This aspect of Indian export trend needs to be analysed in order to understand the trend. The following may be some of the reasons for this shift towards South.

1. The appreciation of the rupee has made Indian exports more expensive in markets where transactions are designated in US dollars while making imports relatively inexpensive.

2. The people of the fast growing economies of China and other Asian nations have found more interest in Indian goods than in other countries' goods.

3. The steps taken by Indian industries to improve quality of their goods and bring down the cost have yielded necessary benefits to them leading to a surge in exports to China and ASEAN nations.

4. Trade agreements with Asian countries like APTA, AFTA, SAFTA, and BIMSTEC have spurred exports to these countries.

INDO-US TRADE

Indo-US trade, which shot up almost three-fold from $13.7 billion in 2001 to $41.4 billion in 2007, suffered a sharp setback after the global slowdown, with growth slowing down from 30.5% in 2007 to 7.4% in 2008. While initial trends show that Indian imports from the US bore the brunt of the recession, recent numbers show that Indian exports have dropped more sharply than imports indicating some resonance in domestic demand.

Statistics show that the growth of Indian exports to the US slowed down from 10.1% in 2007 to 8.4% in 2008, while that of Indian imports dropped from 74.3% to 6.1%. But, most recent figures for the first two months of 2009 show that Indian exports have dropped by 23.2%, while imports declined by 18.9%.

India's exports to the US markets are concentrated across 12 major products, which account for three-fourth of the total exports. The major Indian exports include jewellery (21.7%), non-knitted clothing and apparel (6.9%), iron and steel products (6.5%), pharmaceuticals (5.7%), non-electrical machinery and appliances (5.7%), organic chemicals (5.6%), electrical machinery (5.4%), knitted apparel and clothing (5.1%), textile made ups (4.9%), iron and steel (3.6%), vehicles (2.5%), and carpets (2.2%).

In 2008, nine of these twelve products registered positive growth with the highest increase in iron and steel (105.1%), followed by pharmaceuticals (75.7%), iron and steel (36.8%), non-electrical machinery and appliances (30.2%), organic chemicals (16.3%) and electrical machinery (12.2%), all of which posted a higher growth than average. Indian exports that declined, included jewellery (9.7%), non-knitted clothing and apparel (6.2%) and carpets (8%).

In case of Indian imports from the US, bulk of the earnings came from a dozen products that accounted for 85% of the total imports into the country. Topping the list of Indian imports from the US were fertilisers, which accounted for 16% of the total Indian imports, followed by aircraft (14.7%), non-electrical machinery and appliances (13%), jewellery (11.2%), electrical machinery and equipments (6.3%), mineral fuels (5%), optical and precision equipment (4.8%), organic chemicals (3.4%), iron and steel products (3.3%), plastic articles (2.9%), chemical products (2.1%), and inorganic chemicals (2.1%).

The highest increase in Indian imports from the US markets in 2008 were from inorganic chemicals (275.5%), fertilisers (258.1%), mineral fuels (121.4%), jewellery (65.5%), aircraft (57.1%), chemical products (39.5%), plastic products (34.7%), iron and steel (13.8%), and non-electrical machinery and appliances (6.3%). Indian imports that declined in the year included aircraft (57.1%) and organic chemicals (2.8%). These facts can be noted from Table 2.5.

Table 2.5 US trade with India (2008) (In US$ million)

Month	Exports	Imports	Balance
January	1,078.4	2,306.7	−1,228.3
February	1,505.5	2,118.5	−613.0
March	1,644.7	2,254.7	−610.0
April	1,105.3	2,125.8	−1,020.4
May	1,493.5	2,190.3	−696.8
June	2,047.3	1,869.2	178.1
July	1,986.6	2,069.7	−83.1
August	1,864.4	2,210.6	−346.2
September	2,032.8	2,398.5	−365.7
October	1,640.5	2,452.4	−811.8
November	1,205.4	1,907.5	−702.0
December	1,062.0	1,858.2	796.1
Total	18,666.5	25,761.9	−709.5

Source: US Census Bureau.

Despite other contenders on the horizon, India would like to expand trade with the USA. While the US continues to be the largest economy in the world, India represents a growing knowledge power. The trade figure of US–Japan and US–China indicate the future potential for Indo–US trade. There is no reason why India cannot become as big a trade partner of the USA as Japan and China currently are.

Box 2.1   US and Indian Exports

Trade and commerce form a crucial component in the rapidly expanding and multi-faceted relations between India and the US. From a modest $ 5.6 billions in 1990, the bilateral trade in merchandise goods has increased to $ 41.62 billion in 2007 representing an impressive 743% growth in a span of 17 years. India's merchandise exports to the US grew at 10.05% from US$ 21.83 billion in 2006 to US$ 24.02 billion in 2007. US exports of merchandise to India increased from US$ 10.06 billion in 2006 to US$ 17.59 billion in 2007, an increase of 74.94%. During the period January–October 2008, merchandise exports from India to US increased by 10% to $ 22 billion and merchandise exports from US to India increased by 16% to US$ 16.4 billion.

A tabular profile of the bilateral trade during recent years is given below.

Bilateral Merchandise Trade (2004 to 2008) *(In US$ millions)*

Item	2004	2005	2006	2007	Jan–Oct 2008
India's export to US	15,572	18,808	21,826	24,024	21,966
US exports to India	6109	7958	10,091	17,592	16,399
Total Bilateral Trade	**21,681**	**26,766**	**31,917**	**41,616**	**38,365**

Source   US Department of Commerce.

A profile of growth trends of some major items of bilateral trade in merchandise during the past two years, is given below:

India's Exports to US

The major items of export from India are: Cut and polished diamonds and Jewellery is a major item of India's exports to the US, accounting for 25.81%. Exports of this item grew from US$ 5.87 billion in 2006 to US$ 6.20 billion in 2007.

Textiles exports to the US grew from US$ 5.38 billion in 2006 to US$ 5.45 billion in 2007.

Engineering goods and machinery including electrical machinery grew sharply from US$ 2.20 billion in 2006 to US$ 2.36 billion in 2007. Mineral and fuel oils export grew from US$ 400 million in 2006 to US$ 967 million in 2007. Export of organic chemicals to the US grew from US$ 880 million in 2006 to US$ 1209 million in 2007. Export of vehicles and parts (excluding railway) to the US grew from US$ 487 million in 2006 to US$ 623 million in 2007.

US Exports to India

The major items of export from the US to India are: Engineering goods and machinery including electrical machinery which contribute to over 20% of the total US exports to India. US exports of these items grew from US$ 2.76 billion in 2006 and to US$ 3.51 billion in 2007.

Export of precious stones and metals from the US to India grew from US$ 924 million in 2006 to US$ 1891 million in 2007.

Optical and medical instruments grew from US$ 688 million in 2006 to US$ 867 million in 2007.

Export of aircraft, aviation machinery and parts grew from US$ 1623 million in 2006 to US$ 6058 million in 2007.

INDO-CHINA TRADE

India–China trade relations are the most important part of bilateral relations between the two nations. From a temporary decline in the the influx of Chinese imports in the Indian markets, the scenario seems to have changed; India at one point enjoyed a positive balance of trade with China. The India–China trade relations are regulated by the India–China JBC (Joint Business Council), which ensures a free exchange of products and services between the two nations. India and China signed a Trade Agreement in 1984 which provided for Most Favoured Nation treatment and later in 1994, the two countries signed an agreement to avoid double taxation. In the first six months of the year 2010, the bilateral trade figure stands at US$ 32 billion and was all set to achieve the target of 60 billion. Thus China will become India's single largest trading partner in the world. The bilateral trade has seen a drastic jump from a modest US$ 3 billion in 2000 to an impressive US$ 52 billion in 2008 and was all set to touch US$ 60 billion by end of the year 2010, as agreed by the Prime Ministers of the two countries in 2008. The government has decided to set up an economic wing in its diplomatic mission in Beijing in the next six months, signifying the growing financial clout of China which is set to become India's largest trading partner by the end of 2010. Already considerable ground has been covered towards reaching an understanding that would in many ways be the first-ever comprehensive bilateral trade agreement expected to be signed during 2010–11 between the two Asian giants.

Indian Exports to China

The principal items of Indian exports to China are ores, slag and ash, iron and steel, plastics, organic chemicals, and cotton. In order to increase the extent of exporting Indian goods to China, however, there should be a special emphasis on investments and trade in services and knowledge-based sectors. The other potential items of trade between India and China are marine products, oil seeds, salt, inorganic chemicals, plastic, rubber, optical and medical equipment, and dairy products. Great potential also exists in areas like biotechnology, IT and ITES, health, education, tourism, and financial sector.

One of the important concerns for India is that its IT and pharmaceutical companies have failed to obtain major Chinese contracts over the past several years. This has largely been due to stringent conditions which often restrict bidding to only Chinese companies. Bid documents either don't reach Indian companies, or reach them late.

Chinese Exports to India

The main items that comprise Chinese exports to India are electrical machinery and equipment, cement, organic chemicals, nuclear reactors, boilers, machinery, silk, mineral fuels, and oils. Value added items like electrical machinery dominates Chinese exports to India. This exhibits that Chinese exports to India are fairly diversified and includes resource-based products, manufactured items, and low and medium technology products. It is said that if India is to capture the markets of China and enjoy profits, then it would have to discover new merchandise and branch out its exports to China. China is already the largest trading partner of India and it is expected that bilateral Indo-China trade would reach US$ 60 billion by the end of 2010, said, Shen Wenping, Vice Director of Jiaxing Municipal Bureau of Foreign Trade and Economic Cooperation at the Seminar with the Business Delegation from Jiaxing, China organised by the Confederation of Indian Industry (CII), in New Delhi.

Chinese firms were initially keen on exporting cheap electronic items, garments, and toys to the Indian markets. But recently, Chinese exporters have been focusing on the cement market. Two Chinese cement companies, Yingde Dragon Mountain Cement Company Ltd. and Longkou Fanlin Cement Company have been authorised to sell cement in Indian market. The prospects for Chinese exports to India have been enhanced from 2006, with the opening of the prospective Indo-China border trade. Trade has been initiated between Tibet, an autonomous region of China, and India through Nathu La Pass, reopened after 44 years. From then onwards, nearly 15 items are being exported from China to India.

INDIA–JAPAN TRADE

Trade between India and Japan has the potential to double in the next two years if issues like trade facilitation and non-tariff barriers are addressed, according to the CII. It also declared that India–Japan trade can reach 15 billion dollars by 2010 from 7.5 billion dollars in 2006–07 and added that new areas of trade in services, higher investment flows into India from Japan, promoting people-to-people contact are other ways through which the level of bilateral trade can increase.

Bilateral trade has more than doubled since 2002–03 with trade balance in favour of Japan. According to a study by the CII, "While import duties on most goods in Japan are low at present, the India–Japan Comprehensive Economic Partnership Agreement (CEPA) can raise the level of India's exports." There is need for greater focus on agricultural exports to Japan since the share of agricultural items in India's exports to Japan has declined by about 22% over the last 10 years, although export of processed food increased by 4% during this period. Further, export of Indian agricultural goods, chemicals and pharmaceuticals face various NTBs (Non-tariff barriers). Exporters also have difficulties in understanding guidelines and regulations, since they are mostly in the Japanese language.

The CII further said that there is a need to relax visa norms for Indian medical, paramedical workers and engineers similar to the liberalised entry its nurses have to Philippines and Indonesia as a part of free trade deals. "There should be liberalisation of trade in services with regard to movement of professionals in the CEPA," it said. The Japanese government should also provide Validated End User (VEU) certificate on the lines of the US policy for the Indian buyers.

Major items of export to Japan include fish and crustaceans, molluscs and other aquatic invertebrates, iron, coffee, tea, mate and spices, LAC, gums, resins and other vegetable saps and extracts, salt, sulphur, earths and stone, plastering materials, lime and cement, organic chemicals, cotton, iron and steel, miscellaneous goods, and the like. The major commodities being imported by India include mineral fuels, mineral oils and products of their distillation, bituminous substances, mineral waxes, organic chemicals, photographic or cinematographic goods, plastics, nuclear reactors, project goods, electrical machinery and equipments, vehicles other than railway or tramway rolling stock, and the like.

INDIA–EUROPE TRADE

European countries account for about 22.5% of India's total trade while India's exports to Europe during 2008–09 were US$ 40.73 billion. While India's export to Europe recorded a growth of 17%, India's import from Europe grew by 33%. The top five items of India's exports to Europe are readymade garments including accessories, gems and jewellery, machinery and instruments, petroleum (crude and products) and transport equipment. The top five items of India's imports from Europe are machinery (except electrical and electronics), pearls/precious, semi-precious stones, electronic goods, transport equipments and iron and steel.

Trade and Investment Relations with European Union

The European Union (EU) presently consists of 27 countries: Austria, Belgium, Cyprus, Czech Republic, Denmark, Estonia, Finland, France, Germany, Greece, Hungary, Ireland, Italy, Latvia, Lithuania, Luxembourg, Malta, The Netherlands, Poland, Portugal, Slovak Republic, Slovenia, Spain, Sweden, UK, Bulgaria and Romania.

India and EU enjoy healthy economic relations. These relations have been built on the foundation of (i) India–EU Corporation Agreement on Partnership and Development which came into effect in August, 1994 and (ii) India–EU Strategic Partnership which was announced in September, 2005. India also has bilateral economic agreements with a number of individual EU countries in the areas of trade, investments and avoidance of double taxation. India has agreements for investments and promotions/protections with 22 countries of Europe, including 17 countries of EU. Similarly, agreements for avoidance of double taxation exist with 26 countries in EU.

India–EU bilateral relations are reviewed at the official level by the India–EC Joint Commission. This had its last meeting in July 2008. Three Sub-Commissions on Trade, Economic Cooperation and Development Cooperation and nine Joint Working Groups on agriculture and marine products, textiles, information technology and communications, consular matters, environment, steel, food processing industries, pharmaceuticals and biotechnology and technical barriers to trade (TBT)/sanitary and photo sanitary (SPS) issues are functioning and their reports are considered by Joint Commission.

INDIA–AFRICA TRADE

There are more than 50 countries in the Sub-Saharan Africa (SSA) region. Traditionally relations between India and countries of the African continent have remained close and cordial. In spite of various constraints such as distance, language barriers, lack of information, and the like. India's trade with the region has grown rapidly. The trade between India and SSA region has grown from US$ 7572.65 million in 2004–05 to US$ 197,053.37 million in 2007–08 registering a growth of 32.34%.

Even as India's exports declined during 2009, India-African bilateral trade was projected to grow by over nine times from $ 26 billion now to $ 150 billion by 2012, according to an estimate by a leading business chamber. The Associated Chambers of Commerce and Industry of India (Assocham), in a report on Africa, projected that in the next four years the continent will have greater business significance and drive two-way trade to over $ 150 billion. According to Assocham, bilateral trade grew over five times from $ 5.2 billion to $ 26 billion from 2002–03 to 2007–08. "The governments in African continent have also been encouraging industries to intensify their ties with India because it has already announced Duty Free Tariff Preference Scheme for all LCDs (Least Developed Countries) including Africa so that imports from them become easier and increase by manifold," said Assocham secretary general D.S. Rawat.

India's exports to the region have increased by 30.85% from US$ 16.41bn in 2007–08 to US$ 19.14 bn in 2008–09 and the imports from the region have increased by 42.70% from US$ 9.11 bn in 2004–05 to US$ 26.20 bn in 2008–09.

TRADE WITH ASEAN

Since its beginning about a decade ago, the partnership between India and the Association of South East Asian Nations (ASEAN) comprising Brunei, Cambodia, Indonesia, Laos, Malaysia, Myanmar, the Philippines, Singapore, Thailand and Vietnam has been developing at quite a fast pace. The deepening of ties between India and ASEAN is reflected in the continued buoyancy in the trade figures. The trade grew by 13% during April–September 2007–08 to US$ 17.02 billion as against US$ 15.06 billion during the same period last fiscal. ASEAN is India's fourth largest trading partner after the EU, the US, and China. Indo–ASEAN trade, which has been growing at a compounded annual growth rate (CAGR) of 27% since 2000, stood at US$ 38.37 billion in 2007–08.

However, India's trade balance with the 10-member ASEAN countries has deteriorated sharply over the first eight years of the decade, despite a six-fold increase in total trade, an industry study has revealed. India-ASEAN bilateral trade increased to $ 46.1 billion in 2008 from $ 6.9 billion in 2000, points out a study done by industry body Assocham, but the overall trade deficit with ASEAN countries also increased to $ 7.3 billion in 2008 from $ 1.6 billion in 2000.

The ASEAN countries with large populations and consumption patterns are important drivers of growth. With a combined Gross Domestic Product (GDP) of US$ 2.3 trillion as of now, they together will create a new free trade area of 1.7 billion people and cover 11 countries.

Summing up the future prospects, the Indonesian Trade Minister, Marie Pangestu, said that the FTA in goods paved the way for more economic cooperation between ASEAN countries and that "it will lead to a greater integration between ASEAN and its dialogue partners."

Singapore

The growing bilateral economic relationship is reflected in the rapidly rising bilateral trade between Singapore and India. While Singapore continues to be among the top four investors for India, Indian investments in Singapore are also growing. The cumulative FDI inflow to India from Singapore during April 2000–November 2008 was around US$ 6.34 billion. The total bilateral trade during 2007–08 was US$ 15.49 billion as compared to US$ 11.54 billion in 2006–07. India exported goods worth US$ 7.37 billion in 2007–08, as compared to US$ 6.06 billion exported in 2006–07.

During April–June 2008, India exported goods worth US$ 3.26 billion to Singapore. This included US$ 1.79 billion worth of mineral fuels and mineral oils, US$ 679 million worth of ships and boats and US$ 194.95 million worth of nuclear reactors and boilers. In 2005, India and Singapore signed the Comprehensive Economic Cooperation Agreement (CECA), an integrated package comprising a free trade agreement, a bilateral agreement on investment promotion and protection, an improved double taxation avoidance agreement and a work programme for cooperation in healthcare, education, media, tourism, customs, e-commerce, intellectual property, and science and technology.

MALAYSIA

The bilateral economic relationship between India and Malaysia has been steadily moving ahead. Malaysia has been a huge source of FDI for India. In fact, Malaysia was the twenty-third largest overall investor and second largest investor among ASEAN countries with a total inflow of US$ 105.54 million during April 2000–December 2007. Bilateral trade among the two countries amounted to US$ 8.57 billion during 2007–08, an increase of 30.07% over 2006–07 when it was US$ 6.59 billion.

In 2008–09, India exported goods worth US$ 3.4 billion to Malaysia, registering growth of 32.8% over 2007–08 when the country exported goods worth US$ 2.6 billion. During the first three quarters of 2009–10, India exported goods worth US$ 2.1 billion to Malaysia.

Further, India and Malaysia are working on a Comprehensive Economic Cooperation Agreement and there is a big opportunity for trade in goods, services such as medical, healthcare, computers, and investment in construction, telecommunications, civil aviation and tourism, among others.

In January, 2009 India and Malaysia signed an agreement for the "orderly" recruitment and deployment of workers and the procedures for monitoring recruiting agents and employers. The deal would delineate the responsibility of recruiting agents, workers and employers. There are officially 133,000 Indian workers in Malaysia. The majority of them—nearly 55%—are in the services sector and another substantial number is in the plantation industry.

Indian investments in Malaysia

1. As a part of its expansion plans in Malaysia, Vinayaka Missions University, an Indian education group has earmarked to invest ₹264 crore (US$ 52.84 million) by 2015 to open its engineering, management and technical campuses in Iskandar.

2. Two companies from South India are in the final stages of establishing pre-clinical trial facilities in Malaysia, which has been aggressively promoting biotechnology. A high-level delegation from the two firms have visited and identified certain areas in Malaysia and each of the company is taking up 10 acres to build their units. They would be investing a sum of US$ 30 million.

3. Reliance Money, part of the Reliance Anil Dhirubhai Ambani Group, has announced its debut in Malaysia, by joining hands with Infinity Financial Solutions, one of Malaysia's major financial products and services distribution company as part of its plans to expand its global footprint.

THAILAND

Bilateral trade between the two countries touched US$ 4.11 billion in 2007–08, as compared to US$ 3.18 billion in 2006–07, registering a growth of 28.97%. Exports grew by 7.04% to US$ 1.93 bn. in 2008–09 from US$ 1.81 bn. in 2007–08. During the period April to December 2009–10, exports to Thailand recorded a figure of US$ 1.81 bn. These chiefly comprised of copper, prepared animal fodder, gems and jewellery, iron and steel, and organic chemicals.

Thailand and India have had an "early harvest" agreement for 82 items since 2003. After the FTA (Free Trade Agreement), Thailand is expected to make it simpler for Indian companies to invest in Thailand. Indian firms are on the lookout for partners, and companies like Tata Motors, Tata Consultancy and Tata Steel already have a presence in Thailand. Thailand's Central Group has tied up with DLF Group, and the Charoen Pokphand Group plans to have cold-storage operations across India, with the possibility to start retail operations.

VIETNAM

Bilateral trade grew to US$ 1.77 billion in 2007–08 from US$ 1.14 billion in 2006–07. During 2007–08 exports to Vietnam were worth US$ 1.60 billion, which grew at 63.28% over 2006–07 (US$ 982 million). During 2008–09, India exported goods worth US$ 1.73 billion to Vietnam. This included animal fodder worth US$ 135.57 million and meat worth US$ 50.35 million. During 2009–10 (April–December), exports were US$ 1.25 billion.

The Vietnamese Embassy in India is promoting trade and tourism programmes in India to draw Indian corporations to operate in Vietnam. In 2007, India was the sixth largest foreign investor in Vietnam.

There are many big investment projects from India to Vietnam. These include the US$ 527 million steel refinery project in Ba Ria-Vung Tau Province, the Indian Essar group's US$ 600 million oil exploration project and Tata Steel's joint venture to build an integrated steel plant in Vietnam at a cost of US$ 5 billion.

Recently, McLeod Russel India (MRIL), the largest integrated tea conglomerate in the world that was controlled by the Biji Mohan Khaitan group, announced the group's plans to buy 100% stake in Phu Ben Tea Company of Vietnam for ₹32 crore (US$ 6.39 million).

PHILIPPINES

Bilateral trade between India and Philippines was worth US$ 823.69 million in 2007–08, up from US$ 730.16 million in 2005–06. India exported goods worth US$ 618.95 million in 2007–08 comprising chiefly of meat, rubber, fruits, grains, and iron and steel. During 2008–09, exports totalled US$ 743.77 million and they were US$ 534.8 million during 2009–10 (April–December).

CAMBODIA

Trade between India and Cambodia is rising significantly in percentage terms although in absolute terms it is still a small amount. During 2006–07, bilateral trade between the two countries jumped 115.09% to US$ 53.70 million. It increased to US$ 56.32 million in 2007–08. India exported goods worth US$ 53.45 million in 2007–08, chiefly comprising pharmaceuticals, coffee, tea, spices and cotton. During 2008–09, exports to Cambodia were US$ 46.90 million and US$ 30.53 million during the first three quarters of the FY 2009–10 (April–December).

IMPACT OF RECESSION ON INDIAN EXPORTS

The official data showed that merchandise exports grew at only 3.4% in dollar terms for 2008–09 to touch US$168.70 billion. It was also the first time in nearly a decade that merchandise exports recorded a single-digit growth. The export performance for 2008–09 was a little bit short of the scaled down target of $ 170 billion for the year. India had pegged the export target for 2008–09 at $ 200 billion. In the first half of 2008–09, exports recorded a robust 30.9% growth at $ 94.97 billion.

It was evident that the global financial turmoil, especially after the collapse of Lehman Brothers in September 2008, badly dented the country's merchandise export growth performance in 2008–09. On the outlook for 2009–10, the official sources said that there might be flat or near-zero growth in the wake of the depressed economic environment in the developed countries. It was commented that "The 30% kind of growth rate that we saw in the first half of 2008–09 is some years away". A majority of the exporters surveyed expected sectors like engineering goods, gems and jewellery, chemicals, marine products and tyres to see negative or zero growth in the current fiscal that ended March 31, 2010. A weakening rupee had no major impact for exports, with a bulk of the respondents saying the sliding rupee had a only moderate positive impact on their businesses. Table 2.6 tells the story.

Table 2.6   The falling trend in Indian exports during the 2nd half of 2008–09

Month	2008–09	2007–08	Decline (in%)
October	12.82	14.59	12.13
November	11.51	12.77	9.87
December	12.69	12.83	1.09
January	12.38	12.83	15.89
February	11.91	15.22	21.75
March	11.52	17.25	33.22

BALANCE OF PAYMENTS

Balance of Payment (BoP) of a country is one of the important indicators for international trade, which significantly affects the economic policies of a government. As every country strives to a have a favourable BoP, the trends in, and the position of, the BoP will significantly influence the nature and types of regulation of export and import business in particular. BoP is a systematic and summary record of a country's economic and financial transactions with the rest of the world over a period of time. BoP is a statistical statement that systematically summarises, for a specific time period, the economic transactions of an economy with the rest of the world. Transactions, for the most part between residents and non-residents, consist of those involving goods, services, and income, and those involving financial transactions.

The Reserve Bank of India (RBI) is responsible for compiling the balance of payments for India. It obtains data on the BoP primarily as a byproduct of the administration of the exchange control. In accordance with the Foreign Exchange Management Act (FEMA) of 1999, all foreign exchange transactions must be channelled through the banking system, and the banks that undertake foreign exchange transactions must submit various periodical returns and supporting documents prescribed under the FEMA. In respect of the transactions that are not routed through banking channels, information is obtained directly from the relevant government agencies, other concerned agencies, and other departments within the RBI. The information is also supplemented by data collected through various surveys conducted by the RBI. Data are prepared on a quarterly basis and are published in the Reserve Bank of India Bulletin.

Goods current account   The balance of the current account tells us if a country has a deficit or a surplus. If there is a deficit, does that mean the economy is weak? Does a surplus automatically mean that the economy is strong? Not necessarily. But to understand the significance of this part of the BOP, we should start by looking at the components of the current account: goods, services, income and current transfers. Let us now study these four components of the current account.

The RBI compiles data on merchandise transactions mainly as a byproduct of the administration of exchange control. Data on exports are based on export transactions and the collection of export proceeds as reported by the banks. In the case of imports, exchange control records cover only those imports for which payments have been effected through banking channels in India. Information on payments for imports not passing through the banking channels is obtained from other sources, primarily government records and borrowing entities in respect of their external commercial borrowing. Since 1992–93, the value of gold and silver brought to India by returning travellers is being added to the imports data with a contra-entry under current transfers, other sectors. Exports are recorded on an f.o.b. basis, whereas imports are recorded c.i.f. The IMF adjusts imports, for publication, to an f.o.b. basis by assuming freight and insurance to be 10% of the c.i.f. value.

Services   Under the exchange control rules, authorised dealers (that is, banks authorised to deal in foreign exchange) are required to report details in respect of transactions other than exports when the individual remittances exceed a stipulated amount. For receipts below this amount, the banks report only aggregate amounts without indicating the purpose of the incoming remittance. The balance of payments classification of these receipts is made on the basis of the Survey of Unclassified Receipts conducted by the Reserve Bank of India (RBI). This sample survey is conducted on a biweekly basis. The following are examples of how data are collected in respect of transportation and travel.

- *Transportation*   This category covers all modes of transport and port services; the data are based mainly on the receipts and payments reported by the banks in respect of transportation items. In addition to the exchange control records, the survey of unclassified receipts is also used as a source. These sources are supplemented by information collected from major airline and shipping companies in respect of payments from foreign accounts. A benchmark Survey of Freight and Insurance on Exports is also used to estimate freight receipts on account of exports.

- *Travel*   Travel data are obtained from exchange control records, supplemented by information from the surveys of unclassified receipts. The estimates of travel receipts also use the information on foreign tourist arrivals and expenditure, received from the Ministry of Tourism as a cross-check of the exchange control and survey data.

Income   Income is the money going in or out of a country from salaries, portfolio investments (in the form of dividends, for example), direct investments or any other type of investment. Together, goods, services and income provide an economy with fuel to function. This means that items under these categories are actual resources that are transferred to and from a country for economic production.

Current transfers   Current transfers are unilateral transfers with nothing received in return. These include workers' remittances, donations, aids and grants, official assistance and pensions. Due to their nature, current transfers are not considered real resources that affect economic production.

FINANCIAL ACCOUNT

In the financial account, international monetary flows related to investment in business, real estate, bonds and stocks are documented. Also included are government-owned assets such as foreign reserves, gold, special drawing rights (SDRs) held with the International Monetary Fund, private assets held abroad, and direct foreign investment. Assets owned by foreigners, private and official, are also recorded in the financial account.

Direct investment   Basic data are obtained from the exchange control records, but information on non-cash inflows and reinvested earnings is taken from the Survey of Foreign Liabilities and Assets, supplemented by other information on direct investment flows. Up to

1999/2000, direct investment in India and direct investment abroad comprised mainly equity flows. From 2000/2001 onward, the coverage has been expanded to include, in addition to equity, reinvested earnings, and debt transactions between related entities. The data on equity capital include equity in both unincorporated business (mainly branches of foreign banks in India and branches of Indian banks abroad) and incorporated entities.

Portfolio investment Basic data are obtained from the exchange control records. These are supplemented with information from the Survey of Foreign Liabilities and Assets. In addition, the details of the issue of global depository receipts and stock market operations by foreign institutional investors are received from the Foreign Exchange Department, RBI.

Other investments Most of the information on transactions in other investment assets and liabilities is obtained from the exchange control records, supplemented by information received from the departments of the RBI and various government agencies. Entries for transactions in external assets and liabilities of commercial banks are obtained from their periodic returns on foreign currency assets and rupee liabilities. Data on nonresident deposits with resident banks are obtained from exchange control records, the survey of unclassified receipts, and information submitted by the relevant banks to the RBI.

Reserve assets Transactions under reserve assets are obtained from the records of the RBI. They comprise changes in its foreign currency assets and gold, net of estimated valuation changes arising from exchange rate movement and revaluations owing to changes in international prices of bonds/securities/gold. They also comprise changes in special drawing rights (SDRs) balances held by the government and a reserve tranche position at the IMF, also net of revaluations owing to exchange rate movement.

India's BoP

India's trade deficit on a BoP basis has widened significantly by 52.04% to $ 105.33 26 billion in the nine months (April–December) of fiscal year 2008–09 from $ 68.28 billion in the comparable period in previous fiscal. The widening trade deficit is attributed to the significant growth in imports. During the nine-month period (April–December, 2008) imports were up 30.60% to $ 238.86 billion from $ 182.89% in the comparable period in fiscal 2007–08. This is revealed in a report of the country's central banking authority Reserve Bank of India (RBI) on India's Balance of Payments Developments during the third quarter (April–December 2008) of fiscal 2008–09.

The key features of India's BoP that emerged at the end of Q3 of fiscal 2008–09 were:

1. widening of trade deficit led by high growth in imports and slowdown in exports,

2. increase in invisibles surplus, led by remittances from overseas Indians and software services exports, which financed about 65% of trade deficit,

3. higher current account deficit due to large trade deficit,

4. lower net capital flows mainly led by large net outflows under portfolio investment and large repayments under short-term trade credit, and

5. sharp decline in reserves. The major items of Indias BoP are given in Table 2.7.

Table 2.7   India's Overall Balance of Payments from FY 2006–07 to FY 2008–09

Item	Rupees in crores		
	2006–2007	**2007–08 (PR)**	**2008–09 (P)**
A. Current Account			
1. Exports, f.o.b.	5,82,871	6,67,757	7,98,956
2. Imports, c.i.f.	8,62,833	10,36,289	13,41,069
3. Trade Balance	−2,79,962	−3,68,532	−5,42,113
4. Invisibles, Net	2,35,579	2,99,618	4,09,842
a) "Non-Factor" Services *of which*:	1,33,064	1,51,059	2,28,778
a) Software Services	1,41,356	1,62,020	2,15,588
b) Income	−33,234	−19,888	−21,116
c) Private Transfers	1,34,608	1,67,495	2,01,050
d) Official Transfers	1,141	952	1,130
5. Current Account Balance	−44,383	−68,914	−1,32,271
B. Capital Account			
1. Foreign Investment, Net (a+b)	66,791	1,80,788	11,760
a) Direct Investment *of which*:	34,910	61,793	76,822
i) In India:	1,02,652	1,37,434	1,58,579
Equity	73,969	1,07,320	1,25,362
Re-invested Earnings	26,371	28,859	29,705
Other Capital	2,312	1,255	3,512
ii) Abroad:	−67,742	−75,641	−81,757
Equity	−56,711	−57,936	−63,478
Re-invested Earnings	−4,868	−4,363	−4,985
Other Capital	−6,163	−13,342	−13,294
iii) Portfolio Investment:	31,881	1,18,995	−65,062
In India	31,630	1,18,348	−64,206
Abroad	251	647	−856

(Contd.)

Table 2.7 (Continued)

Item	Rupees in crores		
	2006–2007	2007–08 (PR)	2008–09 (P)
2. External Assistance, Net:	7,973	8,465	12,435
Disbursements	16,978	17,022	23,535
Amortisation	–9,005	–8,557	–11,100
3. Commercial Borrowings, Net:	72,365	91,180	38,009
Disbursements	93,932	1,22,270	71,626
Amortisation	–21,567	–31,090	–33,617
4. Short Term Credit, Net	30,096	68,878	–31,160
5. Banking Capital, *of which:*	8,477	47,148	–19,868
NRI Deposits, Net	19,574	706	20,431
6. Rupee Debt Service	–725	–488	–476
7. Other Capital, Net @	18,696	37,802	21,681
8. Total Capital Account	2,03,673	4,33,773	32,381
C. Errors and Omissions	4,344	4,830	2,775
D. Overall Balance [A(5)+B(8)+C]	1,63,634	3,69,689	–97,115
E. Monetary Movements (F+G)	–1,63,634	–3,69,689	97,115
F. IMF, Net	0	0	0
G. Reserves and Monetary Gold (Increase –, Decrease +)	–1,63,634	–3,69,689	97,115

P: Provisional.   PR: Partially Revised.   @: Includes delayed export receipts, advance payments against imports, net funds held abroad and advances received pending issue of shares under FDI.

Notes:

1. Gold and silver brought by returning Indians have been included under imports, with a contra entry in private transfer receipts.
2. Data on exports and imports differ from those given by DGCI and S on account of differences in coverage, valuation and timing.

Source: Reserve Bank of India Annual Report 2009.

INVISIBLES

The account of invisibles includes remittances by expatriate compatriots, especially those working in West Asia, as also remittances for software services, which have become increasingly important, and provide for payment of interest and dividends. Let us study the important aspects of the invisibles as they are seen in the recent Balance of Payments.

INVISIBLES RECEIPTS

The decline in invisibles receipts, which started in the Q4 of 2008–09, continued during Q3 of 2009–10. Invisibles receipts registered a decline of 3.1% during the quarter (as against an increase of 5.4% in Q3 of 2008–09) mainly on account of decline in business, communication and financial services, and investment income receipts. Although, software exports recorded a robust growth of 15.3%, services exports as a whole witnessed a decline of 12.3% during the quarter as against an increase of 11.8% during the corresponding quarter of 2008–09.

Invisible receipts recorded a decline of 7.7% during April–December 2009, as compared with an increase of 22.2% in the corresponding period of the previous year, mainly due to the lower receipts under almost all components of services coupled with lower investment income receipts.

INVISIBLES PAYMENTS

Invisibles payments recorded a growth of 12.9% during Q3 of 2009–10, as compared with a low growth of 2.4% in Q3 of 2008–09, mainly led by increase in payments under almost all components of services. Invisibles payments witnessed a positive growth of 3.7% in April–December 2009 (10.4% in April–December 2008) mainly supported by higher business, communication and financial services, and increase in payments under investment income account.

INVISIBLES BALANCE

The size of invisibles surplus in Q3 of 2009–10 was, however, lower than Q3 of preceding year. Therefore, despite low trade deficit, the current account deficit was higher at US$ 12.0 billion in Q3 of 2009–10 (US$ 11.7 billion in Q3 of 2008–09). Net invisibles (invisibles receipts minus invisibles payments) stood at US$ 59.2 billion during April–December 2009 as compared with US$ 70.9 billion during April–December 2008. At this level, the invisibles surplus financed 66.1% of trade deficit during April–December 2009 as against 72.0% during April–December 2008.

CURRENT ACCOUNT

The balance of the current account tells us if a country has a deficit or a surplus. To understand the significance of this part of the BOP, it is necessary to study its components: goods, services, income and current transfers.

1. **Goods**   Goods are movable and physical in nature. For a transaction to take place, a change of ownership from/to a resident (of the local country) to/from a non-resident

(in a foreign country) has to take place. Movable goods include general goods, goods used for processing materials and other goods, and non-monetary gold. An export is marked as a credit and an import is noted as a debit. Credit means "money coming in." Debit means "money going out."

2. **Services** Services are the transactions that result from an intangible action such as transportation, business services, tourism, royalties, licensing, and so on. If money is being remitted for a service it is recorded like an import, and if money is received it is recorded like an export.

3. **Income** Income is money coming in. It may take the form of dividends, profit from foreign business investments, and so on.

4. **Current transfers** Current transfers are unilateral transfers with no receipts in return. These include workers' remittances, donations, aids and grants, pensions, and so on. However, current transfers are not considered real resources that affect economic production due to their nature.

India's balance of payments on current account worsened by $ 26 billion to $ 69.2 billion in the first six months (April–September) of 2008 fiscal year. This reflects deterioration in the balance of trade with imports rising faster than exports.

Measures to Improve BoP

The following measures are suggested to improve the Balance of Payments position of India:

Reduce domestic consumption Domestic consumption in India is proving resilient as rest of the world slips into recession. This is causing imports to rise faster than exports. Reducing consumer spending would reduce imports, but it may be deemed inappropriate as economic growth may be more important than balance of payments.

Encourage depreciation of rupee Depreciation of rupee would make Indian exports more competitive and imports more expensive. The problem is that with a global recession many other countries will be wanting to help their exporters through encouraging a weaker currency.

Structural improvements Long term supply side policies aimed at increasing the competitiveness of exports should help improve the balance of payments for India. However, they will take a long time to work.

SUMMARY

- India's foreign trade has undergone a sea change since the time of liberalisation of the economy and the government's new economic policy of 1991. The exports and imports have shown a phenomenal growth after 1991.

- The new foreign trade policy that came into being on August 27, 2009 has taken an integrated view of the overall development of the country's foreign trade.

- The country allowed imports liberally and relaxed many requirements for imports into the country.

- India's principal commodities of imports are broadly categorised as follows:
    - bulk imports,
    - machinery,
    - pearls, precious and semi-precious stones,
    - project goods, and
    - others.

- Due to recession in major parts of the world, Indian exports declined by 33% in March 2009 to $11.5 billion compared to $17.2 billion in the same month the previous year.

- USA, UAE, China, Singapore, UK, Hong Kong, Netherlands, Germany, Belgium, and Italy are India's top markets.

- India's software exports registered a remarkable growth to US$ 47.3 billion during 2008–09 from $7.7 billion during 2002–03. Indian exports show a clear shift towards south from the developed regions of the world.

- India's trade relations with USA, China, Japan, EU, Africa, and ASEAN countries are vital to the country's foreign trade growth.

REVIEW QUESTIONS (SHORT)

1. What are the objectives of the new Foreign Trade Policy of India?

2. What are the main parameters of India's foreign trade?

3. Explain briefly the key strategies of India's foreign trade policy.

4. Explain the direction of India's foreign trade.

5. Which are India's top foreign markets?

6. Explain briefly the status of India's foreign trade with the US.
7. Explain briefly the status of India's foreign trade with China.
8. Explain the impact of recession on India's exports.
9. What is Balance of Payments?
10. What is a Financial Account?
11. What is a Current Account?
12. What are invisibles in the BoP?

REVIEW QUESTIONS (DETAILED)

1. What are the principal commodities of India's exports and imports? State also their destination.
2. Explain the status of India's foreign trade with ASEAN countries.
3. Explain in detail the various accounts found in the Balance of Payments.

REFERENCES

1. India's New Foreign Trade Policy Statement 2009–2014.
2. Export Import Data Bank, Department of Commerce, Government of India.
3. National Portal Content Management Team.
4. Department of Commerce (Targets) DGCI&S.
5. eximkey.com.
6. The U.S Census Bureau—Foreign Trade Statistics and CIA World Factbook.
7. Embassy of Japan's news release in April 2007.
8. Reserve Bank of India Report 2009.

BASIC EXPORT PRACTICES

3

LEARNING OBJECTIVES

After reading this chapter, you will be able to

* recognise the need for exporting

* understand the types of risks associated with exporting

* plan and organise for global marketing

* recognise the significance of coordination in global business

* understand the relevance of a firm's export decision and policy

* understand the key points in the market selection process

* understand the significance of market channel selection

* understand the significance of business negotiations

* understand about production planning and packaging, and

* recognise the role of freight forwarders

INTRODUCTION

In general, organisations follow several market entry formulas. Among them, important are: going alone, acquisitions, joint ventures, franchising, concessions and licensing. These entry formulas apply not only to national markets but also to international market. Successful export business is beneficial not only to the country but also to help business thrive in the long-run. Even though export business involves its own benefits and risks, the businessman has to be alert to avert losses in his business. For this purpose, he has to be very careful in selecting the products, buyers and the country of import. Successful entry into international market requires well-planned strategy, well-formulated action plan, proper market research and careful assessment of the advantages and challenges associated with international markets.

INDIA FACTS

Before proceeding to the subject matter of the chapter, it is important to know some of the facts about our country. India:

- is the world's second largest small car market.
- is one of only three countries that makes its own supercomputers.
- is one of six countries that launches its own satellites.
- is a country in which one hundred of the Fortune 500 companies have R&D facilities.
- has the second largest group of software developers after the US.
- lists 6,500 companies on the Bombay Stock Exchange (only the NYSE has more).
- is the world's largest producer of milk, and second largest producer of food, including fruits and vegetables.
- is a world economic power, with growth over the past few years averaging 8%.
- is the world's fourth largest economy, based on purchasing power parity.
- sends more students to the colleges in USA than any other country in the world. (In 2009, 1,03,260 Indian students enrolled in the colleges in USA).
- has the world's second largest pharmaceutical industry after China.
- has a middle class population estimated at 300 million out of a total population of 1 billion.
- with its large base of English-speaking skilled human resource, it is the most sought-after destination for business process outsourcing, and knowledge processing.
- is the second largest English-speaking scientific, technical and executive manpower in the world.
- produces more than 900 movies a year—significantly more than the US.
- has become increasingly attractive to foreign investors in various sectors.

- with its low costs and huge, English-speaking, workforce have made it popular with multinationals for work including manufacturing and call centres.
- provides many tax exemptions to companies set up in Special Economic Zones.
- provides many tax incentives available to IT companies, business process outsourcing and KPO companies.
- has a stable political system based on parliamentary democracy.
- has a common legal system with English as a court language.
- is emerging as a major market and investment destination.

NEED FOR EXPORTING

The responsibility of making a decision regarding the shift in the policy of extending its frontiers to the foreign countries solely rests upon management. It involves new management culture, multi-lingually equipped at all management levels, computer and logistical equipment, a good knowledge of regulations of foreign countries, a knowledge of international environment and a true commitment to developing and adaptation to the needs of the importer coupled with continued commitment to the buyer. Now let us list out the benefits of exporting.

1. *Market diversification* By exporting, you avoid dependency on the domestic market. In times of tough market conditions or a long economic recession, any business may be affected. The best way to avoid those types of risks is the strategy of market diversification.

2. *Additional source of revenues* Selling abroad to a reliable distributor for a long period of time, will provide you additional steady streams of revenues.

3. *Use of excess production capacity* Increased production to achieve an efficient level of production will reduce fixed costs.

4. *Leverage on purchasing power* Increased negotiation power at the time of purchasing higher volume of raw materials will certainly bring several economies.

5. *Business operation stability* If business operation of a company is subject to revenue fluctuations due to season factors, exporting to countries with opposite seasons will allow your company gain stability in its operations.

6. *Product life cycle extension* When products reach the maturity stage, many companies replace them with new products investing significant amount of resources in their development. However, exporting them to specific target markets, such mature products may still have potential abroad.

7. *Product Improvement* Competing in international markets is an excellent source of learning to gain more competitiveness in the domestic market.

8. *Exploit technology and expertise* Exporting can also enable businesses to exploit unique or niche advantages in technology and other areas such as pricing, packaging, delivery and after-sales service.

9. *Increased customer base*   You can expand your customer base, potentially boosting sales, productivity and profits.

10. *Long term planning*   Exporting helps to create a long-term plan for their future.

11. *New knowledge, experience and enhanced domestic competitiveness*   Expand your horizons! Often, new ideas, new approaches, new marketing techniques learned from exposure to the international market place can be successfully applied domestically.

EXPORT RISKS

International transactions can involve different risks from those encountered domestically. These include foreign exchange risk exposure, political risk (which may result in the buyer's inability to remit foreign currency), shipping risks (loss, damage or delay), customs clearance delays, quarantine, local legal issues and standards regulations. These risks can generally be readily identified and assessed. Many export risks will be country-specific. For example, exporting to New Zealand, Singapore or Hong Kong on letter of credit or secured terms has low risk if a company performs and its buyer is reputable, while open account (no payment guarantee) deals in the US can be high-risk especially when the company has limited recourse to recover debts.

Export business can be a great opportunity, but at the same time it is risky and challenging. These risks, totally different from those encountered domestically, are unavoidable, but you can minimise them taking proper precautions. Risks are always associated with business. It is especially true with foreign trade. There can be no business in the world without risk. Even every human being's life is risky each day. But risks are more common in business. A businessman enjoys risk-taking and considers it a challenge before him. Let us now discuss briefly the various risks involved in the export business.

1. *Longer payment schedule*   Export market involves a longer schedule of repayment by the importer. When it is a maximum of 60 days in the domestic market (sometimes it is still lower), the export market may involve 90 or 120 days or even years. This may pose a cash-flow problem for a smaller company. Factoring, cash in advance, or operating an open account may be some of the possible solutions.

2. *Economic/political risk*   Export risks can be classified as economic and political risks involving a country. However, financial risks such as foreign exchange, interest rates and working capital, or commercial risks such as buyer default or contractual disputes, also may have to be faced by the exporter.

3. *Trade barriers*   Trade barriers are politically and economically manipulated. These may include both customers' tariff and non-tariff barriers.

4. *Corruption, and other antisocial elements*   Corruption, crime, expropriation and fraud are regretfully on the increase despite government's and international agencies' efforts to counter them.

5. *New talents*   New skills are required which average from the foregoing items including methods of financing and skills to cope with cash management. Issues such as the collection of receivables, repatriation of funds and foreign exchange will arise and they have to be confronted by new talents only. Realistic financial plans should be identified and much of the above-mentioned risks can be minimised by consulting the company's bank.

6. *Product launch is costly*   A product launch in the overseas market is more costly and complex in comparison with a domestic launch. The product specification must comply with all the overseas market legislations and the legal environment of the market in which it is to be sold. Good research and visits to the intended market can serve to reduce risk.

Businesses must recognise that exporting will initially involve expenditure which may impact on cash flow. They must also be aware of export financing/currency issues and the added risk of potential non-payment for goods and services supplied to foreign buyers. Exporting may impact on a business's domestic activities. It may reveal capacity constraints and productivity constraints and highlight the need for specific skills. Exporters will need to address more cultural, political and legal issues than when operating in Australia. These may include more complex documentation and administration, protection of intellectual property and geographical remoteness from markets and customers.

PLANNING AND ORGANISING FOR GLOBAL MARKETING

Planning involves where the organisation would like to be and how to get there, which involves goal setting and strategy determination. Planning involves three main activities:

1. *Situation analysis*—where are we now?

2. *Objectives*—where do we want to be?

3. *Strategy and tactics*—how can we best reach our goals?

    Planning gives a number of advantages. It

    1. gives rise to systematic thinking;

    2. helps coordinate activities;

    3. helps prepare for exigencies;

    4. gives activity continuity;

    5. integrates functions and activities; and

    6. helps in a continuous review of operations.

The planning task depends on the level of involvement in a country. Exporting and licensing give minimum country involvement but joint ventures involve more in-country activity and give a greater degree of integration and control. Wholly owned subsidiaries give the organisation almost total control. Because of the "external uncontrollables," international planning is rather more difficult than domestic planning. Planning can be standardised, decentralised or interactive.

Factors like distance, culture, language and practices create barriers to effective control. Yet without control over international operations, the degree to which they have or have not been successful cannot be judged. Plans are the prerequisite to control, yet these are developed in the midst of uncertain forces both internal and external to the firm. Basically, control involves the establishment of standards of performance, measuring performance against standards and correcting deviations from standards and plans. In international marketing, the ability to control is disturbed by the distance, cultural, and political and other factors. Figure 3.1 shows the organisation chart of a typical medium-sized global organisation.

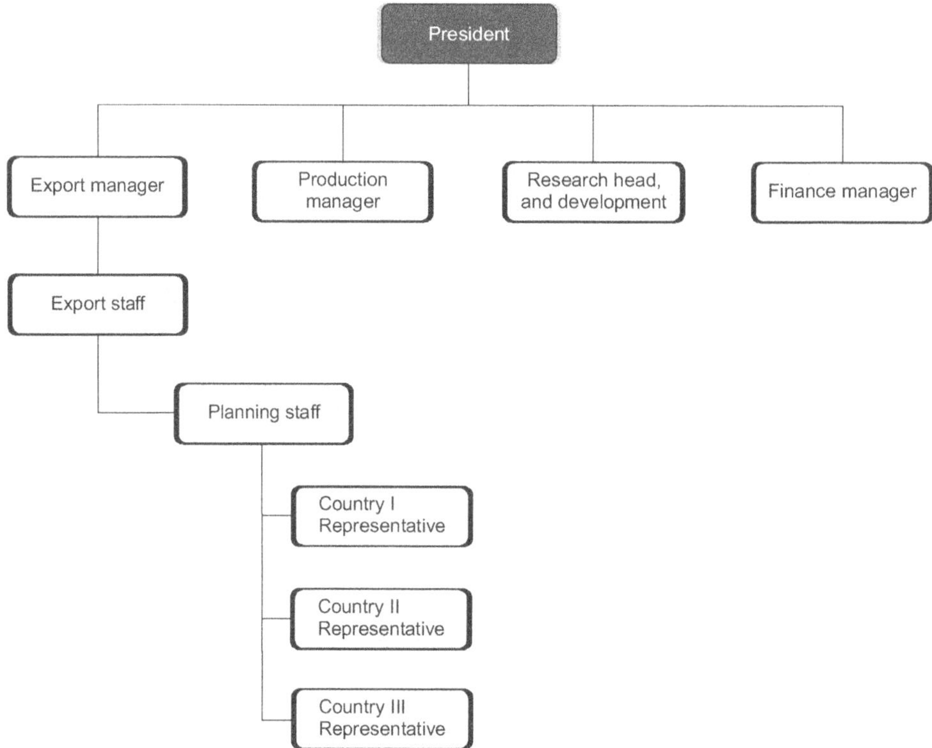

Figure 3.1   A typical organisation chart of a medium-sized global organisation

EXPORT DIMENSIONS

Foreign markets increasingly have become more volatile in the past two decades. Therefore, it is important to identify the key factors influencing the export marketing performance of export market ventures. Eight distinctive features should be noted at the outset. These dimensions are:

- Inventory replenishment
- Merchandising/promotions

- Export agreements
- Ownership
- Type of product
- Export variables
- Stock location
- Transaction mode and channel to market

Figure 3.2 shows these dimensions in a diagrammatic representation.

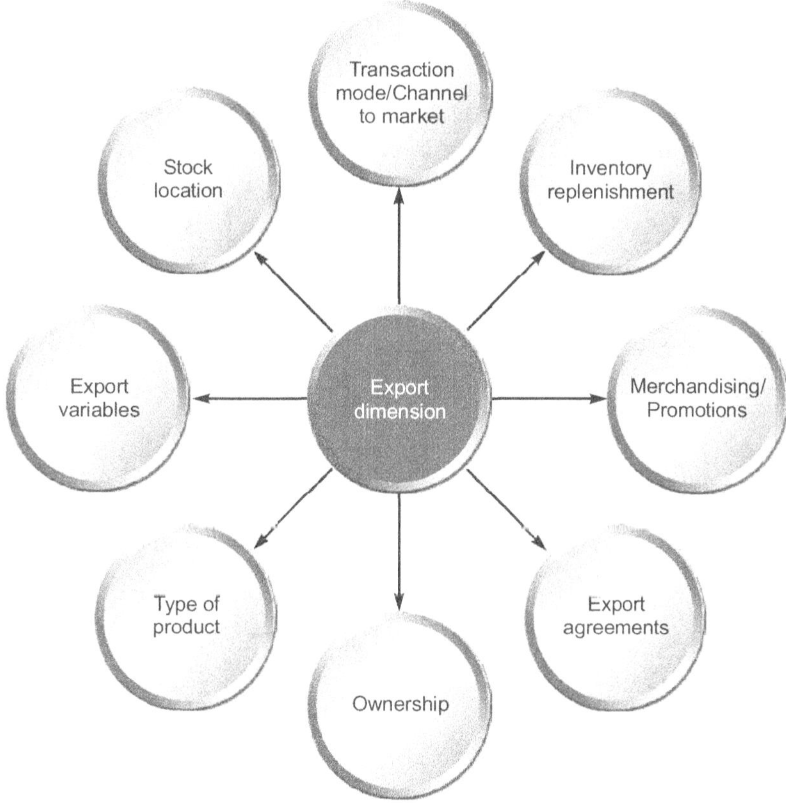

Figure 3.2 Important export dimensions

COMPETITIVE ADVANTAGE

An export organisation must possess some competitive advantages as given below.

Agreed and aligned strategy with key goals The strategies being adopted in the export organisation, must be in conformity with the organisational goals. Any deviation will lead to inefficiency of the personnel. Therefore, care should be taken in this matter.

Superior product research, development, and quality   There cannot be two opinions on this aspect. An international marketing organisation must be conscious to the requirements of the international customers. Today, customers are after quality products and good after-sales service of the products. Therefore, care should be taken to see that there is no let-up in this priority.

World class order satisfaction and stock efficiency at the lowest processing costs   The order execution and delivery of goods must be in accordance with the agreed schedules. At the same time, the stock availability is also a major factor. The executive in charge of the operations should see that the stock is ready well before time.

Networks   The global organisation's network should possess the requisite qualities of a good network. Loving people is the number one trait among successful network marketers. The second most important quality is persistence. A successful network marketer takes the good with the bad and persists until success is achieved. This persistence is necessary in any business, because nothing is ever completely easy. The third quality essential to network marketing is freedom and independence. Network marketing enables one to be his own boss.

End-to-end flow of information   Information should flow freely without any break. If there is nothing to tell, it should be conveyed to the superior. There must be a regular flow of information from the market. In a global market, information must be available in plenty. An effective researcher must be able to gather valuable information for the organisation somehow or other.

Continuous process improvement   It's all about collecting feedback to set the right priorities for changing the process. Feedback is needed to drive the change process. The more feedback is got the better will be the change process. The change process needs to include:

1. Feedback records with deficiency notations

2. Trend analysis

3. Corrective action process and criteria for action

4. Audit process, and

5. Management review process.

The following questions about the change process need to be considered:

    i. Are process feedback records created?

    ii. Have the feedback records been analysed for process deficiencies?

    iii. Does management review all findings to ensure the change process is working?

    iv. Are the deficiencies analysed for statistical significance?

    v. Are the deficiencies of statistical significance written up for corrective action?

    vi. Is corrective/preventive action implemented?

    vii. Is there an objective review of all processes to ensure the change process is working?

    viii. Are processes evolved to meet or exceed organisational requirements?

GLOBAL ORGANISATION: COORDINATION IS THE KEY

Coordination is considered as an essential element of administration. Coordination is the integration, synchronisation or orderly pattern of group efforts in the institution towards the accomplishment of common objectives. To ensure a harmonious and smooth working of an organisation with a number of its divisions, department or its units, and the activities in all the areas are required to be pulled together, unified and blended, so as to give them a commonness and purpose. For a global organisation, coordination is very much required. As the thinking function of management precedes the doing function, coordination endeavour must start at the planning stage, otherwise it becomes impossible to secure coordination of activities and efforts in the execution of work. There is need for importance of direct personal contact in removing misunderstanding and conflict between departments. Coordination is a continual activity that permeates through each managerial function. There should be an integration of all efforts, actions and interests toward a common purpose. For this coordination, one should call for the establishment of a reciprocal relationship among all pertinent factors by way of balancing, blending and joining together the factors with one another.

NEED FOR COORDINATION

Coordination is essential for any organisation, more importantly for a global organisation. Let us see in what ways, it is essential:

Diverse and specialised activities The activities of an organisation are divided into several units and subunits on the basis of product specialisation. Every manager tends to concentrate his attention on activities and objectives of his own department. Coordination prevents and discourages too much of such concentration on one aspect of work.

Empire building To project self importance and personal motive is deeply ingrained in human nature. This causes an individual department to get isolated from others, thus turning it as a separate entity. So coordination is needed to curb the growing tendency towards the empire building.

Personal rivalries and prejudice Human organisation gives rise in due course to the development of personality politics among members. Under such situation, coordination is deliberately damaged by the members of the rival group. The perceptual conflict between line and staff positions or between personnel is a pointer to this problem. Therefore, perfect coordination will smoothen the relationships in the organisation.

Conflict of interests   Subordination of individual interest to general interest acts as a bar to coordination. This subordination may arise from a number of causes such as laziness, incompetence and ambition, apart from a lack of loyalty, integrity or initiative on the part of employees. There is a need for coordination to avoid conflicts or overlapping in the work of employees or units or as organisation.

TECHNIQUES OF COORDINATION

Let us now discuss briefly the techniques that may be adopted in bringing coordination for the organisation.

Communication   Effective communication is possible not only by building a network of communication systems but also by allowing wide participation in the decision making on the part of the affected persons.

Orderly plans   Standing plans like policies and procedures, standing orders and instructions communicate the expected pattern of behaviour required for any coordinated action.

Supervision   Effective supervision aids in coordination much in developing coordinated effort by checking, observation and guidance.

Leadership   Leadership provides individual motivation and persuades any group to have identity of interests and outlook in group efforts.

Departmentation   Departmentation arranges for necessary correlation and interconnection of activities in an analytical manner by assigning duties and delegating authority in different positions.

Direct contact   It permits the management members to exchange their ideas, prejudices and problems as well as to understand each others.

GLOBAL TEAMS

To implement global marketing projects which in return enable global coordination, the most common organisational change is the creation of global teams. The qualities of global teams are as follows:

1. The teams consist of members from different country subsidiaries and from different functional fields.

2. Responsibilities vary from launching specific programmes or activities, such as the advertising campaign for a new product, to more wideranging responsibilities, including the whole marketing mix.

3. Successful teams strive to build trust and overcome barriers of geography, language and culture.

Tools for Global Coordination

The following are the tools for global coordination:

1. Globally standardised planning systems

2. Globally standardised management systems

3. Globally standardised sales reports

4. Coordinating committees and staff

5. Cross-functional and cross-country teams

6. Informal coordination, people-to-people.

Skills of the Global Manager

Effective global managers generally have the ability to

1. develop and use global strategic skills;

2. manage change and transition;

3. manage cultural diversity;

4. design and function in flexible organisation structures;

5. work with others and in teams;

6. communicate clearly; and

7. learn and transfer knowledge in an organisation.

EXPORT DECISION AND POLICY OF A FIRM

Exporting is the most common way for manufacturers to conduct business in foreign markets. Even firms long involved in international business, still export on a regular and permanent basis. Exporting will always be a major factor in the economy, and an important ingredient in the growth of many firms. In exporting its products, a firm has to make two strategic decisions:

1. choose the target country market; and

2. identify the most suitable type of export distribution channel structure to use.

The types of organisational systems employed to distribute products into the market can be viewed along varying degrees of channel integration. At one extreme, the firm can integrate forward and perform all the marketing and distribution functions itself by establishing a sales subsidiary in a foreign market. At the other extreme, a firm can choose not to perform any of these functions, and instead, leave the tasks to independent firms. A firm may also use intermediate options such as act as an export management company or form distribution oriented alliances of various types with foreign firms. Different degrees of integration in international distribution channel give a firm varying degrees of control as well as require different resource commitments, responsibilities and attendant risks. Therefore, it is important for firms to consider the alternative structural arrangements, evaluate the alternatives and select the most appropriate structure relative to the firm and the market when exporting. Although such decisions are very important, researchers have not paid much attention to investigating factors influencing exporters' choice of international channels.

The chief concern of a company will be to combine stability with the highest financial return available. In many industries, this is achieved by a balance or a mixture between home and overseas markets, but much depends on the product. This is important where:

1. exports may rely on the continued existence of one or two foreign markets,

2. markets which may be cut off by changes in import licensing laws, etc., in the countries concerned; and

3. overseas enthusiasm for a product may depend on the fact that it is in use in the home market.

Some businesses virtually exist solely for export with no significant home market. In such a situation, it is prudent, where possible, to have the export markets broadly based and extending to several countries, thereby lessening the impact of a change of export demand in any one of the countries. Export marketing research is an important function and involves fact-finding enquiry on which marketing policy is then based. In all, there are three basic areas to focus on constantly. They are:

Statistical This involves the determination of the total existing market factors like the quantity bought, the price range and then locations. Additionally, it should indicate, where relevant, a comparison with the company's own sales in the area, and whether total market is expanding or otherwise.

Economic This involves evaluation of the product's market potential and its acceptable market price bearing in mind the competition.

Social This includes the public attitude towards the products and their adequacy in terms of design, durability, and so on.

Other internal factors that have a motivating influence on companies to export have been found by researchers as:

1. Production of a (domestically) seasonal product

2. Availability of excess capacity

3. Management's familiarity with the countries to be exported to

4. Management's familiarity with the language of the foreign market

5. Entry of domestic rivals into exporting.

The results of research in the export market can be correlated with parallel activities on the home market, and the international marketing plan projections so that an overall marketing policy may be formulated. However, the divergence of treatment called for by home and overseas markets makes a fusion of the export department with the home marketing organisation under a general marketing manager most unwise. Today much statistical and economic data is available as countries worldwide develop their information resources.

MARKET SELECTION

One of the most important decisions in international marketing is market selection. The global market, made up of well over 200 independent nations, with their own distinctive characteristics, is too vast indeed. Also are the studies about marketing objectives, firm-related factors, market related factors and parameters for market selection. Based on these, a firm would take various marketing decisions. When a company makes the commitment to expand internationally, one of the first, critical challenges it faces is that of market selection. Success or failure in the first foreign foray will often determine whether the effort should continue, or whether it is more prudent to sound the retreat and withdraw to the safety of more familiar surroundings. In deciding where to start, there is often a tendency to equate market size with market potential. This is a fallacy sometimes referred to as the "Chinese Market Share Theory". With more than a billion people, all you really need is 2% to be hugely successful. Unfortunately, the largest markets for technology products such as software have significant hurdles that can make them quite a challenge.

The market selection is normally based on two sets of factors, viz., the firm-related factors and the market-related factors. Firm related factors refer to such factors as the objectives, resources, product mix, and international orientation, and so on of the firm.

Firm-Related Factors

A firm whose export objective is only to sell out a marginal surplus will select a foreign market suited to serve this purpose. Market selection may also be influenced by an objective like growth. A planned business strategy may also influence the market selection. A company that has plans for large expansion of foreign business may choose a market, to start with, which can serve as a hub of international business. Market selection is also influenced by the international orientation of the company. The dynamism and philosophy of the top management and the internal power relations may also influence the market selection decision.

MARKET-RELATED FACTORS

There are a number of market-related factors, which need to be carefully evaluated for market selection. Such factors might be broadly grouped into general factors and specific factors. General factors are factors general to the market as a whole, whereas specific factors are factors those which are specific to the industry concerned.

General factors   There are nine general factors that influence the market selection. They are:

1. economic factors,
2. economic policy,
3. business regulations,
4. currency stability,
5. political factors,
6. ethnic factors,
7. infrastructure,
8. bureaucracy and procedures, and
9. market hub.

Specific factors   These are the factors which are industry-specific. Examples of specific factors are given below:

1. competition in the international market,
2. trade practices,
3. foreign trade trends,
4. nature of domestic production and consumption,
5. raw material availability,
6. government policy on foreign trade,
7. international price levels in the industry,
8. international labour supply.

Box 3.1   Chand International

Chand International was established in 1987 to explore, develop, make and merchandise textile exports from India. They are a professional group of companies active in exports, imports and investments managed by an experienced set of decision-makers.

Needless to say, the company has carved out a reputable niche for itself in the International Business Community with its impressive track record for providing quality products and services. The company has gained the recognition of being a government recognised export house since 1999.

The company has a highly qualified staff to evaluate customers' requirements and can accordingly arrange production that matches buyers' quality parameters, within the specified timelines.

Chand International is also a recipient of the silver trophy awarded by Texprocil (Cotton Textiles Export Promotion Council of India, a Government of India Organisation), being the second highest exporter for cotton made-ups for the year 2004–2005. It has also won awards in the year 2001–2002 and 2002–2003. The company also partners with other industrial units located across the Indian Subcontinent for different processes.

The following are the sales figures of Chand International for the period 2001–09.

2001–02	₹1,112.75 crores	2005–06	₹1,501.56 crores
2002–03	1,328.32 crores	2006–07	1,532.43 crores
2003–04	1,399.98 crores	2007–08	1,509.34 crores
2004–05	1,453.18 crores	2008–09	1,367.43 crores

The management of Chand International is worried over the sales figures of the organisation after 2006–07. The company's major buyers are located in Europe and South-East Asia. Its manager in charge of sales attributes the drop in sales to the economic recession that is taking away a major portion of company's exports. But he is unable to explain the reasons for the fall in sales in 2007–08. However, he is of the opinion that competition may be the reason for fall in sales in 2007–08.

Discussion Questions

Now, analyse the reasons for this setback taking into account India's exports in 2007–08 and the prevailing economic conditions then.

MARKET SELECTION PROCESS

The market selection process is a lengthy one. It can be divided into three stages: Stage I, Stage II and Stage III.

STAGE I—PRELIMINARY STAGE

In the preliminary stage, the foreign trade statistics has to be analysed, and we have to understand thoroughly the international trade situation. For this purpose, a good amount of time has to be spent. But, it is easy to understand the international scenario once the necessary information are collected.

STAGE II—STUDYING MARKET INDICATORS

One has to consider the relevant indicators for studying the market. The indicators are classified into two groups—external and internal.

- External indicators relate to the market such as obstacles to trade, growth rate, competition, price level, and so on while the internal indicators show the information available with the firm.

- The internal indicators include financial strength of the organisation, talents of the executives, and knowledge on international environment.

STAGE III—SELECTION OF TARGET MARKET

In the final stage, the target market has to be selected. It requires lengthy discussion with company executives and executives of export consultancy organisation. After this discussion, a clear picture will emerge about the export possibilities to a foreign destination.

EXPORT PRICING

Price is one of the elements of marketing mix and marketing plan. Enough care should be taken when it is international trade. However, in today's international trade, a good export manager can handle all the problems tactfully and he can overcome most of the risks except the uncontrollable ones, many of which, however, are taken care of by insurance companies. Let us now see the international processing strategies which are more or less similar to the domestic pricing methods, except that the export pricing has to take into account the risk factors associated with export trade.

COST-ORIENTED PRICING

Normally, the exporter starts with his figures of cost of production. Then he adds a certain margin which has been fixed by the management plus a small allowance for risk factors.

RETROGRADE PRICING

Retrograde pricing is fixed taking into account all the deductions like expenses, markings, taxes and duties from the ceiling. This can be compared with the cost at the gate.

MARKET-PRACTICE PRICING

There is an exclusive procedure followed by the exporters of a particular product line. The market practice has to be found out by the new exporter and the same procedure may be followed.

SALES VISITS

If the company is a large one, and if it proposes to carry on a big export business, then sales trips abroad to meet the buyers will be useful. This has many advantages. First, you meet the buyer and find out his strengths and weaknesses. Second, you can understand the regulations of the importing country. Third, you can make personal bank enquiries on the basis of information provided by the prospective importers.

PROMOTION

Public relations, sales force and publicity are the three principal aspects of overseas promotion. An exporter has to decide on the priority of national or regional markets and target promotional activities to importers, agents or distributors to various markets. Europe was considered as a single market previously. But it is not so today. There are cultural differences, differences in languages and many other differences. To avoid the problems in export business, the exporter has to have a long term approach, which has to consider the following:

1. Establishing long-term relationships with agents of importers
2. Maintaining these with regular contacts and personal visits
3. Visiting important customers with the representatives
4. Answering all queries promptly
5. Adapting the product to the market trends
6. Competitive pricing
7. Supporting agents, importers and distributors sales promotion efforts.

SALES PROMOTION LITERATURE

Sales literature performs many functions. It

1. introduces or creates interest in the company and its products;
2. provides details of the products;
3. explains the use of products;

4. serves as references for use by customers;

5. creates a favourable image about the company;

6. stimulates inquiries; and

7. answers queries.

TRADE FAIRS

Participation in trade fairs does promote exports. However, this alone does not ensure success. Success rather depends on the action taken by exporters on key factors such as:

1. getting products ready at competitive prices;

2. having clear objectives;

3. effective representation at the stand;

4. following up promptly after the fair; and

5. exhibiting at a fair repeatedly.

MARKET CHANNEL SELECTION

A new entrant feels under-equipped to handle export procedures and prefers indirect exporting. Sometimes, the exporter wants to confirm about the demand for his products and tries to establish intermediaries before going for direct marketing. There are many types of export intermediaries. The major decision regarding distribution is the selecting of the intermediary. There are many options and each has its own merits and demerits. The exporter wants to analyse them and finally selects the suitable intermediary. The types of intermediaries in the order of their increasing involvement in distribution operations are:

1. Export merchants

2. Combination export managers

3. Export agents

4. Travelling buyers

5. Import merchants

6. Import agents

7. Importers or distributors

DIRECT AND INDIRECT EXPORTING

In direct marketing, the exporter need not use the intermediaries, if he himself possesses sufficient knowledge on this issue. If there are knowledgeable executives in the organisation, the exporter may resort to direct marketing. As exports increase, the firm sets up a separate export department. This approach is the most ambitious and difficult, since the exporter personally handles every aspect of the exporting process from market research and planning to foreign distribution and collections. Consequently, a significant commitment of management time and attention is required to achieve good results. However, this approach may also be the best way to achieve maximum profits and long-term growth. With appropriate help and guidance from the Department of Commerce, state trade offices, freight forwarders, international banks, and other service groups, even small or medium-sized firms can export directly if they are able to commit enough staff time to the effort. For those who cannot make that commitment, the services of an EMC (Export Management Company), ETC (Export Trading Company), trade consultant, or other qualified intermediary are indispensable.

Indirect exporting is frequently used to enter new markets. Businesses selling products enter into an agreement with an agent, distributor or a trading house for the purpose of selling (or marketing and selling) the products in the target market. Due diligence is critical when selecting an agent or distributor for indirect exporting.

Another market entry strategy involves strategic partnerships with other companies or individuals with complementary skills and capabilities. A partner can often provide the insight, contacts and expertise that fills the gap in your export readiness. A strategic alliance with a company selling a complementary product or service can provide more effective market access, resulting in more foreign sales in less time. As with indirect exporting relationships, contractual agreements with partners must be stated in clear terms.

OVERSEAS AGENT

There are two types of foreign representatives—the commission agent and the distributor. The agent solicits orders for a product and then passes them on to the exporter. On the other hand, the distributor buys the product directly from the manufacturers on his own account at an agreed discount. He maintains stocks and sells through his own salespersons. Normally, the discount is higher than the commission of an agent. Selecting an agent or distributor takes time. It is to be made sure that any agreement with an agent or distributor is formalised in a clear written contract. This will reduce the chances of disagreements or problems arising later. It is worth seeking expert advice, for example, from a lawyer with trade-related experience or a local team. Satisfaction with every part of the contract is a must.

The following key points should be covered by the contract:

1. *Parties*—the names and addresses of the businesses involved, and the nature of the relationship, for example, agency or distributorship.
2. *Products*—a clear description of company's goods.
3. *Territory*—the geographic area within which, the agent or distributor will sell your goods.
4. *Exclusivity*—possessing the sole rights to sell a particular company's goods.

5. *Exceptions to exclusivity*—for example, can a company sell direct to customers it already has in the market?

6. *Pricing*—what price will the company receive from a distributor for its goods? What price will an agent charge their customers?

7. *Commission*—what commission will an agent receive?

8. *Payment terms*—when will payments be made, in what currency, and at what exchange rate?

9. *Period*—a termination date set for the agreement, which includes clear provisions for ending the agreement before that date.

10. *Confidentiality*—make sure that sensitive information about a business or products is to be protected.

11. *Intellectual property*—what rights will the agent or distributor have to use a company's business name, brand names, trade marks, and so on?

12. *After-sales care*—for example, product liability, insurance and warranties. Who is responsible at each stage of the trading process?

13. *Marketing*—what promotional activities will support a company's products and who will pay for them?

14. *Rights*—it should be ensured that rights assigned can't be transferred to a third party.

15. *Jurisdiction*—which country's rules will apply to the contract? This can affect the employment, performance and termination provisions of agency contracts.

If a company is contracting with an overseas agent, it may also want to set clear weekly or monthly sales targets that are realistic and measurable. The action to be taken if these targets are not met should also be dealt with in the contract. If the company can't agree on terms with its agent or distributor, or if a contractual dispute arises, the issue should be resolved through the International Chamber of Commerce (ICC), International Court of Arbitration or a similar body.

BUSINESS NEGOTIATIONS

Let's begin with a definition of negotiation, the first part in understanding how to be a more effective negotiator, to manage conflict, and to get what you want. Here we define what negotiation is and is not. Negotiation is any activity that influences another person. Here's how some of the leading thinkers define the topic:

Negotiating is the process of getting the best terms once the other side starts to act on their interest

Mark H. McCormack

... negotiating is... a means of achieving one's goals in every relationship regardless of the circumstances

Gerard I. Nierenberg

Negotiation is a field of knowledge and endeavour that focuses on gaining the favour of people from whom we want things

Herb Cohen

Business negotiation skills are very important in export marketing. There is only one reason to engage in business negotiation. You want the other person to do something—to say "Yes"; to do more; to do less; or stop doing it altogether. Precisely, because they are not doing what we want is why you should negotiate. The exporter has to negotiate the terms and conditions of sales or terms of appointment of agency system overseas, etc. There may be differences between the exporter and buyer/agent regarding terms and conditions of sales. In such a situation, exporter should be aware of the negotiation process involved and be prepared for handling such eventualities. Export negotiation is a service offering by which the exporter's corresponding bank receives and authenticates the full set of export documents submitted by the exporter, before paying for the bills and documents.

Jens Thang, the negotiation guru, gives his views on negotiation skills which are valuable as well as useful for negotiators.

.......If you are better prepared than the other party you are negotiating with, you will almost always do better. Knowledge is really power at the negotiating table. Whether you are on the buying side or selling side, you will have an edge over the other party if you are better informed. Being better prepared will give you more confidence at the table that will definitely help you improve your negotiation results.

Evaluate the information you collect and decide on the factors that will have an effect on your negotiation. Keeping your eyes and ears open for additional information during the negotiation can assist you in the end result. Before you sit down at the table, know the real goal that you have. Understand what your limits on all aspects of the deal are. When you are better prepared, you will be able to accelerate every step of the process.

Do not get distracted and rush to close a deal. There is simply no need to say yes all the time during the negotiation. If you find yourself eager to close a deal, take a step back and give yourself a time-break. Sometimes we move so fast to close a deal that we trip ourselves, only to regret our decision later. Learn to project forward before making a decision. Look before you take the plunge. Many people are so eager to close a deal that they forget that they are there for a specific reason or a specific goal. Never rush to make a decision which you will later regret.

What is really going to matter in a team negotiation is the quality of your team. Always go into a negotiation with a winning team. Do not start to think that it's all about you. You will never know everything. No matter how good you are or how good you think you are, it is your team which will determine the success of your negotiation. Make sure that your team is better (or at least better prepared) than the other party.

We always take things for granted. Failing to understand the terms and conditions thoroughly can cost you dearly. Always make sure that all the terms are properly negotiated during the process. If possible, make it a habit to document all the terms discussed. Having the terms documented (and may be signed) is a form of commitment both sides have. This will help you avoid the problem of the other party going against an agreement that they have originally agreed to."

PRODUCTION PLANNING AND PREPARATION

The production plan initially needs to address specific key elements well in advance of production, in order to ensure an uninterrupted flow of work as it unfolds. It includes the following.

1. *Material ordering*   Materials and services that require a long lead time or are at an extended shipping distance, also known as blanket orders, should be ordered in advance of production requirements. Suppliers should send you materials periodically to ensure an uninterrupted pipeline.

2. *Equipment procurement*   Procuring specialised tools and equipment to initiate the production process may require a longer lead time. One should keep in mind that the equipment may have to be custom-made or simply difficult to set up. This type of equipment may also require special training.

3. *Bottlenecks*   These are the constraints or restrictions in the process flow and should be assessed in advance so you can plan around them or eliminate them before you begin production. When you assess possible bottlenecks, be aware that they may shift to another area of the process. Dealing with bottlenecks is a continual challenge for any business.

4. *Human resources acquisition and training*   Key or specialised positions may demand extensive training on specialised equipment, technical processes or regulatory requirements. These employees should be interviewed thoroughly about their skills. When hiring them, allow sufficient time for training and be sure that they are competent in their work before the job begins. This will ensure that your process or service flows smoothly.

The production plan provides a foundation to schedule the actual work and plan the details of day-to-day activities. As sales orders come in, you will need to address them individually based on their priority. The importance of the sales order will determine the work flow and when it should be scheduled. After this, you should evaluate whether or not you are ready for production or to offer the service. You will need to determine:

1. If the inventory is available at the point where work is to start. If not, then the work needs to be rescheduled when supplies become available. There is no point in scheduling work that you will not be able to complete.

2. Are your resources available? Do you have the necessary staff to complete the task? Are the machines being used?

3. Does the standard time fit within the open time allowed? If not, then the work should be rescheduled.

4. You should be careful to minimise risk factors; allowing too many what-ifs can delay delivery and be counter productive.

One of the many challenges of production planning and scheduling is following up with changes to orders. Changes happen every day; you may lack materials; delivery time is moved up or work parameters have to be adapted. You will need to adjust your plan in line with these changes and advise the plant. Dealing with change is not always easy and may take as much effort as creating the original production plan. You will need to follow up with the various departments involved in order to rectify any problems. Also, computer software can be helpful in tracking changes, inventory, employees and equipment.

New product development for foreign markets involves the combined efforts of market, process and product development research. The initial development costs might not be recoverable in the short. This discourages many exporters to develop new products. However product modification is essential to comply with rules and regulations in foreign markets. The export product policy includes adaptation of existing products to target market needs. There are four alternatives:

1. *Standardisation of product*   Same product for both domestic and export markets.

2. *Modification of the product image*   Same product caters to the different needs in different markets.

3. *Modification of product specification*   Same product but usage varies in different markets.

4. *Modification of specification and image*   Slight modification in specification and image of the product in different markets.

PACKAGING

Packaging is the science, art and technology of enclosing or protecting products for storage, distribution, and sale. Packaging also refers to the process of design, evaluation, and production of packages. Packaging requirements today are becoming increasingly sophisticated to meet.

It can be described as a coordinated system of preparing goods for transport, warehousing, logistics, sale, and end use. Packaging contains, protects, preserves, transports, informs, and sells products. It is fully integrated into government, business, institutional, industry, and personal use. Package design and development are often thought of as an integral part of the new product development process. Alternatively, development of a package (or component) can be a separate process, but must be linked closely with the product to be packaged. Package design starts with the identification of all the requirements like structural design, marketing, shelf life, quality assurance, logistics, legal, regulatory, graphic design, end-use, and environmental conditions.

Package design may take place within a company or with various degrees of external packaging engineering: contract engineers, consultants, vendor evaluations, independent laboratories, contract packagers, total outsourcing, and the like. Some sort of formal Project Planning and Project Management methodology is required for all except the simplest package design and development programmes. An effective quality management system, and verification and validation protocols are mandatory and recommended for all exporters for some types of packaging.

Package development involves considerations for sustainability, environmental responsibility, and applicable environmental and recycling regulations. It may involve a life cycle assessment which considers the material and energy inputs and outputs to the package, the packaged product (contents), the packaging process, the logistics system, waste management, and others. It is necessary to know the relevant regulatory requirements for point of manufacture, sale, and use.

The design criteria, time targets, resources, and cost constraints need to be established and agreed upon a market which is seeking continuous improvements in the following areas:

1. *Improved standards to reduce risk, damage and pilferage* This, in turn, encourages competitive cargo insurance premiums and maintains good relations with the importer. Cargo received in a damaged condition seriously impairs the exporter's products' overseas market prospects as it loses goodwill with the importer. Moreover, the exporter is ultimately obliged to replace the damaged goods, which can be a costly task.

2. *Better utilisation of transport capacity to lower distribution cost* This is particularly relevant to ISO container use when suitably sized packaged cargo can be firmly stowed in it with no broken stowage. Full advantage should be taken of high capacity containers for volume cargoes, and use made of a stowage plan. This reduces the risk of damage, and ensures all container capacity is utilised, subject to the total weight limitations not being exceeded.

3. *Improved cargo handling* Cargo packaging in design, namely dimension and configuration, should facilitate the most economical method of handling. This is particularly relevant to awkwardly shaped cargo. Moreover, it is applied, from the time goods are

packaged, which may be in the factory, until it reaches the importer's warehouse/distribution centre.

4. *Competitive packaging costs* Packaging costs amongst various manufacturers are now very competitive. The shipper is very conscious of containing packing costs and the exporter is well advised to engage a specialist packaging company to obtain professional advice and gain the best results.

Factors Influencing the Nature of Packaging

Let us now examine the various factors influencing the nature of packaging for an international consignment.

Value of goods In the main, the high-value consignment usually attracts more extensive packaging than low-value merchandise. Much, of course, depends on the nature of the commodity. If packing is inadequate, bearing in mind the transit and declared cargo valuation, problems could be experienced in carrier's liability, acceptance and adequate cargo insurance coverage.

Nature of transit The type and length of transit is about whether the movement of cargo is national, international or transglobal. What form of transport will be used during the transit—road, rail, short sea, deep sea or air? All have varying characteristics which make varying demands of the packaging of the goods.

Nature of cargo This concerns the characteristics of the goods concerned and their susceptibility to various losses or damage. It is important to bear in mind that packaging offers protection against pilferage as well as damage. Cargo shipped in bulk requires little or no packing, while general merchandise needs adequate packing.

Compliance with customs or statutory requirements This is particularly relevant to dangerous cargo, where strict regulations apply both by air and sea concerning the carrier's acceptance, packing, stowage, documentation, marking, and carrier's liability. Statutory regulations also apply to the transportation of foodstuffs involving the temperature requirements of the food.

Resale value Resale value, if any, of packaging material in the importer's country is also important. In some developing countries, large drums, wooden cases, or bags have a modest resale value. This helps to offset the packaging cost.

General fragility of the cargo In the main, the more fragile the cargo becomes, the greater the degree of packaging required. This is very much related to the mode of transport, particularly air freight, which has only limited packaging needs and low value of consignment. A judgment must be made on the most acceptable form of packaging to adopt and, if in doubt, advice must be sought.

The international consignment delivery terms of sale Again, the actual packaging specifications may be contained therein and it is important to take into account who will bear the cost. Usually it is the exporter.

Variation during the course of the transit Temperature variations can be quite extensive during transit and packaging must take into account of this to permit the cargo to breathe and avoid excessive condensation/sweating. Again, advice should be sought, when necessary, from the airline or the ship owner. For example, jaggery needs very careful packaging.

Ease of handling and stowage Cargo stowage and obtaining the maximum practical utilisation of available transport unit capacity are areas worthy of study to lower unit distribution cost. Likewise, if awkwardly shaped cargoes are conveniently packed, this will speed up cargo handling.

Packaging, therefore, is not only designed as a form of protection to reduce the risk of goods being damaged in transit, but also to prevent pilferage and aid marketing. It is, of course, essential to see not only that right type of packing is provided, but also that the correct quality and form of container/material is used.

ROLE OF FREIGHT FORWARDERS

An international freight forwarder is an agent for the exporter in moving cargo to an overseas destination. These agents are familiar with the import rules and regulations of foreign countries, the export regulations of various governments, the methods of shipping, and the documents related to foreign trade. Export freight forwarders are licenced by the International Air Transport Association (IATA) to handle air freight and the International Maritime Organisation to handle ocean freight.

Freight forwarders assist exporters in preparing price quotations by advising on freight costs, port charges, consular fees, costs of special documentation, insurance costs, and their handling fees. They recommend the packing methods that will protect the merchandise during transit or can arrange to have the merchandise packed at the port or containerised. If the exporter prefers, freight forwarders can reserve the necessary space on a vessel, aircraft, train, or truck. The cost for their services is a legitimate export cost that should be included in the price charged to the customer.

Once the order is ready for shipment, freight forwarders should review all documents to ensure that everything is in order. This is of particular importance with letter of credit payment terms. They may also prepare the bill of lading and any special required documentation. After shipment, they can route the documents to the seller, the buyer, or to a paying bank. Freight forwarders can also make arrangements with customs brokers overseas to ensure that the goods comply with customs export documentation regulations. A customs broker is an individual or company that is licenced to transact customs business on behalf of others. Customs business is limited to those activities involving transactions related to the entry and admissibility of merchandise; its classification and valuation; the payment of duties, taxes, or other charges assessed or collected; or the refund, rebate, or drawback thereof.

FINDING A LOCAL FREIGHT FORWARDER

Freight forwarders are located in most metropolitan areas. Yellow pages of telephone directories often have a freight forwarder, or transportation, and headings. Shippers must know the legal nature of the contract between them and their forwarding agents. Agents are supposed to carry out their principals' instructions and have no authority to choose sub-contractors. The exporter should be clean about the nature of activities offered by the forwarding agent in his own country. The types of forwarding agents are:

Multimodal transport operators   They offer door-to-door service using different modes of transport. The duties include handling customs clearance, warehousing, arranging cargo insurance, final storage, and responsible for meeting deadlines.

Port or airport agents   They act as a link in the international physical distribution from one mode of transport to another. They are referred to as 'cargo consignees' as the goods are addressed to him. Their status is of agents who oversee the movement of goods through ports and airports.

Cargo consolidators   They negotiate group rates with the carriers and consolidate the small shipments from their clients into groups to give full loads for railway freight cars, trucks, containers or pallets. They have authority to forward by any carrier of their choice.

Airfreight agents   These agents assemble freight for airlines and have the power to make out and sign airway bills on their behalf. They act as customs brokers and freight consolidators.

Road haulage agent brokers   They bring together the road carriers and shippers of goods.

Customs brokers   They carry out customs formalities for exporters and importers. They will have written authorisation from the customers' administration concerned. They take the place of exporters and importers in customer's import and export formalities.

INCOTERMS

Incoterms are standard trade definitions most commonly used in international sales contracts. Devised and published by the International Chamber of Commerce, they are at the heart of world trade. Among the best known Incoterms are: EXW (Ex Works), FOB (Free on Board), CIF (Cost, Insurance and Freight), DDU (Delivered Duty Unpaid), and CPT (Carriage Paid To).

ICC introduced the first version of Incoterms—short for "International Commercial Terms"—in 1936. Since then, ICC expert lawyers and trade practitioners have updated them six times to keep pace with the development of international trade. Most contracts made after 1 January 2000 will refer to the latest edition of Incoterms, which came into force on that date. The correct reference is to "Incoterms 2000". Unless the parties decide otherwise, earlier versions of Incoterms—like Incoterms 1990—are still binding if incorporated in contracts that are unfulfilled and dated before 1 January 2000. Versions of Incoterms preceding the 2000 edition may still be incorporated into future contracts if the parties so agree. However, this is not recommended, since the latest version is designed to bring Incoterms into line with the latest developments in commercial practice.

The English version is the original and the official one of Incoterms 2000, which have been endorsed by the United Nations Commission on International Trade Law (UNCITRAL). Authorised translations into 31 languages are available from ICC national committees. Correct use of Incoterms goes a long way to providing the legal certainty upon which mutual confidence between business partners must be based. To be sure of using them correctly, trade practitioners need to consult the full ICC texts, and be aware of the many unauthorised summaries and approximate versions that abound on the web. Some of the commonly used Incoterms are as follows:

EXW—Ex Works (named place)	The seller makes the goods available at his premises; the buyer is responsible for all the charges.
FCA—Free Carrier (named place)	The seller hands over the goods, and they are cleared for export.
FAS—Free Alongside Ship (named loading port)	The seller must place the goods alongside the ship at the loading port.
FOB—Free On Board (named loading port)	This is a classic maritime trade term meaning which the seller must load the goods on board the ship nominated by the buyer, cost and risk being divided at ship's rail. The seller must clear the goods for export. This is used for maritime transport only.
CFR—Cost and Freight (named destination port)	The seller must pay the costs and freight to bring the goods to the port of destination. However, risk is transferred to the buyer once the goods have crossed the ship's rail. This is suitable for maritime transport only.
CIF—Cost, Insurance and Freight (named destination port)	It is exactly the same as CFR except that the seller must in addition procure and pay for insurance for the buyer. This is mostly used for maritime transport.
CPT—Carriage Paid To (named place of destination)	It is the general/containerised/multimodal equivalent of c.f.r. The seller pays for carriage to the named point of destination, but risk passes when the goods are handed over to the first carrier.
CIP—Carriage and Insurance Paid to (named place of destination)	It is the containerised transport/multimodal equivalent of c.i.f. The seller pays for carriage and insurance to the named destination point, but risk passes when the goods are handed over to the first carrier.

DAF—Delivered At Frontier (named place)	It can be used when the goods are transported by rail and road. The seller pays for transportation to the named place of delivery at the frontier. The buyer arranges for customs clearance and pays for transportation from the frontier to his factory. The passing of risk occurs at the frontier.
DES—Delivered Ex Ship (named port)	Where goods are delivered ex ship, the passing of risk does not occur until the ship has arrived at the named port of destination and the goods made available for unloading to the buyer. The seller pays the same freight and insurance costs as he would under a c.i.f arrangement. Unlike CFR and CIF terms, the seller has agreed to bear not just cost, but also Risk and Title up to the arrival of the vessel at the named port. Costs for unloading the goods and any duties, taxes, and the like are for the buyer. A commonly used term in shipping bulk commodities, such as coal, grain, dry chemicals—where the seller either owns or has chartered, their own vessel.
DEQ—Delivered Ex Quay (named port)	It means the same as DES, but the passing of risk does not occur until the goods have been unloaded at the port of destination.
DDU—Delivered Duty Unpaid (named destination place)	It means that the seller delivers the goods to the buyer to the named place of destination in the contract of sale. The goods are not cleared for import or unloaded from any form of transport at the place of destination. The buyer is responsible for the costs and risks for the unloading, duty and any subsequent delivery beyond the place of destination. However, if the buyer wishes the seller to bear the cost and risks associated with the import clearance, duty, unloading and subsequent delivery beyond the place of destination, then this all needs to be explicitly agreed upon in the contract of sale.
DDP—Delivered Duty Paid (named destination place)	It means that the seller pays for all transportation costs and bears all risk until the goods have been delivered and pays the duty. Also used interchangeably with the term "Free Domicile".

TIPS FOR EXPORT SUCCESS

When a company gets into export trade, it stands to gain in a number of ways. Its business will be cushioned against fluctuations in local demand. It positions yourself to utilise its excess capacity and gain a share of global markets. The organisation stands a chance to increase its sales and profits. It also contributes to the growth of the country's economy.

The following tips can be useful for becoming successful in the export business:

- Know what markets to export to, consider how attractive they are in terms of demand, size and profits, purchasing power. Consider also the activities of competitors and whether they can be a problem to your entry.

- Establish the potential of the market by undertaking some desk research to establish the size of the population, growth rate and distribution channels.

- Also establish the existence of products similar to yours, the value of their imports, import tariffs, market requirements, per capita income, availability and cost of transport, and contacts in the target market.

- Talk to potential importers and trade promotion organisations in the target market.

- If possible, visit the target market to verify your desk research and undertake assessment on the ground.

- Finally, develop a marketing plan.

- You do not need to be a giant manufacturer to get into the export trade. All you need is a market, the right information and the right skills.

- You will also need a product which can be adapted to meet the market standards and requirements, the right price to make your goods competitive in the export market, and financial and human resources to develop your export business.

- You also need a focused, dedicated, and competent trade promotion organisation to provide you with the necessary market information and marketing skills.

- Ensuring right quality increases chances for the success of products in world markets.

- Proper packaging protects, shapes and makes products attractive to consumers. You communicate with your customer through packaging.

- The nature of the product you are marketing, the markets you are targeting and the mode of shipment will determine the type of packaging to use. Thus, packaging should take into consideration the customer's requirements, international standards, and regulations applicable in markets.

- Branding gives product identity and enhances recognition. If a brand is well known and liked, it wins consumer loyalty. Known brands are hard to get displaced in the market place.

- Timely delivery of your products is also a major plus point.

- Like all other businesses, export marketing carries its own risks. Exporters should be aware of these risks and guard against them.

- Because of distance barriers, an exporter may not understand fully, the requirements of the target market. Therefore, he must possess knowledge of risks related to these barriers.

SUMMARY

- The benefits of exporting are 1. increased company business, 2. increased company exposure, 3. the presence of high quality staff, 4. dilution of risk, 5. economies of scale, 6. increased competitiveness, and 7. increase in profitability.

- The export risks are 1. longer payment schedule, 2. economic/political, 3. trade barriers, 4. corruption, 5. paucity of new talents, and 6. high cost of product launch.

- Planning and organising are the key elements for global marketing. Coordination is considered as an essential element of global organisation.

- Coordination is the integration, synchronisation or orderly pattern of group efforts in the institution towards the accomplishment of common objectives.

- The market selection is normally based on two sets of factors: the firm-related factors and the market-related factors. Firm related factors refer to such factors as the objectives, resources, product mix, and international orientation of the firm. Market related factors may be general or specific.

- The export pricing methods are cost-oriented pricing, retrograde pricing and market-practice pricing.

- Overseas promotion is a difficult function which must be performed by the exporters. Specialised knowledge is required for overseas sales promotion and market channel selection.

- Business negotiations and production preparation are important stages in the export process.

- Packaging is a very important function because the goods have to reach the destination safely. Freight forwarders also play a vital role in this task.

- Incoterms are standard trade definitions most commonly used in international sales contracts. Devised and published by the International Chamber of Commerce, they are at the heart of world trade.

▶ Review Questions (Short)

1. Give any six important facts about India.

2. Explain briefly the need for export.

3. What are the important export risks?

4. What are the competitive advantages that an export organisation must possess?

5. Explain the process of production planning and preparation for export.

6. Discuss briefly about the art of business negotiations.

7. What are the different types of export pricing?

8. Distinguish between direct exporting and indirect exporting.

9. Explain the role of freight forwarders in exporting.

▶ Review Questions (Detailed)

1. Explain the need for and techniques of coordination for a global organisation.

2. Explain the process of market selection for exporting.

3. Explain the process of market channel selection for exporting.

4. Explain the importance of export packaging.

5. State the Incoterms with sufficient explanation.

6. Draw a typical organisation chart of a medium-sized global organisation and explain the positions and their functions.

7. Discuss the important points of an export contract.

8. What are the different dimensions of export? Explain them in detail.

REFERENCES

1. Entering overseas markets *businesslink.gov.uk*.

2. Jens Thang's "10 Commandments of Negotiations".

3. www.bdc.ca/en/advice_centre/articles/Pages/production_planning_plan.aspx.

4. Soroka. (2002). *Fundamentals of Packaging Technology*. Institute of Packaging Professionals. ISBN 1-930268-25-4.

5. Zabaniotou, A., Kassidi. (August 2003). "Life cycle assessment applied to egg packaging made from polystyrene and recycled paper". *Journal of Cleaner Production*. 11(5): 549–559. doi:10.1016/S0959-6526(02)00076-8.

6. Franklin (April 2004). "*Life Cycle Inventory of Packaging Options for Shipment of Retail Mail-Order Soft Goods*" (PDF). Retrieved December 13, 2008.

7. www.gxnube.com for "Factors Influencing the Nature of Packaging".

8. www.shipping-worldwide.com/freight-forwarder.htm for "Role of freight forwarders".

THE PROCESS OF EXPORTING

4

LEARNING OBJECTIVES

After reading this chapter, you will learn the steps involved in the process of exporting:

* Deciding to export
* Obtaining IEC Number from the Regional Licensing Authority
* Obtaining Business Identification Number
* Obtaining registration cum membership certificate (RCMC)
* Registering your company with State and Central Sales Tax Departments
* Obtaining Enrolment Number
* Getting Identity Cards countersigned by the Regional Licensing Authority
* Finalising the export sales contract
* Commencing production/procurement for export
* Arranging for export finance
* Obtaining the EXIM Digital Signature Certificate
* Arranging the freight forwarders and shipping the cargo, and
* Preparing the packing list.

KEY TERMS

* Feasibility study
* Regional Licensing Authority
* Importer Exporter Code Number
* Directorate General of Foreign Trade
* Business Identification Number
* Export Promotion Council
* Commodity Board
* Federation of Indian Exporters Associations
* Registration-cum-membership certificate
* Enrolment number
* Identity Card
* Export contract
* Production/procurement
* EXIM Digital Signature Certificate
* Freight forwarders
* Packing list

INTRODUCTION

Exporting involves several steps. They are:

1. deciding to export

2. adhering to guidelines given in the legislations

3. finalising the export contract with the foreign buyer

4. taking steps to production or procurement

5. arranging for export finance

6. the shipping formalities; and

7. taking steps for collection.

In addition, a prudent exporter has to consider many aspects like nature of risks involved, and continuous market research. These activities together may be called as the export process. Let us now discuss these steps in detail.

DECIDING TO EXPORT

Making a decision whether to export or not is a very basic decision of the firm. In addition to the positive and significant influence of a history of exporting (indicating the presence of sunk costs), a number of other plant characteristics are found to impact the probability of being an exporter. Factors such as plant size, age and ownership by a corporation are found to increase the probability of exporting. Location, particularly in terms of distance to a port, is also found to be significant. Business councils, chambers of commerce, and other organisations can be very helpful to learn about the international markets.

There are a number of differences between doing business in India and doing business abroad. A key to your learning process will be talks and seminars where you can both gain information and network with persons familiar with the markets you are considering. As an exporter, you must take advantage of the many events sponsored by your industry association, the Bilateral Trade Councils, the Boards of Trade and Chambers of Commerce around the country.

You have to have sufficient internal capacity to handle extra demand, internally efficient systems to respond to customers quickly, an ability to respond both online and offline, senior managers and marketing staff with culturally-sensitive marketing skills, and senior management support for export objectives.

Figure 4.1 gives clearly the factors that are key for making the decision whether to export or not. The businessman must possess all the four qualities for making a decision to export. These qualities include

1. Desire to export,

2. Resources,

3. Knowledge, and

4. Export skills.

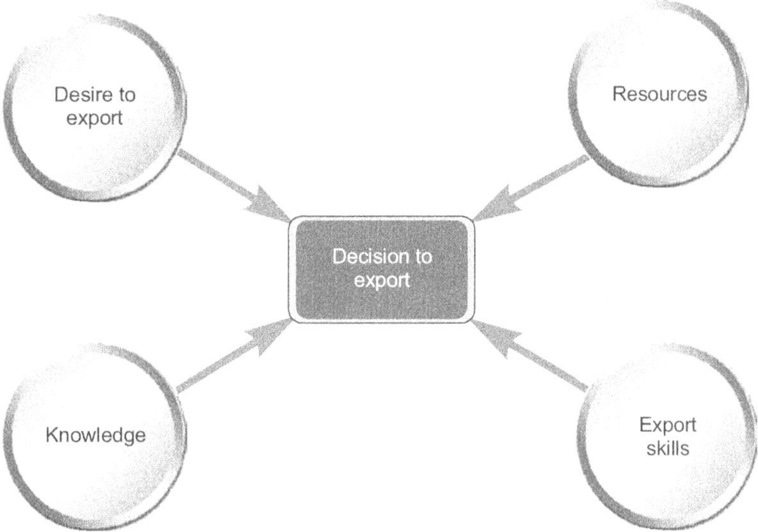

Figure 4.1   Determinants of the decision to export

You have to have a product or service that is unique and/or competitive in the type of market you are targeting, sophisticated market entry methods creative ways to use the internet in promotion and delivery, and market research demonstrating the viability of your product or service abroad. You must have clear and achievable export objectives, a realistic idea of what exporting entails, open-mindedness to new ways of doing business, and realism about what will be necessary to be profitable abroad. When all these conditions are satisfied you become ready to export. "Export readiness" refers to a firm's capacity for success in an export market. Being "export ready" includes having capabilities that are well-matched to the particular market in which you wish to do business.

For fast-paced, competitive economies like the US, Australia, the UK, and other developed countries, efficient service delivery, excellent quality assurance, and a media profile are critical to success. For relationship-based relatively affluent economies like Hong Kong, Japan, South Korea, Malaysia, Singapore, and Taiwan, inter-personal communication skills, cultural sensitivity, and linguistic fluency are critical in developing a good relationship with a local partner with whom one can do business. For donor-funded economies, market development takes time, requires flexibility, and needs swift but flawless action. Donor-funded economies are a good match for a firm which have:

1. Senior managers who are politically well connected with donor agencies;

2. Staff with good interpersonal communications skills;

3. Resources to support a long planning cycle;

4. Experience in satisfying several customers at once;

5. Experience in working with government agencies;

6. A service delivery system that can adapt to low technology.

Senior management support is absolutely critical to successful exporting. Therefore, the CEO of the organisation should rope in all the senior executives in the task of exporting. They, however, cannot be always forced to do this and that. Once the task is entrusted to them, they must work with full involvement.

The export process has three stages:

1. Feasibility study

2. Determining foreign market entry strategy

3. Execution.

The steps in these stages can now be focused.

FEASIBILITY STUDY

Any new endeavour needs a feasibility study. When a proposal has come up for doing business in a hitherto unknown market, a feasibility study becomes doubly important. Feasibility study includes the following:

1. *Assess the firm's capability*   The business firm which wants to enter into a foreign market must first assess its own capability. The financial background, contacts in the foreign market, and most importantly, the man power availability in the exporter's organisation are a few important considerations.

2. *Analysis of foreign environment*   The exporter must analyse the demographics, social, political, economic, and other factors of target markets.

3. *Seek the opinions of experts*   It is necessary to obtain the opinions of experts in the field. It will help the organisation greatly and will lead to a concrete proposal and, then, a decision.

4. *Select target market*   The final step in the feasibility study is the selection of the target market. The exporter must study the risk perceptions in the target market.

5. *Seek the advice of other friendly exporters*   It is necessary that a company venturing into export must know about the target market from sources very well known to it.

DETERMINING FOREIGN MARKET ENTRY STRATEGY

Any business organisation must first decide whether to undertake direct marketing or indirect marketing. Details of important contacts in the foreign soil must be collected with care and from reliable sources. It is important to study the need for applying for any patent rights, and the like. If it is felt necessary, the company must take necessary steps in this respect.

EXECUTION OF THE PLAN

The final step is to execute the proposal for export. It needs the following tasks:

1. Comply with domestic formalities like obtaining IEC number

2. Negotiate with the importer

3. Finalise the export contract

4. Begin production or procurement of the product

5. Obtain necessary insurance policies

6. Take utmost care in packaging the product

7. Ship the product.

FORMALITIES BEFORE THE ACTUAL EXPORT PLAN

Let us discuss now some of the important formalities to be completed before executing the actual export plan.

REGISTER WITH REGIONAL AUTHORITY AND OBTAIN THE IEC NUMBER

An application for grant of Importer Exporter Code (IEC) number shall be made by Registered/Head Office of applicant, except Export Oriented Units and Special Economic Zone units, to concerned Regional Licensing Authority (RLA) in Aayaat Niryaat Form (ANF) 2A with documents prescribed therein. Only one IEC would be issued/allowed against a single Permanent Account Number which is to be obtained from the Income Tax Department. A copy of such IEC number shall be endorsed to concerned banker. An IEC number allotted to an applicant shall be valid for all its branches/divisions/units/factories. Where an IEC Number is lost or misplaced, issuing authority may consider requests for grant of a duplicate copy of IEC number, on an affidavit. If an IEC holder does not wish to operate allotted IEC number, he may surrender the same by informing issuing authority. On receipt of such intimation, the issuing authority shall immediately cancel it and electronically transmit it to the DGFT and the customs authorities.

The customs authorities will not allow a company to import or export goods into or from India unless it holds a valid IEC number. For obtaining IEC number, it should apply to Regional Licensing Authority in duplicate, in the prescribed form. Before applying for IEC number it is necessary to open a bank account in the name of the company/firm with any commercial bank authorised to deal in foreign exchange. The duly signed application form should be supported by the following documents:

1. Bank Receipt (in duplicate)/Demand Draft for payment of the fee of ₹1,000/-.

2. Certificate from the Banker of the applicant firm in the format given in Appendix 18A.

3. Two copies of passport size photographs of the applicant duly attested by the banker to the applicants.

4. A copy of Permanent Account Number issued by Income Tax Authorities. If PAN has not been allotted, a copy of application of PAN submitted to Income Tax Authorities.

5. In case the application is signed by an authorised signatory, a copy of the letter of legal authority may be furnished.

6. If there is any non-resident interest in the firm and NRI investment is to be made with repatriation benefits, a simple declaration indicating whether it is held with the general/ specific permission of the RBI on the letter head of the firm should be furnished. In case of specific approval, a copy may also be furnished.

7. Declaration by the applicant that the proprietors/partners/directors of the applicant firm/company, as the case may be, are not associated as proprietor/partners/directors with any other firm/company which has been caution-listed by the RBI. Where the applicant is so associated with a caution-listed firm/company the IEC number is allotted with a condition that he can export only with the prior approval of the RBI.

8. Exporter's Profile.

The Regional Licensing Authority concerned will, on merit, grant an IEC number to the applicant. The number should normally be given within 3 days provided the application is complete in all respects and is accompanied by the prescribed documents. An IEC number allotted to an applicant shall be valid for all its branches/divisions as indicated on the IEC number.

The following categories of importers or exporters are exempted from obtaining IEC number:

1. Importers covered by clause 3(1) [except sub-clauses (e) and (l)] and exporters covered by clause 3(2) [except sub-clauses (i) and (k)] of foreign trade (Exemption from application of Rules in certain cases) Order, 1993.

2. Ministries/Departments of Central or State Government.

3. Persons importing or exporting goods for personal use not connected with trade or manufacture or agriculture.

4. Persons importing/exporting goods from/to Nepal, Myanmar through Indo-Myanmar border areas and China (through Gunji, Namgaya Shipkila and Nathula ports), provided CIF value of a single consignment does not exceed Indian ₹25,000. In case of Nathula port, the applicable value ceiling will be ₹100,000. However, exemption from obtaining IEC number shall not be applicable for export of Special Chemicals, Organisms, Materials, Equipments and Technologies (SCOMET) as listed in Appendix 3, Schedule 2 of ITC (HS) except in case of exports by category (ii) above.

The list of IEC licensing authorities is given in Appendix 1. Appendix 2 gives the Application Form for Issue of/Modification in Importer Exporter Code (IEC) Number. The format of IEC number certificate is given in Appendix 8.

File your Profile with the Regional Authority

Each importer/exporter shall be required to file importer/exporter profile (given here as Appendix 10) once with the Regional Authority in Part 1 of "Aayaat Niryaat Form (ANF) 2A". The Regional Authority shall enter the information furnished in Part 1 of "Aayaat Niryaat Form (ANF) 2A" in their database so as to dispense with the need for asking the repetitive information. In case of any change in the information given in Part 1 of "Aayaat Niryaat Form (ANF) 2A", importer/exporter shall intimate the same to the Regional Authority.

Obtain Business Identification Number from the DGFT

Any exporter who wants to export his goods needs to obtain PAN based Business Identification Number (BIN) from the Directorate General of Foreign Trade prior to filing of shipping bill for clearance of export goods. The exporters must also register themselves to the authorised foreign exchange dealer code and open a current account in the designated bank for credit of any drawback incentive.

Registration with Export Promotion Council/Commodity Board

In order to enable the company to obtain benefits/concession under the export–import policy, it is required to register itself with an appropriate export promotion agency by obtaining registration-cum-membership certificate. Most of the Export Promotion Councils do online registration only. However, it should be noted that registering with the export promotion councils is not compulsory to export the company's goods.

An application for registration should be accompanied by a self certified copy of the Importer–Exporter code number issued by the Regional Licensing Authority concerned and a bank certificate in support of the applicant's financial soundness. In case an exporter desires to get registration as a manufacturer–exporter, he should furnish evidence to that effect. In the case of a manufacturer–exporter the licensing authority may seek copy of registration with SSI/any other sponsoring authority in addition to the application in the prescribed form for the Import Export Code Number.

If the application for registration is granted, the Export Promotion Council (EPC) or Federation of Indian Export Organisations (FIEO) shall issue the registration cum membership certificate (RCMC) indicating the status of the applicant as merchant exporter or manufacturer exporter. The RCMC shall be valid for five years ending 31st March of the licensing year. The certificate shall be deemed to be valid from 1st April of the year in which it was issued.

In the case of Cashew Export Promotion Council, registration is made online. Membership in the Council is not mandatory to take up exports of Cashew Kernels/Cashewnut Shell Liquid. Membership, however, is granted to those who are "engaged" in export of Cashew kernels/Cashewnut Shell Liquid and have obtained Approval of Name from the Council.

The first step is to get the name approved by sending the following particulars:

1. Name and nature of the firm

2. Name(s) of Proprietor/Partners

3. Association with any other organisation

4. IEC Number

The second step is the submission of application. Application for membership, after name approval may be submitted to the council along with the following:

1. Proof of having engaged in export of cashew kernels/cashewnut shell liquid during the previous financial year/current year viz. copies of bill of lading/invoice duly certified by a chartered accountant.

2. Entrance Fee (₹1,000/-), Membership Subscription (₹20,000/-) and Minimum Trade Contribution (₹7500/-) by way of a Demand Draft in favour of the Cashew Export Promotion Council, payable at Ernakulam/Cochin.

3. The renewal of membership subscription for the subsequent years will be ₹5000/- at the current rates, but subject to revision every year.

GET REGISTERED WITH STATE AND CENTRAL SALES TAX AUTHORITIES

Goods which are to be shipped out of the country for export are eligible for exemption from both Sales Tax and Central Sales Tax. For this purpose, the company should get itself registered with the Sales Tax Authority of its State after following the procedure prescribed under the Sales Tax Act applicable to its State.

The list of Export Promotion Councils is available in Appendix 3. The specimen for EPCG authorisation application is given in Appendix 4, while application for registration cum membership with EPCG is available in Appendix 11 to this chapter. Instructions for filling up various forms are available in Appendix 9.

OBTAIN ENROLMENT NUMBER

In order to obtain various licences from the Licensing Authority, it is essential to have the enrolment number. The Regional Authority, on application being made, issues it to the exporter.

OBTAIN IDENTITY CARD FROM REGIONAL AUTHORITY

To facilitate collection of authorisation and other documents from the DGFT head quarters and the RLA (Regional Licensing Authority), identity cards which are valid for 3 years may be issued to the proprietor/partners/directors and authorised employees (not more than three), of importers and exporters, upon application as in Appendix 20A in the Handbook of Procedures. In addition, Identity Card may also be issued by the applicant firms on their letter head to the concerned employees. These Identity Cards may be countersigned by the concerned RLA. However, application for identity card in Appendix 20B of the Handbook of Procedures will require to be made by the applicant and all other parameters would need to be met. However, in case of limited companies, the RLA may approve allotment of more than three identity cards per company.

In case of loss of an identity card, a duplicate card may be issued on the basis of an affidavit. Common directors/partners, of a group company or in any other similar cases, the RLA may issue multiple identity cards after recording reasons in writing. Officers may grant interview at their discretion to the authorised representative of the importer/exporter. Interviews/clarifications may also be sought through e-mails. Units other than small scale units are permitted to expand or create new capacities in respect of items reserved for small scale sector, subject to condition that they obtain an Industrial Licence under the Industries (Development and Regulation) Act, 1951, with export obligation as may be specified. Such licencee is required to furnish a LUT (Legal Undertaking) to the RLA and the DGFT in this regard. The DGFT/RLA concerned shall monitor export obligation.

Box 4.1   Writing the Export Contract

Giri Engineering Ltd.

Giri Engineering Limited is a company based in Coimbatore. The company manufactures general-purpose lathes, drilling machines, and other basic machinery. The company has a good domestic market as well as export market. The company exports these machinery to the US and the EU. Sixty per cent of the company's sales revenue is generated through the exports.

The company's agent in the US buys the company's products in bulk and he undertakes to sell them in the foreign market. Since the company's machinery are of high quality, the US agent does not find it difficult to sell them in the American market. But in the wake of current recession in the US, the agent has demanded a reduction in the prices of the company's products. He has also voiced his concern about the quantity of goods to be purchased by him in future, as he was afraid whether he will be able to sell the same number of products in the American market.

The US agent is coming to India to sign the next contract with Giri Engineering Limited in the next month. Raghav, the Export Manager, is busy preparing documents for signing the contract with the American agent. He has a meeting the next day with the Managing Director about the expected visit of the American agent.

Before the arrival of the agent, Raghav has to decide on several points so that there will not be any hitch during the negotiations with the agent. The issues before Raghav are the following:

- The recession in the US,
- Its effects on the company's sales,
- Possibility of any reduction in the prices of the company's products,
- If there is no possibility, what are the other options?, and
- Exploring new foreign markets.

Discussion Question

Assuming yourself as Raghav, analyse how would you go about on the abovesaid issues, as well as other issues that may crop up at the time of the meeting with the American agent.

Finalising an Export Contract

It is the most important step in the process of exporting because any mistake in this process will cost a company heavily and its efforts will be in vain. Therefore, while dealing with the importer, the exporter must take utmost care in finalising the export contract. There is no standard format of export contract as the elements of export contract may vary from individual to individual, transaction to transaction and country to country. The elements of an export contract also depend upon the nature of the product being exported.

Export sales contract can be informal or formal, depending on the foreign buyer. An offer to sell may be made over the telephone by the exporter, covering the type of good, quantity to be sold, per unit price, and delivery and payment terms accepted by the foreign buyer or an offer to buy from the importer. Such a contract may be preceded by a series of offers and counter-offers before the final offer and acceptance. Such a contract may or may not be confirmed in writing. It usually occurs between branches of the same company or between long-standing trade partners or between reputed companies dealing in commodities subject to rapid price changes. An offer to sell may also be made by airmail, courier, telex, cable, facsimile or e-mail by the exporter and accepted by the foreign buyer. A pro-forma invoice by facsimile may be despatched by the exporter, to the buyer and confirmed by the foreign buyer. A formal typewritten contract setting out all the conditions of the sale must be signed by both the buyer and the seller. When the export contract is made quickly and informally, some of the conditions are either assumed or clarified later which, of course, may lead to dispute and misunderstanding.

A formal export sales contract will contain the following clauses:

- Names and addresses of the parties
- Product, standards and specification
- Quantity
- Inspection
- Total value of the contract
- Terms of delivery
- Taxes, duties, and charges
- Period of delivery, shipment, and so on.
- Post-shipment, trans-shipment, and marking
- Terms of payment, amount, mode, and currency
- Discounts and commission
- Licences and permits

- ❂ Insurance

- ❂ Documentary requirements

- ❂ Product guarantee

- ❂ Force majeure or excuse for non-performance of contract

- ❂ Remedy

- ❂ Applicable law

- ❂ Arbitration

- ❂ Signature of the parties

PRODUCTION OR PROCUREMENT FOR EXPORT

Once signing of the export contract is over, the exporter has to prepare for export of the contracted goods. An exporter may be a supplier or manufacturer. It may be manufacturing or procuring. Depending on the time availability, and nature of contract and the product, the exporter will start production of the product. Sometimes the exporter may not possess the production facility. In this case, he will enter into subcontracts with the local manufacturers. If the goods are readily available in the market, the exporter will arrange for procurement of the goods in the market. In any case the exporter must see to it that all the contract requirements are satisfied by him.

ARRANGING FOR EXPORT FINANCE

Financing exports can involve a number of scenarios and objectives. Typically, trade finance products and services focus on:

1. Providing cash flow or working capital

2. Facilitating or expediting the remittance of funds

3. Obtaining finance, based on the expected completion of an export sale or shipment

4. Providing credit to a buyer to make the transaction more attractive

5. Mitigating against a variety of complex risks inherent in international trade, such as non-payment, political or foreign exchange risk, loss or damage of goods in transit, and many others.

Box 4.2 Deccan Exporters Limited

Deccan Exporters Ltd. is a company engaged in the export of agricultural commodities to destinations like South-East Asia, Gulf countries, the US and the EU. The company exports horticultural commodities like flowers, mangoes, grapes, and oranges and other agricultural commodities like onions. In general, the company exports all agricultural commodities which are available on particular seasons.

The buyers have a good rapport with the company, as the company provides all the documents required by the importers. The company, in its existence for the past 20 years, has only five cases of rejection of its goods. Therefore it enjoys very good name among the importers of these countries.   India's agri-exports can be divided into three broad categories, that is, export of

1. raw products,
2. semi raw products
3. processed and ready-to-eat products.

Raw products exported are essentially of low-value, high-volume nature, while semi processed products are of intermediate value and limited volume, and processed ready-to-eat products are of high-value but low-volume nature. Deccan Exporters concentrate on export of the first category.

India's agri-exports face certain constraints that arise from conflicting domestic policies relating to production, storage, distribution, food security, pricing concerns, and the like. Unwillingness to decide on basic minimum quantities for export makes Indian supply sources unreliable. Higher domestic prices in comparison to international prices of products of bulk exports like sugar, wheat, rice and the like make our exports commercially less competitive. Market intelligence and creating awareness in international market about quality of products need to be strengthened to boost agricultural exports. Deccan Exports Limited is also facing problems now and then on these matters. The monsoon failures also affect the exports of Deccan Exporters Limited. During such years, the company's financial performance has also showed a dismal figure.

Of late, monsoon failures have become very common and the company has been considering some alternatives such as

- Diversification of its area of operation,
- Exploring new businesses.

Discussion Question

You are required to assist the management of Deccan Exporters Limited to make a wise decision.

OBTAINING EXIM DIGITAL SIGNATURE CERTIFICATE

The Ministry of Company Affairs (MCA), Government of India, is going live with its flagship e-governance project MCA-21. This project will make it possible for company directors, professionals, financial institutions and other authorised signatories to do e-filing with the MCA, using a secure mode of communication. (Complete details are available at www.dca.nic.in or www.mca.gov.in).

To facilitate electronic filing, all companies registered with the Registrar of Companies have to procure legally valid Digital Signature Certificates. The DGFT has offered 50% discount on application licence fees for any application made online using (n)eXIM. (n)eXIM is a complete solution in itself and does not require any additional software buying exclusive to the online application at the DGFT. (n)eXIM can also be used as the legal online identity for any organisation. It can also be used elsewhere where Digital Certificate is required. For example, it can be used for online tendering, online form filling, and the like. (n)eXIM is a special kind of DGFT Digital Signature Certificate exclusively for the EXIM community of India. It is issued to organisations/people who have obtained a valid IEC. These (n) Code Digital Signatures are approved by the Directorate General of Foreign Trade.

Digital certificates serve as your identity in the digital world. Just as a passport or a driver's licence is used to uniquely identify individuals in the physical world, digital certificates are used to identify entities in digital transactions. Based on public key cryptography, these digital certificates associate every entity with a unique pair of credentials—the public key and the private key. Only the owner of a Digital Certificate can have access to the private key and can use it to digitally sign and encrypt any digital information such as e-mails, forms, and files.

Documents required and to be submitted by the applicant for application of Digital Signature Certificate for DGFT:

1. Certified true copy (from Company Secretary/Director/Partner/Proprietor of the organisation) of any one of the following:

   ○ Certificate of Incorporation,

   ○ Memorandum and Articles of Association,

   ○ Registered Partnership Deed,

   ○ Valid business licence document.

2. Certified true copy of any one of the following:

   ○ Annual Report,

   ○ Income Tax Return,

   ○ Statement of Income,

   ○ Letter from the bank giving bank details of the organisation.

3. Authorisation letter in favour of the certificate applicant from the applicant organisation (as per the format)

4. Latest photograph of the applicant

5. IEC Certificate photocopy

6. Declaration giving Director details duly attested by a CA/CS as per the format given in form.

You will find below some of the authorised signatories to EXIM Digital Certificate

- SafeScrypt Ltd.
- Gromax Infonet Ltd.
- PKI solutions
- SAFESCRYPT Ltd.
- *n*Solutions
- DigiSolutions and services

The specimens of EXIM Digital Certificate Application Form (Appendix 5), and Signature Verification Letter (Appendix 6) are available at the end of this book.

ARRANGING FREIGHT FORWARDERS AND SHIPPING THE CARGO

An international freight forwarder is an agent for the exporter in moving cargo to an overseas destination. These agents are familiar with the import rules and regulations of foreign countries, the export regulations of the Government of India, the methods of shipping, and the documents related to foreign trade. Export freight forwarders are licenced by the International Air Transport Association (IATA) to handle air freight and the Federal Maritime Commission to handle ocean freight. Freight forwarders assist exporters in preparing price quotations by advising on freight costs, port charges, consular fees, costs of special documentation, insurance costs, and their handling fees. They recommend the packing methods that will protect the merchandise during transit or can arrange to have the merchandise packed at the port or containerised. If the exporter prefers, freight forwarders can reserve the necessary space on a vessel, aircraft, train, or truck. The cost for their services is a legitimate export cost that should be included in the price charged to the customer.

Once the order is ready for shipment, freight forwarders should review all documents to ensure that everything is in order. This is of particular importance with letter-of-credit payment terms. They may also prepare the bill of lading and any specially required documentation. After shipment, they can route the documents to the seller, the buyer, or to a paying bank. Freight forwarders can also make arrangements with customs brokers overseas to ensure that the goods comply with customs export documentation regulations. A customs broker is an individual or company that is licenced to transact customs business on behalf of others. Customs business is limited to those activities involving transactions related to the entry and admissibility of merchandise; its classification and valuation; the payment of duties, taxes, or other charges assessed or collected; or the refund, rebate, or drawback thereof.

For a port to efficiently send and receive cargo, it requires some infrastructure. Harbours, and seaports host watercraft, and consist of components such as piers, wharfs, docks and roadsteads. A port is a facility for receiving ships and transferring cargo to and from them. They are usually situated at the edge of an ocean or sea, river, or lake. Ports often have cargo-handling equipment such as cranes (operated by stevedores) and forklifts for use in loading/unloading of ships, which may be provided by private interests or public bodies. Often, canneries or other processing facilities will be located very close by. Harbour pilots, barges and tugboats are often used to safely maneuver large ships in tight quarters as they approach and leave the docks. Ports, which handle international traffic, will have customs facilities.

Access to other transport systems such as rail and truck terminals can contribute to a port's efficiency. Some ports feature canals, which allow further movement inland. The presence of deep water in channels or berths, the provision of protection from the wind, waves and storm surges and access to intermodal transportation such as trains or trucks are critical to a good port. A port must also have navigational aids such as lighthouses, buoys and sea marks.

PREPARING THE PACKING LIST

When goods are prepared for shipment, a detailed export packing list should also be prepared. This is a formal document that itemises quite a number of details about the cargo such as:

- The name of the exporter (referred to as the *shipper*) and their contact details (telephone, fax, cell, e-mail), including physical (not postal) address

- The name of the importer (referred to as the *consignee*, meaning the person or firm to whom the goods are to be sent) and their contact details (telephone, fax, cell, e-mail), including physical (not postal) address

- The gross (that is, the weight of the product and packaging—that is, the total weight), tare (that is, the weight of the packaging without any contents) and net (that is, the weight of the product only) weights of the cargo

- The nature, quality and specifications of the product being shipped

- The type of package (such as pallet, box, crate, drum, and carton)

- The measurements/dimensions of each package

- The number of pallets/boxes/crates/drums, and the like

- The contents of each pallet or box (or other container)

- The package markings, if any, as well as shipper's and buyer's reference numbers

- Reference to the associated commercial invoice such as the invoice number and date

- A purchase order number or similar reference to correspondence between the supplier and importer

- An indication of who the carrier is (airline, shipping line or road hauler)

- Reference to the bill of lading or airwaybill number

It is also important that the details on the packing list (such as shipper's/importer's details, number of items involved, and the like), match exactly what is stipulated on the commercial invoice and bill of lading/airway bill. A mismatch between the packing list and the other transport/export documents may lead to closer scrutiny of the cargo and may ultimately result in delays in the cargo arriving at its destination. Note that pricing information is not required on the packing list.

PURPOSE OF THE PACKING LIST

The packing list should be attached to the outside of a package in a waterproof envelope or plastic sheath marked "Packing list enclosed". The list is used by the shipper or forwarding agent to determine 1. the total shipment weight and volume, and 2. whether the correct cargo is being shipped. In addition, the customs officials (both local and foreign) may use the list to check the cargo. Packing lists come in fairly standard forms and can be obtained from your freight forwarder.

COMBINING PACKING LISTS AND COMMERCIAL INVOICES

It is also not uncommon to find combined commercial invoices/packing lists. In such instances, the commercial invoice simply contains more packing information than it might normally have on it. This makes sense, as the commercial invoice already contains most of the packing and packaging information on the invoice; just a little more detail and it becomes a full-blown packing list. The title might also state; "Commercial Invoice/Packing List"

DON'T MAKE ERRORS WITH THE PACKING LIST

It is essential that the packing list agrees exactly with all the terms and conditions of the export sale. It is important to realise that any error on the packing list may cause a delay in clearance at the port of destination. Customs authorities in the target country have the right to delay the clearance of the shipment until the importer provides a packing list reflecting the real contents of the container. If all the information required for the packing list is already stated in the commercial invoice, then the packing list may be unnecessary. It is better to provide it anyway–you don't want the consignment delayed, simply because a customs official demands to see a packing list.

A specimen of the packing list is available in Appendix 7.

SUMMARY

❀ The first step in the process of exporting is deciding to export. Making a decision whether to export or not is a very basic decision of the firm. There are a number of differences between doing business in India and doing business abroad. A key to your learning process will be talks and seminars where you can both gain information and network with persons familiar with the markets you are considering.

❀ The second step is registering with the Regional Authority (RA). An application for grant of Importer Exporter Code (IEC) number shall be made by Registered/ Head Office of applicant, except EOUs and SEZ units, to the concerned Regional Authority in Aayaat Niryaat Form (ANF) 2A with documents prescribed therein.

❀ The third step is registering with the Export Promotion Councils/Commodity Boards. In order to enable you to obtain benefits/concession under the export-import policy, you are required to register yourself with an appropriate export promotion agency by obtaining registration-cum-membership certificate. Most of the Export Promotion Councils do online registration only. However, it should be noted that registering with the export promotion councils is not compulsory to export your goods.

❀ The next step is to obtain Identity Cards from the Regional Authority. To facilitate collection of Authorisation and other documents from the DGFT Head Quarters and the RA, identity cards which are valid for 3 years may be issued to proprietor/ partners/directors and authorised employees (not more than three), of importers and exporters, on application.

❀ Finalising export contract is the most important step in the process of exporting because any mistake in this process will cost you heavily and your entire efforts will be in vain. Therefore, while dealing with the importer, the exporter must take utmost care in finalising the export contract.

❀ Once signing of the export contract is over, the exporter has to prepare for export of the contracted goods.

❀ To facilitate electronic filing, all companies registered with the Registrar of Companies have to procure legally valid Digital Signature Certificates. The DGFT offers a 50% discount on application licence fees for any application made online using (n)eXIM.

❀ Finance may be arranged in any of the two stages: pre-shipment and post-shipment depending on the requirement of funds to the exporter.

❀ The exporter must arrange freight forwarders and the cargo to be shipped with their assistance.

REVIEW QUESTIONS (SHORT)

1. Discuss briefly the significance of export decisions.
2. Explain the procedure to be followed for obtaining the IE Code number.
3. Explain the procedure of registration with Export Promotion Council.
4. What is an Identity Card in exporting? As an exporter, how would you obtain it?
5. What are the important clauses of an export contract?
6. Can an invoice do the function of a packing list? Explain your point.

REVIEW QUESTIONS (DETAILED)

1. As an exporter, what are the steps you would follow in the process of exporting?
2. How would you make your decision to export?
3. What is an IEC number? Explain the procedure of obtaining it. Which categories of exporters/importers are exempted from obtaining it?
4. What is packing list? How would you prepare it?
5. Explain in detail the contents of an export contract.

REFERENCES

1. Asia-Pacific: A Small Business Guide to Exporting, A note on *Deciding to Export*.
2. www.dca.nic.in or www.mca.gov.in

5

EXPORT PROMOTION SCHEMES

LEARNING OBJECTIVES

To know about various schemes of the Indian Government available to promote exports of the country, viz.

* Duty Drawback Scheme

* Duty Exemption Schemes

* Duty Remission Schemes

* Export Promotion Capital Goods Scheme

* ASIDE

* "Served from India" Scheme

KEY TERMS

* EXIM policy
* Duty drawback scheme
* All Industry Rate (AIR)
* Brand rate
* Duty exemption scheme
* Standard input-output norms (SIONs)
* Advance licences
* Export obligation (EO)
* Duty remission scheme
* DFRC scheme
* DEP scheme
* DEPB scheme
* Present Market Value (PMV)
* EPCG scheme
* Special economic zones
* Export-oriented units
* Domestic Tariff Area (DTA)
* Service exports
* Agri export zone
* Status holders
* Quantitative restrictions

INTRODUCTION

The new Foreign Trade Policy was announced on August 27, 2009. This FTP shall cover a 5-year period of 2009–2014. Several new announcements were made to give a fillip to Indian foreign trade which has been showing poor performance for the last 10 months of fiscal year 2008–09. Of course, this is mainly due to the economic melt down experienced by developed economies of the world. The Government of India took note of this trend and made necessary changes in its foreign trade policy announcement. Let us now discuss briefly the important export promotion schemes under the banner of the Government.

DUTY DRAWBACK (DBK) SCHEME

Under the Duty Drawback Scheme, relief of customs and central excise duties, paid on the inputs used in the manufacture of export product, is allowed to exporters. The admissible duty drawback amount is paid back to exporters by depositing it into their nominated bank accounts. Section 75 of the Customs Act, 1962 and Section 37 of the Central Excise Act, 1944, empower the Central Government to grant such duty drawback. Customs and Central Excise Duties Drawback Rules, 1995 have been framed outlining the procedure to be followed for the purpose of grant of duty drawback by the customs authorities processing export documentation.

Under the scheme, an exporter can opt for either All Industry Rate (AIR) of Duty Drawback Scheme or Brand Rate of Duty Drawback Scheme. Major portion of Duty Drawback is paid through AIR duty of Duty Drawback Scheme, which essentially attempts to compensate exporters of various export commodities for average incidence of customs and central excise duties suffered on the inputs used in their manufacture. Brand rate of duty drawback is granted in terms of rules 6 and 7 of Customs and Central Excise Duties Drawback Rules, 1995 in cases where the export product does not have any AIR or duty drawback rate, or where the AIR duty drawback rate notified is considered by the exporter, insufficient, to compensate for the customs/central excise duties suffered on inputs used in the manufacture of export products. For goods having an AIR, the brand rate facility to particular exporters is available only if it is established that the compensation by AIR is less than 80% of the actual duties suffered in the manufacture of the export goods.

Duty Drawback facilities on re-export of duty paid goods is also available in terms of Section 74 of Customs Act, 1962. Under this Scheme, part of the customs duty paid at the time of import is remitted on re-export of the goods subject to identification and prescribed procedure being followed.

SCHEME FOR ALL INDUSTRY RATE (AIR) OF DUTY DRAWBACK

The government of India announces on May 31 every year, the rates of Duty drawback in respect of scheduled items. All such rates are called All Industry Rates (AIR). The rates indicated custom and excise duty allocation. These rates are generally made effective for one year from June 1 each year. In case duty drawback rates are not announced for a product, then the exporter can submit an application in the prescribed form for determination of specific rate of duty drawback for the particular product. Such a rate is known as Brand rate. If the rate of duty drawback is less then 80% of the duties paid then the exporter can apply for its upward revision in the prescribed form.

All Industry Rates (AIRs) of Duty Drawback for a large number of export products are notified every year by the Government after an assessment of average incidence of customs and central excise duties suffered on inputs utilised in the manufacture of export products. This facility is generally availed by the exporters as no proof of actual duties suffered on inputs used is required to be produced.

After the announcement of the Union Budget every year, new AIRs of drawback are notified every year usually with effect from 1st of June, after factoring in the changes in duty rates effected by the budget. The Directorate of Drawback requests all Export Promotion Councils and Associations to collect, collate and furnish representative data in respect of the existing export products as also for any new product which the Councils feel have sufficient export from the country. After the announcement of the Budget, various Export Promotion Councils/Associations are also consulted by the Joint Secretary (Drawback), and their suggestions as well as their requests and justification for suitable enhancement of rates and also any changes sought in the scheme of the Drawback Table or the entries therein are taken note of while finalising and announcing new AIRs.

The AIRs are generally fixed as a percentage of FOB price of export product. Often very good export prices are obtained for a product or class of products—which have no co-relation with the actual duties suffered on inputs used—which is sought to be refunded to exporters as drawback. In order to safeguard Government revenue and also be fair to exporters, reasonable duty drawback conditions have been imposed in respect of many export products having rates on FOB basis. These caps essentially reflect the average duty incidence suffered on the inputs used in the manufacture of the particular goods exported by several exporters with different prices and they are fixed on the basis of data supplied by the export promotion councils and collected by Directorate from other sources.

The duty drawback claim scrutiny, sanction, and payment in 23 Customs Houses are now done through the Electronic Data Interchange (EDI) System. This system facilitates credit/disbursal of drawback within 72 hours from the date of shipment and electronic filing of Export General Manifest (EGM) in respect of related aircraft/vessel, directly to the exporter's, accounts in the specified bank branches.

BRAND RATE OF DUTY DRAWBACK SCHEME

In respect of export products where AIR of duty drawback is not notified or where the AIR of duty drawback is considered by the exporter to be insufficient to fully neutralise incidence of duties suffered on the inputs utilised in the production/manufacture of the export product, the exporters opt for Brand Rate Duty Drawback Scheme. Under this Scheme, the exporters are compensated by paying the amount of customs and central excise duty incidence which is actually incurred on the inputs used in the manufacture of export products. For this purpose, the exporter has to produce documents/proof about the actual quantity of inputs utilised in the manufacture of export product along with evidence of payment of duties thereon.

The exporter has to make an application to the Directorate of Drawback in the prescribed format along with enclosures (in the form of 3 drawback statements called DBK-I, II and III), within 60 days from the date of export of goods. The application has to be submitted to the Directorate of Drawback with copies to the concerned Central Excise Commissionerate which has jurisdiction over the factory of production of export product. The Central Excise Authorities conduct verification of the authenticity/fact of utilisation of inputs/payments of duties on the inputs on the basis of records maintained by the factory of the exporter, current production of identical goods, if being effected, and the like. A verification report has to be sent to the Directorate of Drawback. The Directorate of Drawback, on the basis of verification report and other relevant documents submitted by the exporter, processes and issues drawback Brand Rate Letter to the exporter on the basis of which the concerned Customs House (from where the goods were exported) makes payment of duty drawback. The Brand Rate Letter may be valid for particular export shipment or series of shipment and may also be extended for future shipments for one or more ports on request, subject to proof of availability of related raw materials and duty evidence, etc., when verification was carried out.

SIMPLIFIED SCHEME OF BRAND RATE

Under Brand Rate of Duty Drawback Scheme, a "Simplified Scheme" is also available to limited companies and registered partnership firms. Under this Scheme, a rate letter for duty drawback is issued prior to receipt of verification report from the jurisdictional central excise authorities on the basis of application made by the exporter subject to certain certification. For this purpose, besides application in the prescribed format along with enclosures, the exporter is also required to submit Chartered Accountant/Chartered Engineer's certificate about the authenticity of consumption pattern and duty payments as claimed. An indemnity bond undertaking to pay back the duty drawback being claimed by him, if it is found later on verification that the drawback amount paid to him is in excess of the admissible amount, has also to be furnished. In all cases where duty drawback is paid under Simplified Scheme, after receipt of the verification report from jurisdictional Central Excise Authority, the veracity of the application is counter checked with the said verification report and recovery action taken, wherever found necessary.

Section 74—Drawback

In case of goods which were earlier imported on payment of duty and are later sought to be re-exported within a specified period, customs duty paid at the time of import of the goods with certain cut can be claimed as duty drawback by the exporter at the time of export of such goods. Such duty drawback is granted in terms of Section 74 of the Customs Act, 1962 read with Re-export of Imported Goods (Drawback of Customs Duty) Rules, 1995. For this purpose, at the time of import, the identity particulars of the goods are recorded at the time of examination of import goods; at the time of export, cross verification of the goods under export is done with the help of related import documents to ascertain whether the goods under export are the very ones which were imported earlier.

Where the goods are not put into use after import, 98% of duty drawback is admissible at the maximum under Section 74 of the Customs Act, 1962. In cases where the goods are put into use in India after import (and prior to its export), duty drawback is granted on a sliding scale basis depending upon the extent of use of the goods. No duty drawback is available if the goods are put into use for a period exceeding 36 months after import. Application for duty drawback is required to be made within 3 months from the date of export of goods.

Limitations on Drawback Admissibility

The Customs Act lays down certain limitations and conditions, which exporters claiming drawback have to meet/fulfil. Thus, no drawback is admissible under Section 75 if the market price is less than the amount of drawback claimed. Drawback is also not admitted if the claim **is less than** ₹50/– in individual shipments.

The government has powers to deny or admit drawback claim subject to laid down conditions where there is likelihood of goods exported being smuggled back. These powers are used for exports to Nepal where normal provisions of duty drawback are not applied. The Drawback Rules also lay down in Rule 8, some further limitations, where the rate is less than 1%, and this may be referred to. The government has also powers to deny drawback facility in such cases where export of goods is less than the value of imported material used in their manufacture. If necessary, certain minimum value addition over the value of imported materials can also be prescribed before granting drawback.

It is also pertinent to note that the drawback is permitted to encourage exports and essentially there must be export proceeds repatriation. Though prior repatriation of export realisation is not a prerequisite, the law prescribes that if sale proceeds are not received within the stipulated period, the drawback paid will be recoverable by the Government as per procedure laid down in drawback.

Procedure for Claiming Drawback

Under the Duty Drawback Scheme, relief of customs and central excise duties suffered on the inputs used in the manufacture of export product is allowed to exporters. The admissible duty drawback amount is paid to exporters by depositing it into their nominated bank account. Section 75 of the Customs Act, 1962 and Section 37 of the Central Excise Act, 1944, empower the Central Government to grant such duty drawback. Customs and Central Excise Duties Drawback Rules, 1995 have been framed outlining the procedure to be followed for the purpose of grant of duty drawback (for both kinds of duties suffered) by the customs authorities processing export documentation.

The drawback on export goods, whether under AIR or Brand Rate, is to be claimed at the time of export, and requisite particulars have to be filled in the prescribed format of shipping bill/bill of export under Drawback. The triplicate copy of the Shipping Bill is treated as a claim for Drawback. The claim is also to be accompanied by certain documents as laid down in the Duty Drawback Rules. If the requisite documents are not furnished or there is any deficiency, the claim may be returned after shipment for complying with the requirements and furnishing requisite information/documents (for example, Brand Rate letter which may not be available at the time of export but becomes available after shipment).

DUTY EXEMPTION SCHEMES

Duty exemption schemes enable duty free import of inputs required for export production. Duty Exemption Schemes consist of

1.   Advance Authorisation scheme, and

2.   Duty-Free Import Authorisation (DFIA) scheme.

Advance Authorisation Scheme

An Advance Authorisation is issued to allow duty free import of inputs, which are physically incorporated in the export product (making normal allowance for wastage). In addition, fuel, oil, energy, catalysts which are consumed/utilised to obtain export product, may also be allowed. The DGFT, by means of Public Notice, may exclude any product(s) from the purview of Advance Authorisation. Duty free import of mandatory spares up to 10% of CIF value of Authorisation which are required to be exported/supplied with resultant product are allowed under Advance Authorisation. Advance Authorisations are issued for inputs and export items given under Standard Input Output Norms (SION).

These can also be issued on the basis of adhoc norms or self-declared norms as per para 4.7 of HBP volume 1. Advance Authorisation can be issued either to a manufacturer exporter or merchant exporter tied to supporting manufacturer(s) for:

1. Physical exports (including exports to SEZs); and/or

2. Intermediate supplies; and/or

3. Supply of goods to the categories mentioned in paragraph 8.2 (b), (c), (d), (e), (f), (g), (i) and (j) of FTP;

4. Supply of 'stores' on board of foreign going vessel/aircraft subject to condition that there is specific SION in respect of item(s) supplied.

In addition, in respect of supply of goods to specified projects mentioned in paragraph 8.2 (d), (e), (f), (g) and (j) of FTP, an Advance Authorisation can also be availed by a sub-contractor to such projects provided the name of subcontractor(s) appears in the main contract. Such Authorisation can also be issued for supplies made to the United Nations Organisation or under any Aid Programme of the United Nations or other multilateral agencies and which are paid for in free foreign exchange. However, Advance Authorisation for import of raw sugar, can be issued either to a manufacturer exporter or merchant exporter tied to supporting manufacturer(s). Exports can also be made by procurement of white sugar from any other factory(ies).

Advance Authorisations are exempted from payment of basic customs duty, additional customs duty, education cess, anti-dumping duty and safeguard duty, if any. However, imports for supplies covered under paragraph 8.2 (h) and (i) will not be exempted from payment of applicable anti-dumping and safeguard duty, if any.

Advance Authorisation and/or materials imported thereunder will be with actual user condition. It will not be transferable even after completion of export obligation. However, an Authorisation holder will have option to dispose off product manufactured out of duty free inputs once export obligation is completed. In case where CENVAT credit facility on inputs have been availed for the exported goods, even after completion of export obligation, the goods imported against Advance Authorisation shall be utilised only in the manufacture of dutiable goods whether within the same factory or outside (by a supporting manufacturer), for which the authorisation holder shall produce a certificate from either the jurisdictional Central Excise Superindendent or Chartered Accountant, at the option of the exporter, at the time of filing application for EODC to RA concerned. Further, the manufacturing wastes/scrap, as allowed, can be disposed off with the payment of applicable duty before fulfilment of export obligation.

Advance Authorisations necessitate exports with a minimum value addition of 15%, except for items in gems and jewellery sector, for which value addition would be as per paragraph 4A.2.1 of HBP volume 1. Exports to Special Export Zone (SEZ) Units/supplies to developers/Co-developers, irrespective of currency of realisation, would also be covered. For physical exports for which payments are not received in freely convertible currency, they shall be subject to value addition as specified in Appendix-11 of HBP volume 1. In the case of Authorisation for import of tea, the minimum value addition under Advance Authorisation shall be 50%. Similarly, in the case of spices [covered by Chapter 9 of ITC(HS)], duty free import of spices shall be permitted only for value addition purposes like crushing/grinding/sterilisation or for manufacture of oils and oleoresins and not for simple cleaning, grading, re-packing, etc.

Advance Authorisation shall be issued in accordance with policy and procedure in force on authorisation issue date. The validity period of Advance Authorisation for import shall be as prescribed in HBP volume 1.

Free of cost supply by foreign buyer   Facility of Advance Authorisation shall also be available where some or all inputs are supplied free of cost to the exporter by a foreign buyer. In such cases, for calculation of value addition, notional value of free-of-cost inputs along with value of other duty-free inputs shall be taken into consideration. However, if all inputs are supplied free of cost, the exporter shall also have an option to follow the provisions prescribed by DoR.

Export obligation   The period for fulfilment of export obligation under Advance Authorisation shall be as prescribed in HBP volume 1.

Provision for BIFR units   Any firm/company registered with BIFR or any firm/company acquiring a unit, which is under BIFR shall be allowed Export Obligation Period (EOP) extension as per rehabilitation package prepared, subject to approval of BIFR or 5 years if not specified, without payment of composition fee. The provisions stated above also apply to SSI units as per rehabilitation scheme of the concerned state government.

Advance authorisation for annual requirement   Advance Authorisation can also be issued for annual requirement. The Status Certificate holders and all other categories of exporters having past export performance (in the preceding two years) shall be entitled for Advance Authorisation for annual requirement. Entitlement in terms of CIF value of imports shall be up to 300% of the FOB value of physical export and/or FOR value of deemed export in preceding licensing year or ₹1 crore, whichever is higher.

Advance release orders (ARO) and invalidation letter   The holders of Advance Authorisation, Advance Authorisation for Annual Requirement and Duty Free import Authorisation intending to source inputs from indigenous sources/State Trading Enterprises, in lieu of direct import, have option to source them either against Advance Release Order (ARO) or Invalidation letter denominated in free foreign exchange/Indian rupees. However, supplies may be obtained against Authorisation from EOU/EHTP/BTP/STP/SEZ units, without conversion into ARO or Invalidation letter. Transferee of DFIA shall also be eligible for ARO/invalidation letter facility. Validity period of ARO shall be as prescribed in HBP volume 1.

Back-to-back inland letter of credit   The holder of Advance Authorisation, Advance Authorisation for Annual Requirement and DFIA may, instead of applying for an ARO or Invalidation letter, avail of the facility of Back-to-Back Inland Letter of Credit in accordance with procedure specified in HBP volume 1.

Prohibited items   Prohibited items of imports mentioned in ITC(HS) shall not be imported under Advance Authorisation/DFIA. Further items reserved for imports by STEs cannot be imported against Advance Authorisation/DFIA. However, those items can be procured from STEs against ARO or Invalidation letter. STEs are also allowed to sell goods on High Sea Sale basis to holders of Advance Authorisation/DFIA holder.

In addition, STEs are permitted to issue "No Objection Certificate (NOC)" for import by advance Authorisation/DFIA holder. The Authorisation Holder would be required to file quarterly returns of imports effected against such NOC to concerned STE which would, in turn, submit half-yearly import figures of such imports to the concerned administrative department for monitoring with a copy endorsed to the DGFT. Similarly, prohibited items of exports mentioned in ITC (HS) shall not be exported under Advance Authorisation/DFIA scheme. Export of restricted items shall be subject to all conditions or requirements of export authorisation or permission, as may be required, under Schedule II of ITC (HS).

Admissibility of drawback   In the case of an Advance Authorisation, drawback shall be available for any duty paid material, whether imported or indigenous, used in goods exported, as per drawback rate fixed by DoR, Ministry of Finance (Directorate of Drawback). Drawback allowed shall be mentioned in the Authorisation.

DUTY-FREE IMPORT AUTHORISATION (DFIA) SCHEME

A DFIA is issued to allow duty free import of inputs, fuel, oil, energy sources, catalyst which are required for production of the export product. The DGFT, by means of a public notice, may exclude any product(s) from the purview of DFIA. This scheme has been in force from May 1, 2006.

Entitlement   The provisions of paragraph 4.1.3 of the Handbook of Procedures (volume 1) shall be applicable in case of DFIA. However, these Authorisations shall be issued only for products for which Standard Input and Output Norms (SION) have been notified. In the case of post export DFIA, a merchant exporter shall be required to mention only name(s) and addresses of manufacturer(s) of the export product(s). The applicant is required to file application to the concerned RA before effecting exports under DFIA. Pre-export Authorisation shall be issued with actual user condition and shall be exempted from payment of basic customs duty, additional customs duty/excise duty, education cess, anti-dumping duty and safeguard duty, if any. In case of actual user DFIA and where CENVAT credit facility on inputs have been availed for the exported goods, even after completion of export obligation, the goods imported against such DFIA shall be utilised in the manufacture of dutiable goods whether within the same factory or outside (by a supporting manufacturer).

Value addition   A minimum 20% value addition shall be required for issuance of such authorisation, except for items in gems and jewellery sector, for which value addition would be as per paragraph 4 A.2.1 of HBP volume 1. There are some items for which higher value addition is prescribed under Advance Authorisation Scheme.

Export obligation   Procedure and time period related to fulfilment of Export Obligation have been laid down in Chapter 4 of HBP volume 1.

Transferability   Once export obligation has been fulfilled, a request for transferability of Authorisation or inputs imported against it may be made before the concerned RA. Once, transferability is endorsed, the Authorisation holder may transfer DFIA or duty free inputs, except fuel and any other item(s) notified by the DGFT. However, for fuel, import entitlement may be transferred only to companies which have been granted authorisation to market fuel by Ministry of Petroleum and Natural Gas of Government of India. Once transferability is endorsed, imports/domestic procurement against authorisation or transfer of imported inputs/ domestically procured inputs shall be subject to payment of applicable additional customs duty/excise duty. While endorsing transferability, authorisation would bear a note as to liability of such additional customs duty/excise duty. However, in case where CENVAT facility has not been availed, exemption from additional customs duty/excise duty would be available even after endorsement of transferability on DFIA. Wherever SIONs prescribe actual user condition and in case of Acetic Anhydride, Ephedrine and Pseudo-Ephedrine, DFIA shall be issued with actual user condition for these inputs and no transferability shall be allowed for these inputs even after fulfilment of export obligation. However, for authorisations issued prior to 1 April, 2007, exemption from Additional Customs Duty/Excise Duty shall continue to be available even after endorsement of transferability as provided in the FTP (RE–2006).

CENVAT facility   The CENVAT credit facility shall be available for inputs either imported or procured indigenously.

DUTY REMISSION SCHEMES

A Duty Remission Scheme enables post export replenishment/remission of duty on inputs used in export product. Duty Remission Schemes consist of:

1. Duty Entitlement Passbook (DEPB) Scheme and
2. Duty Drawback (DBK) Scheme.

DUTY ENTITLEMENT PASSBOOK (DEPB) SCHEME

The objective of DEPB is to neutralise the incidence of customs duty on import content of an export product. Component of customs duty on fuel (appearing as consumable in the SION) shall also be factored in the DEPB rate. Component of Special Additional Duty shall also be allowed under DEPB (as brand rate) in the case of non-availing of CENVAT credit. Neutralisation shall be provided by way of grant of duty credit against export product. An exporter may apply for credit, at specified percentage of FOB value of exports, made in freely convertible currency. In the case of supply by a DTA unit to a SEZ unit/SEZ Developer/ Co-Developer, an exporter may apply for credit for exports made in freely convertible currency or payment made from foreign currency account of SEZ Unit/SEZ Developer/Co-Developer. In addition, the exporter shall also be entitled for DEPB benefit in case payment is made in Indian Rupees by SEZ Developer/Co-Developer for supplies received w.e.f 10.2.2006. Credit shall be available against such export products and at such rates as may be specified by the DGFT by way of public notice. Credit may be utilised for payment of customs duty on freely importable items and/or restricted items. The DEPB Scrips can also be utilised for payment of duty against imports under the EPCG Scheme. Further, the DEPB Scrips can also be used/ debited towards payment of customs duty, in the case of EO defaults for Authorisations issued under Chapters 4 and 5 of this Policy. However, penalty/interest shall be required to be paid in cash.

Prohibited items of exports mentioned in ITC (HS) Book (as amended from time to time) shall not be entitled for DEPB credit except for the exports effected under transitional facility, wherever allowed, in terms of paragraph 1.5 of FTP. The DEPB holder shall have option to pay additional customs duty in cash as well.

DEPB rates   Export of cotton yarn including Melange Yarn shall not be entitled for DEPB benefit from immediate effect. For Fish, Crustaceans, Molluscs, Aquatic, Invertebrates and any Aquatic Animal product of marine or fresh water origin in live or chilled or dried form, including Ornamental Fish and any Aquatic Animal product of marine or fresh water origin, the DEPB rate is 4 and the value cap is US $ 2.85 per Kg. (when in dried form). For all other products/commodities, the old rates will prevail unless otherwise stated or amended from time to time.

Validity   The validity period of DEPB for import shall be as prescribed in HBP volume 1.

Transferability   DEPB and/or items imported against it are freely transferable. Transfer of DEPB shall however be for import at specified port, which shall be the port from where exports have been made. Imports from a port other than the port of export shall be allowed under TRA facility as per terms and conditions of DoR notification.

Applicability of drawback   Additional customs duty/excise duty and special additional duty paid in cash or through debit under DEPB may also be adjusted as CENVAT Credit or Duty Drawback as per DoR rules.

Duty Drawback (DBK) Scheme

Duty Drawback Scheme has been discussed in this Chapter as the first export promotion scheme.

EXPORT PROMOTION CAPITAL GOODS (EPCG) SCHEME

Let us study the various schemes under the EPCG Scheme.

ZERO DUTY EPCG SCHEME

Zero duty EPCG scheme allows import of capital goods for pre-production, production and post-production (including CKD/SKD thereof as well as computer software systems) at zero Customs duty, subject to an export obligation equivalent to 6 times of duty saved on capital goods imported under EPCG scheme, to be fulfilled in 6 years reckoned from Authorisation issue-date. The scheme will be available for exporters of engineering and electronic products, basic chemicals and pharmaceuticals, apparels and textiles, plastics, handicrafts, chemicals and allied products and leather and leather products; subject to exclusions as provided in HBP volume 1. Validity period for import of capital goods and provision for extension in export obligation period will be as separately provided in the HBP volume 1. All other provisions pertaining to concessional 3% duty EPCG scheme, to the extent they are not inconsistent with the above provisions of zero duty EPCG scheme, shall be applicable to the zero duty EPCG scheme also. The zero duty EPCG scheme will be in operation till 31 March 2011.

CONCESSIONAL 3% DUTY EPCG SCHEME

Concessional 3% duty EPCG scheme allows import of capital goods for pre-production, production and post-production (including CKD/SKD thereof as well as computer software systems) at 3% customs duty, subject to an export obligation equivalent to 8 times of duty saved on capital goods imported under EPCG scheme, to be fulfilled in 8 years reckoned from Authorisation issue date. In the case of agro units, and units in cottage or tiny sector, import of capital goods at 3% Customs duty shall be allowed subject to fulfilment of export obligation equivalent to 6 times of duty saved on capital goods imported, in 12 years from Authorisation issue-date.

For SSI units, import of capital goods at 3% customs duty shall be allowed, subject to fulfilment of export obligation equivalent to 6 times of duty saved on capital goods, in 8 years, from Authorisation issue-date, provided the landed c.i.f value of such imported capital goods under the scheme does not exceed ₹50 lakhs and total investment in plant and machinery after such imports does not exceed SSI limit. However, in respect of EPCG Authorisation with a duty saved amount of ₹100 crore or more, export obligation shall be fulfilled in 12 years. In case CVD is paid in cash on imports under EPCG, incidence of CVD would not be taken for computation of net duty saved, provided the same is not CENVATed. Capital goods shall include spares (including refurbished/reconditioned spares), tools, jigs, fixtures, dies and moulds. Second hand capital goods, without any restriction on age, may also be imported under EPCG scheme.

However, import of motor cars, sports utility vehicles/all purpose vehicles shall be allowed only to hotels, travel agents, tour operators or tour transport operators and companies owning/operating golf resorts, subject to the condition that:

1. Total foreign exchange earning from hotel, travel and tourism and golf tourism sectors in current and preceding three licensing years is ₹1.5 crore or more;

2. 'Duty saved' amount on all EPCG Authorisations issued in a licensing year for import of motor cars, sports utility vehicles/all purpose vehicles shall not exceed 50% of average foreign exchange earnings from hotel, travel and tourism and golf tourism sectors in the preceding three licensing years;

3. Vehicles imported shall be so registered that the vehicle is used for tourist purpose only. A copy of the registration certificate should be submitted to the concerned RA as a confirmation of import of vehicle. However, parts of motor cars, sports utility vehicles/all purpose vehicles such as chassis cannot be imported under the EPCG Scheme. Import of restricted items of imports mentioned under ITC (HS) shall only be allowed under EPCG Scheme after approval from EFC at headquarters.

Spares (including refurbished/reconditioned spares), moulds, dies, jigs, fixtures, tools, refractory for initial lining and catalyst for initial charge for existing plant and machinery (imported earlier, under EPCG or otherwise) shall be allowed to be imported under the EPCG scheme, subject to an export obligation equivalent to 50% of the normal export obligation prescribed above (for import of capital goods), to be fulfilled in 8 years (6 years for zero duty EPCG scheme), reckoned from Authorisation issue date. This would however be subject to the condition that the c.i.f. value of import of the above spares will be limited to 10% of the value of plant and machinery imported under the EPCG scheme. In the case of plant and machinery not imported under the EPCG scheme, c.i.f. value of import of the spares and so on will be limited to 10% of the book value of the plant and machinery.

EPCG for Projects

An EPCG authorisation can also be issued for import of capital goods under the scheme for project imports notified by the Central Board of Excise and Customs under S.No.441 of Customs Exemption Notification No. 21/2002 dated 01.03.2002. Export obligation for such EPCG authorisations would be eight times (6 times for zero duty EPCG scheme) of duty saved. Duty saved would be the difference between the effective duty under aforesaid Customs Notification and concessional duty under the EPCG Scheme.

EPCG for Retail Sector

To create modern infrastructure in retail sector, concessional duty benefits under EPCG scheme shall be extended for import of capital goods required by retailers having minimum area of 1000 sq. metres. Such retailer shall fulfil export obligation, that is, 8 times of duty saved, in 8 years.

Eligibility   EPCG scheme covers manufacturer exporters with or without supporting manufacturer(s)/vendor(s), merchant exporters tied to supporting manufacturer(s) and service providers. Export Promotion Capital Goods (EPCG) Scheme also covers a service provider who is designated/certified as a Common Service Provider (CSP) by the DGFT or State Industrial Infrastructural Corporation in a Town of Export Excellence subject to provisions of Foreign Trade Policy/Handbook of Procedures with the following conditions:

1. An EPCG licence to be given to the CSP should have a clear endorsement giving the details of the users and the quantum of Export Obligation (EO) which each user would fulfil;

2. Such exports will not count towards fulfilment of other specific export obligations; and

3. Each one of the users of the CSP apart from the CSP should furnish 100% bank guarantee (BG) equivalent to their portion of duty foregone apportioned in terms of quantum of EO to be discharged by them and the BG will be enforced in the event of the obligation not being fulfilled.

Conditions for import of capital goods   Import of capital goods shall be subject to Actual User condition till export obligation is completed.

Export obligation   The following conditions shall apply to the fulfilment of the export obligation:

- Export obligation shall be fulfilled by export of goods manufactured/services rendered by the applicant. Export obligation under the scheme shall be, over and above, the average level of exports achieved by him in the preceding three licensing years for the same and similar products within the overall export obligation period including extended period, if any; except for categories mentioned in paragraph 5.7.6 of HBP volume 1. Such average would be the arithmetic mean of export performance in the last three years for the same and similar products provided that Premier Trading House (PTH) shall have option of fixing average level of exports based, on arithmetic mean of export performance in the last five years instead of three years. Up to 50% export obligation may also be fulfilled by exports of other good(s) manufactured or service(s) provided by the same firm/company, or group company/managed hotel, which has the EPCG authorisation. However, EPCG authorisation issued prior to 1 April 2008 will be governed by earlier policy provisions. However, in such cases, additional export obligation imposed shall be over and above average exports achieved by the unit/ company/group company/managed hotel in preceding three years for both the original and the substitute product(s)/service(s), despite exemptions in Para 5.7.6 of HBP volume 1.

- The shipments under Advance Authorisation, DFRC, DFIA, DEPB or Drawback scheme, or incentive schemes under Chapter 3 of FTP would also count for fulfilment of EPCG export obligation.

- An export obligation can also be fulfilled by the supply ITA-I items to DTA, provided realisation is in free foreign exchange.

- Exports shall be physical exports. However, deemed exports shall also be counted towards fulfilment of export obligation, along with usual benefits available under paragraph 8.3 of FTP. Royalty payments received in freely convertible currency and foreign exchange received for research and development services shall also be counted for discharge under EPCG. Payment received in rupee terms for port handling services, in terms of Chapter 9 of FTP shall also be counted for export obligation discharge.

Provision for BIFR units   Any firm/company registered with BIFR or any firm/company acquiring a unit, which is under BIFR, may be allowed export obligation extension, as per rehabilitation package prepared by operating agency and approved by BIFR/Rehabilitation Department of State Government, up to 12 years if not specified. These provisions apply also to SSI units as per rehabilitation scheme of concerned State government.

EPCG for agro units   LUT/Bond or 15% bank guarantee(as applicable) may be given for EPCG authorisation granted to units in Agri Export Zones provided EPCG authorisation is taken for export of primary agricultural product(s) notified in Appendix 8 or their value added variants.

Indigenous sourcing of capital goods and benefits to domestic suppliers   A person holding an EPCG authorisation may source capital goods from a domestic manufacturer. Such domestic manufacturer shall be eligible for deemed export benefit under paragraph 8.3 of FTP. Such domestic sourcing shall also be permitted from EOUs and these supplies shall be counted for purpose of fulfilment of positive NFE by said EOU as provided in Para 6.9 (a) of FTP.

Fixation of export obligation   In case of direct imports, export obligation shall be reckoned with reference to actual duty saved amount. In case of domestic sourcing, export obligation shall be reckoned with reference to notional customs duties saved on FOR value.

Technological upgradation of existing EPCG machinery   EPCG authorisation holders can opt for technological upgradation of existing capital goods imported under EPCG authorisation. Conditions governing technological upgradation of existing capital goods are as under:

- Minimum time period for applying for technological upgradation of existing capital goods imported under EPCG is 5 years from authorisation issue date.

- Minimum exports made under old capital goods must be 40% of total export obligation imposed on first EPCG authorisation.

- Export obligation would be re-fixed such that total export obligation mandated for both capital goods would be sum total of 6 times of duty saved on both the capital goods, to be fulfilled in 8 years from new authorisation issue-date.

- Facility for technological upgradation shall be available only once and the minimum imports to be made shall be at least 10% of the existing investment in plant and machinery by applicant.

- Capital goods to be imported must be new and technologically superior to earlier capital goods.

Incentives for fast track companies   To incentivise fast track companies with a view to accelerate exports, in cases where an authorisation holder has fulfilled 75% or more of specific export obligation and 100% of Average Export Obligation till date, if any, in half or less than half the original export obligation period specified, remaining export obligation shall be condoned and the authorisation redeemed by RA concerned.

ASSISTANCE TO STATES FOR DEVELOPING EXPORT INFRASTRUCTURE AND ALLIED ACTIVITIES (ASIDE)

The Scheme for Assistance to States for Developing Export Infrastructure and Allied Activities (ASIDE) is formulated to involve the states in the export effort by providing assistance to the state governments for creating appropriate infrastructure for the development and growth of exports. The scheme is administered by the Department of Commerce (DoC). The objective of scheme is to establish a mechanism for involving the state governments to participate in funding of infrastructure critical for growth of exports by providing export performance linked financial assistance to them. The activities aimed at development of infrastructure for exports can be funded from the scheme, provided such activities have overwhelming export content and their linkage with exports is fully established.

The specific purposes for which funds allocated under the scheme can be sanctioned and utilised are as follows:

1. Creation of new Export Promotion Industrial Parks/Zones (SEZs/Agri Business Zones) and augmenting facilities in the existing ones;

2. Setting up of electronics and other related infrastructure in export conclave;

3. Equity participation in infrastructure projects including the setting up of SEZs;

4. Meeting requirements of capital outlay of EPIPs/EPZs/SEZs;

5. Development of complementary infrastructure such as, roads connecting the production centres with the ports, setting up of Inland Container Depots and Container Freight Stations;

6. Stabilising power supply through additional transformers and isolation of export production centre, and so on;

7. Development of minor ports and jetties to serve export purpose;

8. Assistance for setting up common effluent treatment facilities; and

9. Any other activity as may be notified by DoC.

SERVED FROM INDIA SCHEME (SFIS)

Objective The objective of this scheme is to accelerate growth in export of services so as to create a powerful and unique "Served From India" brand, instantly recognised and respected world over.

Eligibility All Indian Service Providers, of services listed in Appendix 10 of HBP volume 1, who have free foreign exchange earning of at least ₹10 Lakh in preceding financial year/ current financial year shall qualify for Duty Credit Scrip for Individual Indian Service Providers, minimum free foreign exchange earnings would be ₹5 Lakh.

Ineligible services and service providers Services and service providers as listed in Para 3.6.1 of HBP volume 1 shall not be entitled for benefits under the SFIS scheme.

Entitlement All service providers shall be entitled to Duty Credit Scrip equivalent to 10% of free foreign exchange earned during current financial year.

Eligible remittances Free foreign exchange earned through international credit cards and other instruments as permitted by the RBI for rendering of service, shall also be taken into account for computation of Duty Credit Scrip

Imports allowed Duty Credit Scrip may be used for import of any capital goods including spares, office equipment and professional equipment, office furniture and consumables that are otherwise freely importable and/or restricted under ITC (HS). Imports shall relate to any service sector business of applicant. Utilisation of Duty Credit Scrip earned shall not be permitted for payment of duty in the case of import of vehicles, even if such vehicles are freely importable under ITC (HS). In the case of hotels, and clubs having residential facility of minimum 30 rooms, golf resorts and stand-alone restaurants having catering facilities, Duty Credit Scrip may also be used for import of consumables including food items and alcoholic beverages.

Non-transferability Entitlement/goods (imported/procured) shall be non-transferable (except within group company and managed hotels) and be subject to Actual User condition.

Procurement from domestic sources Utilisation of Duty Credit Scrip shall be permitted for payment of excise duty in terms of DoR notification issued in this behalf for procurement from domestic sources, of items permitted for imports under SFIS Duty Credit Scrip.

SUMMARY

The Government of India has been executing several schemes for encouraging exports including the following:

- Duty Drawback Scheme
- Duty Exemption Scheme
- Duty Remission Scheme
- Export Promotion Capital Goods Scheme
- ASIDE
- "Served from India" Scheme

REVIEW QUESTIONS (SHORT)

1. What is Duty Drawback Scheme?

2. State the procedure briefly for claiming duty drawback.

3. What is Duty Exemption Scheme?

4. What is DFRC Scheme?

5. What is DEPB Scheme?

6. What is Export Promotion Capital Goods Scheme?

7. State briefly the concessions enjoyed by the units in Special Economic Zones.

8. State briefly the concessions enjoyed by export-oriented units.

9. State the incentives offered to service exports.

10. What do you mean by ASIDE?

REVIEW QUESTIONS (DETAILED)

1. Explain the provisions of the Duty Drawback Scheme.

2. Explain the provisions of the Duty Exemption Scheme.

3. Explain the provisions of the Duty Remission Scheme.

4. Write an essay on export promotion schemes of the Government of India.

REFERENCES

1. Handbook of Export-Import Procedures Vol.1 (2009–14).
2. www.dgft.org
3. www.tradejunction.apeda.com/ready%20reckoner/duty_drawback_schem.aspx
4. www.kolkatacustoms.gov.in/drawback-introduction.html
5. www.smeindia.net/export_schemes
6. www.smeindia.net/export_schemes
7. www.smeindia.net/export_schemes
8. www.exim-policy.com/Duty_Exemption_Remission_Scheme.html
9. www.ganatragroup.net/foreigntrade.html
10. www.exim.locateindia.com/.../export-promotion-capital-goods.html
11. www.mit.gov.in/.../schemes-and-policies-electronic-hardware-dpl-schemes
12. www.simexindia.com/EPCG_Scheme_Eligibility.php
13. www.foreign-trade.in/.../Chapter-3-Promotional-Measures.html

IMPORT POLICY AND PROCEDURES

LEARNING OBJECTIVES

After reading this chapter, you will be able to

* be thorough with the import policy of the Government.

* understand fully the steps involved in the process of import.

* recognise the significance of sufficient knowledge about Letter of Credit.

* become aware of the procedure followed for grant of import licence.

* know the legal provisions regarding imports by post and courier, imports for personal use and import of samples and computer/ computer software.

KEY TERMS

* Prohibited list
* Restricted list
* Canalised list
* Grievance redressal mechanism
* Import licence
* Uniform customs and practice
* Hedging
* Documents against payment (D/P)
* Documents against acceptance (D/A)
* Cash against documents (CAD)
* Postal imports
* Forex remittances
* TT selling rate
* TT buying rate
* Prototype import

INTRODUCTION

The economic needs of the country, effective use of foreign exchange and industrial as well as consumer requirements are the basic factors which influence India's import policy. On the import side, the policy has three objectives:

1. To make necessary imported goods more easily available, including essential capital goods for modernising and upgrading technology.

2. To simplify and streamline procedures for import licensing.

3. To promote efficient import substitution and self-reliance.

There are only four prohibited goods under the new import policy: tallow fat, animal rennet, wild animals and unprocessed ivory. There is also a restricted list, but most of the restrictions are on the grounds of security, health and environmental protection or because the goods are reserved for production by small and micro enterprises, which are home-based or village-based and which require low skills and employ a large number of people. But the policy of restricting import of consumer goods is changing. The Indian government's policy is to achieve, through a series of progressive steps, the average tariff levels prevalent in the ASEAN region. The basic customs tariff rate now ranges from 0 to 40% plus additional duty of 2%; the average rate is about 30%. Imports are allowed free of duty for export production under a duty exemption scheme. Input-output norms have been specified for more than 4200 items. These norms specify the amount of duty-free import of inputs allowed for specified products to be exported. There are no quantitative restrictions on imports of capital goods and intermediates. Import of second-hand capital goods is permitted provided they have a minimum residual life of 5 years. There is an Export Promotion Capital Goods (EPCG) Scheme under which the exporters are allowed to import capital goods (including computer systems) at concessionary customs duty, subject to fulfilment of specified export obligations. Service industries enjoy the facility of zero import duty under the EPCG Scheme. Likewise, hospitals, air cargo, hotels, and other tourism-related industries can make use of the Scheme. Software units can use data communication network to export their products.

IMPORTANT PROVISIONS OF IMPORT POLICY

Let us see briefly the important provisions of the new import policy of the Government of India.

1. *Exports and imports free*   Unless regulated, exports and imports shall be free, except in cases where they are regulated by the provisions of this policy or any other law for the time being in force. The item-wise export and import policy shall be, as specified in ITC (HS), published and notified by Director General of Foreign Trade, as amended from time to time.

2. *Compliance with laws* Every exporter or importer shall comply with the provisions of the Foreign Trade (Development and Regulation) Act, 1992, the Rules and Orders made thereunder, the provisions of this Policy and the terms and conditions of any licence/certificate/permission granted to him, as well as provisions of any other law for the time being in force.

3. *Restricted goods* Any goods, the export or import of which is restricted under ITC (HS) may be exported or imported only in accordance with a licence/certificate/permission or a public notice issued in this behalf.

4. *Importer–exporter code number* No export or import shall be made by any person without an Importer–Exporter Code (IEC) number unless specifically exempted. An Importer–Exporter Code (IEC) number shall be granted on application by the competent authority in accordance with the procedure specified in the Handbook (Vol.1).

5. *Actual user condition* Capital goods, raw materials, intermediates, components, consumables, spares, parts, accessories, instruments and other goods, which are importable without any restriction, may be imported by any person. However, if such imports require a licence/certificate/permission, the actual user alone may import such goods, unless the actual user condition is specifically dispensed with by the licensing authority.

6. *Second hand goods* All second hand goods, excepting second hand capital goods, shall be restricted for imports and may be imported only in accordance with the provisions of this Policy, ITC(HS), Handbook (Vol.1), Public Notice or a licence/certificate/permission issued in this behalf. Import of second hand capital goods, including refurbished/reconditioned spares, shall be allowed freely.

7. *Import of samples and gifts* Import of samples shall be governed by the provisions given in the Handbook (Vol.1). Import of gifts shall be permitted where such goods are otherwise freely importable under this Policy. In other cases, a Customs Clearance Permit (CCP) shall be required from the DGFT.

8. *Import on export basis* New or second hand capital goods, equipments, components, parts and accessories, containers meant for packing of goods for exports, jigs, fixtures, dies and moulds may be imported for export without a licence/certificate/permission on execution of Legal Undertaking/Bank Guarantee with the Customs Authorities provided that the item is freely exportable without any conditionality/requirement of licence/permission as may be required under ITC (HS) Schedule II.

9. *Import of goods used in projects abroad* After completion of the projects abroad, project contractors may import, without a licence/certificate/permission, used goods including capital goods provided they have been used for at least one year.

10. *Clearance of goods from customs* The goods already imported/shipped/arrived, in advance, but not cleared from customs may also be cleared against the licence/certificate/permission issued subsequently.

11. *Private/public bonded warehouses for imports*   Private/public bonded warehouses may be set up in the Domestic Tariff Area as per the terms and conditions of notification issued by Department of Revenue. Any person may import goods except prohibited items, arms and ammunition, hazardous waste and chemicals and warehouse them in such private/public bonded warehouses. Such goods may be cleared for home consumption in accordance with the provisions of this policy and against licence/certificate/permission, wherever required. Customs duty as applicable shall be paid at the time of clearance of such goods. If such goods are not cleared for home consumption within a period of one year or such extended period as the custom authorities may permit, the importer of such goods shall re-export the goods.

12. *Registration-cum-Membership Certificate*   Any person, applying for (i) a licence/certificate/permission to import export, [except items listed as restricted items in ITC (HS)] or (ii) any other benefit or concession under this policy shall be required to furnish Registration-cum-Membership Certificate (RCMC) granted by the competent authorities (EPCs/Commodity Boards) in accordance with the procedure specified in the Handbook of Procedures (Vol. 1) unless specifically exempted under the Policy.

13. *Grievance Redressal Mechanism*   In order to facilitate speedy redressal of grievances of trade and industry, a new grievance redressal mechanism has been put into place by a Government Resolution. The office of the Director General of Foreign Trade has opened a chat window on its website for interacting with the trade and industry to reply to queries on the Foreign Trade Policy. This web-based interface would be held from 3.00 pm to 5.00 pm on the second Wednesday of every month.

14. *EPCG Scheme*   The scheme allows import of capital goods for pre-production, production and post-production (including CKD/SKD thereof as well as computer software systems) at 5% customs duty subject to an export obligation equivalent to 8 times of duty saved on capital goods imported under EPCG scheme to be fulfilled over a period of 8 years reckoned from the date of issuance of licence. Capital goods would be allowed at 0% duty for exports of agricultural products and their value added variants.

However, in respect of EPCG licences with a duty saved of ₹100 crore or more, the same export obligation shall be required to be fulfilled over a period of 12 years.

In case CVD is paid in cash on imports under EPCG, the incidence of CVD would not be taken for computation of net duty saved provided the same is not cenvated. The capital goods shall include spares (including refurbished/reconditioned spares), tools, jigs, fixtures, dies and moulds. EPCG licence may also be issued for import of components of such capital goods required for assembly or manufacture of capital goods by the licence holder. Second hand capital goods without any restriction on age may also be imported under the EPCG scheme. Spares (including refurbished/reconditioned spares), tools, refractories, catalyst and consumable for the existing and new plant and machinery may also be imported under the EPCG scheme.

However, import of motor cars, sports utility vehicles/all purpose vehicles shall be allowed only to hotels, travel agents, tour operators or tour transport operators whose total foreign exchange earning in current and preceding three licencing years is ₹1.5 crore. However, the parts of motor cars, sports utility vehicles/all purpose vehicles such as chassis cannot be imported under the EPCG.

Spares (including refurbished/reconditioned spares), tools, spare refractories, catalyst and consumable for the existing plant and machinery may also be imported under the EPCG scheme subject to an export obligation equivalent to eight times of duty saved to be fulfilled over a period of 8 years reckoned from the date of issuance of licence.

An EPCG licence can also be issued for import of capital goods for supply to projects notified by the Central Board of Excise and Customs under S. No. 441 of Customs Exemption Notification No. 21/2002 dated 1 March 2002 wherein the basic customs duty on imports is 10% with a CVD of 16%. The export obligation for such EPCG licences would be eight times the duty saved. The duty saved would be the difference between the effective duty under the aforesaid Customs Notification and the concessional duty under the EPCG Scheme.

The scheme covers manufacturer–exporters with or without supporting manufacturer(s)/vendor(s), merchant exporters tied to supporting manufacturer(s) and service providers.

15. *Export-oriented units*   An EOU/EHTP/STP/BTP unit may import and/or procure from DTA or bonded warehouses in DTA/international exhibition held in India without payment of duty, all types of goods, including capital goods, required for its activities, provided they are not prohibited items of import under the ITC (HS). Any permission required for import under any other law shall be applicable. The units shall also be permitted to import goods including capital goods required for the approved activity, free of cost or on loan/lease from clients. The import of capital goods will be on a self certification basis. Second hand capital goods, without any age limit, may also be imported duty free.

Other entitlements of EOU/EHTP/STP/BTP units are as under:

    i. Exemption from payment of Income Tax as per the provisions of Section 10A and 10B of Income Tax Act will be given.

    ii. Exemption from industrial licensing for manufacture of items reserved for SSI sector will be given. An Offshore Banking Unit will extend credit on the same terms and conditions as extended to units to SEZ. Export proceeds will be realised within 12 Months.

    iii. They will be allowed to retain 100% of its export earning in the EEFC account.

    iv. The units will not be required to furnish bank guarantees at the time of import or going for job work in DTA, where the unit

       ○ has a turnover of rupees 5 crore or above,

       ○ has been in existence for at least three years, and

       ○ is having an unblemished track record.

   v.   100% FDI investment permitted through automatic route similar to SEZ units.

IMPORT PROCEDURE

With the globalisation of Indian economy and consequent upon comfortable balance of payment position, the Government of India has liberalised the Import Policy and practically all controls on imports have been lifted. Imports may be made freely except to the extent they are regulated by the provisions of Import Policy or by any other law for the time being in force.

Imports into India are governed by Foreign Trade (Development and Regulation) Act 1992. Under this act, imports of all goods are easy, except for the items regulated by the policy or any other law for the time being in force. The present import policy and procedures in respect of various commodities/category of importers, are, inter alia, contained in the following publications issued by the Ministry of Commerce and revised from time to time:

1. Import–Export Policy, 1997–2002 as modified up to 31 March 1999.

2. Handbook of Import–Export Procedures (Volume 1), 1997–2002 as modified up to 31 March 2000.

3. Handbook of Import–Export Procedures: (Volume 2) Input-Output and Value Addition Norms, 1997–2002.

4. ITC (HS) Classification of Import and Export Items.

5. Handbook of Export–Import Procedures (Volumes I and II) 2004–2009.

6. Handbook of Export–Import Procedures (Volumes I and II) 2009–2014.

Notifications and circulars   The Import–Export Policy and Procedure books issued by the government are amended/clarified/explained by the Ministry of Commerce from time to time. The types of notifications/clarifications/instructions issued by the ministry for this purpose are:

   i. Public Notices,

  ii. Notifications, and

 iii. Policy Circulars.

Let us now study the procedure to be followed for importing goods from abroad.

Select the Commodity/Product You Wish to Import

The importer must be aware of the import potential and the commercial viability of the commodity/product. He must check whether the items of his interest fall in the restricted list of ITC (HS) Classifications of Exports and Imports items. Prohibited items are not permitted to be imported at all. List of prohibited items of import are:

- ✪ Tallow, fat or oils rendered, unrendered or otherwise of any animal origin, animal rennet and wild animals including their parts and products and ivory and products, including ivory.

- ✪ For import of items appearing in the restricted list, the importer needs to secure import licence. The third category of items comes under the canalised list of items. Import of items included in the canalised list is permitted to be imported through canalising agencies.

Thus items not appearing in the prohibited list, restricted list, and/or in the canalised list can be imported freely without any import licence. A large number of consumer goods are freely importable without licence.

Registering with Regional Licencing Authority and Obtaining IEC No.

Registration with Regional Licensing Authority is a pre-requisite for import of goods. The customs will not allow clearance of goods unless the importer has obtained IE Code Number from Regional Licensing Authority. However, no such registration is necessary for persons importing goods from/to Nepal, provided the value of a single consignment does not exceed ₹25000/-.

An application for grant of IEC Code Number should be made in the prescribed proforma given at Appendix 3.1. of the Handbook of Export–Import Procedures. The application duly signed by the applicant should be supported by the following documents:

1. A bank receipt (in duplicate)/demand draft for payment of the fee of ₹1000/-.

2. A certificate from the banker of the applicant firm as per Annexure 1 to the form.

3. Two copies of passport size photographs of the applicant, duly attested by the banker of the applicant.

4. A copy of card containing Permanent Account Number issued by Income Tax Authorities.

5. If the PAN has not been allotted, a copy of the letter of legal authority may be furnished.

6. If there is any non-resident interest in the firm and NRI investment is to be made with repatriable benefits, full particulars thereof along with a photocopy of RBI's approval.

7. If there is NRI investment without repatriation benefit, a simple declaration indicating whether it is held with the general/specific permission of the RBI on the letter head of the firm should be furnished. In the case of specific approval, a copy may also be furnished.

8. A declaration by the applicant that the proprietor/partners/directors of the applicant firm/company, as the case may be, are not associated as proprietor/partners/directors with any other firm/company. The IEC No. is allotted with a condition that he can export only with the prior approval of the RBI.

The importer should apply for allotment of the IEC No. However, only one IEC No. is allotted to a company and the same is valid for all its branches/offices/units. The application for grant of the IEC No. should be made to the Regional Licensing Authority concerned. The application fee shall be deposited by way of deposit in an authorised branch of Central Bank of India indicating the head of Account 1453 Foreign Trade and Export Promotion Minor Head 102/Import Licence Application Fee.

The IEC No. is likely to be granted within 3 days of the receipt of the complete application and requisite documents.

How to Fill up IEC Application?

1. An application form should be made in the prescribed form in duplicate along with the enclosures, just listed, also in duplicate.

2. The form should be neatly typed/handwritten in bold capital letters only.

3. Each copy of the application form should be signed in ink by the authorised person.

4. Items of information relevant to applicant should only be filled and remaining items may be marked not applicable.

5. Modification of particulars of the applicant should also be furnished on this form by filling the relevant items.

However, in case an IE Code holder no longer wishes to operate under the allotted code number, the matter should be brought under the notice of the Regional Licensing Authority (RA) to make the Code number inoperative.

Profile of the Exporter/Importer in a Given Format

Each importer/exporter shall be required to file importer/exporter profile once with the Regional Authority in Part 1 of "Aayaat Niryaat Form (ANF) 2A". The Regional Authority shall enter the information furnished in Part 1 of "Aayaat Niryaat Form (ANF) 2A" in their database so as to dispense with the need for asking the repetitive information. In case of any change in the information given in Part 1 of "Aayaat Niryaat Form (ANF) 2A", importer/ exporter shall intimate the same to the Regional Authority.

Procedure to be Followed for Grant of Import Licence

An application for grant of an import licence or CCP for import of the items mentioned as restricted for import in ITC (HS) Classification of Export and Import items may be made to the regional licensing authority concerned.

Fees for Licence Application

Every application for import licence or CCP should be accompanied by 2 copies of a bank receipt from the Central Bank of India or a bank draft from any bank indicating the deposit in accordance with the prescribed scale of fees.

i. ₹200 where the value of goods specified does not exceed ₹50,000.

ii. ₹2 per thousand or part thereof subject to a minimum of ₹200 and a maximum of ₹1,50,000, where the value of goods exceeds ₹50,000.

iii. ₹200 where application is filed for SSI units where the c.i.f. value of goods specified in the application does exceed ₹2 lakh.

iv. ₹200 where application is for grant of duplicate licence.

Licensing Conditionalities

The licence for import is taken into consideration provided,

1. the goods covered by the licence shall not be disposed off except in accordance with the provisions of the EXIM Policy, 2009–2014 or in the manner specified by the licensing authority in the licence; and

2. the applicant for a licence shall execute a bond for complying with the terms and conditions of the licence.

It shall be deemed to be a condition of every licence for import that

1. no person shall transfer or acquire by transfer any licence issued by the licensing authority except in accordance with the provisions of the policy;

2. goods for the import of which a licence is granted shall be the property of the licencee at the time of import of which a licence is granted shall be the property of the licencee at the time of import and up to the time of clearance through the customs;

3. the goods for the import of which a licencee is granted shall be new goods, unless otherwise stated in the licence; and that

4. the goods covered by the licence for import shall not be exported without the written permission of the DGFT.

IMPORTER'S IDENTITY CARD

An application for issuance of an Identity Card may be made in the prescribed form to the RA. In the case of loss of an Identity Card, a duplicate card is issued.

SELECTING THE OVERSEAS SUPPLIER

Imports can be made from any country of the world except Fiji and Iraq. The information regarding overseas supplier can generally be obtained from the following sources: trade directories and yellow pages, like Singapore yellow pages, Japan yellow pages, and US yellow pages available from leading booksellers in India including consulate generals and trade representatives of various countries in India and abroad, friends and relatives in foreign countries, international trade fairs and exhibitions for which you may contact: International Trade Promotion Organisation (ITPO), Pragati Maidan, New Delhi, Chamber of Commerce, Directorate of Industries, and so on and indenting agents of foreign suppliers. The advertisement in foreign newspapers may also be useful.

CAPABILITY AND CREDITWORTHINESS OF OVERSEAS SUPPLIER

Successful completion of an import transaction will mainly depend upon the capability of the overseas supplier to fulfil his contract. The credit worthiness of the overseas supplier, his capacity to fulfil that contract, etc. should, therefore, be properly verified before entering into a contract with him. Confidential reports about the supplier may be obtained through the banks and Indian embassies abroad. Reputed overseas suppliers normally have their indenting agents with offices in India and contract can also be finalised through them for smoother operations. The importer can also take the assistance of credit information agencies for specific commercial information on overseas suppliers. They may also contact trade information centres of the country concerned.

Correct address of these agencies can be obtained from the overseas countries trade representatives posted in India.

ROLE OF AGENTS OF OVERSEAS SUPPLIERS' IN INDIA

Some overseas suppliers have appointed their agents in India. These agents procure orders from the Indian parties and arrange for the supply of goods from their principal abroad. It is advisable to import through such agents as they can be readily contacted in the case of any difficulty with regard to quality of goods, payment and documentation, and the like.

FINALISING THE TERMS OF IMPORT

This is an important subject and should be handled with extreme care and caution. It is advisable that before finalising the terms of import order, you should call for the samples or catalogue and other relevant literatures and the specification of the items to be imported. Import of samples of goods is exempt from import duties under the Geneva Convention of

7 November, 1952. Samples are subject to re-export and other conditions as specified in the Geneva Convention. Besides, vide Customs Notification No. 154/94 dated 13 July, 1994, commercial samples brought into India as personal baggage by bona fide commercial travellers and businessmen or imported into India by post or by air are exempt from the customs duty. Similarly, vide Notification No. 154/94 dated 13 July, 1994, prototype of engineering goods when imported into India as samples for executing or for use in connection with export orders are exept from customs duty. Likewise, the central government has exempted bona fide commercial samples and prototype of engineering goods when imported into India by post or by air or by courier service by manufacturers of export goods.

Once you are satisfied with the samples and the creditworthiness of the overseas supplier, you can proceed to finalise the term of the contract to be entered into. For this purpose, the import contract should be carefully and comprehensively drafted incorporating therein precise terms and all relevant conditions of the trade deal. There should not be any ambiguity regarding the exact specifications of the goods and terms of the purchase including import price, mode of payment, type of packaging, port of shipment, delivery schedule, and so on. The different aspects of an import contract are enumerated below. Some of these may be relevant and others may not be.

- Product, standards and specifications
- Quantity
- Inspection
- Total value of the contract
- Terms of delivery
- Taxes, duties and charges payable at exporting country and payable in India on importation
- Period of delivery/shipment
- Packing, labeling and marking
- Terms of payment—amount, mode and currency
- Discounts and commissions
- Licences and permits
- Insurance
- Documentary requirements
- Guarantee
- Force *majeure* or excuse for non-performance of the contract
- Remedies
- Arbitration

MODE OF PRICING AND INCOTERMS

While finalising the terms of import contract, the importer, should, inter alia, be fully conversant with the mode of pricing and the manner of payment for the imports. As regards mode of pricing, the overseas supplier normally quotes the terms prevailing in international trade. The importer for his benefits should know the meaning of the technical terminology. To avoid ambiguity in interpretation of such terms, International Chamber of Commerce, Paris has given detailed definition of a few standard terms popularly known as Incoterms. These terms have already been discussed in Chapter 3 of this book.

LETTER OF CREDIT VS BANK GUARANTEE

A letter of credit (L/C) differs from a bank guarantee. An issuing or confirming bank's obligation is independent of, and unqualified by, the contract of sale under the transaction. A commercial credit is neither a performance bond; nor it is a guarantee of the quantity or quality of the goods shipped.

The L/Cs are separate transactions. A contract for sale of goods between the seller and the buyer incorporates mode of settlement. L/Cs by their nature are separate from the sale contract, and banks are not concerned or bound by such sale contracts even if the credits bear reference to them. The credits stipulate documents which have to be tendered for payment and it, therefore follows, that in credits, parties deal with documents and not with goods, services or performances to which the documents relate. It is, therefore, in the interest of all the parties concerned that the conditions and terms of credit are complete and precise, and bereft of excessive details. Payment under an L/C does not depend on the performance obligation on the part of the exporter except those which the credit imposes. Banks accept documents under letters of credit for what those documents purport to be on their face. Contract between the buyer and the seller is obligatory between themselves. The seller (beneficiary) cannot take advantage of any contractual terms in between the buyer and the opening bank, and between the opening bank and the advising/confirming bank.

UNIFORM CUSTOMS AND PRACTICE FOR DOCUMENTARY CREDIT

In the course of time, a number of practices, expressions and terms have evolved between banks dealing with documentary credits. To ensure uniformity of interpretation in international trade, the International Chambers of Commerce in Paris has worked out the "Uniform Customs and Practice for Documentary Credit". These have been revised and brought up-to-date several times in the past. The latest revision was approved by the Banking Commission of the ICC at its meeting in Paris on 25 October, 2006. This latest version, called the UCP600, formally commenced on 1 July, 2007.

The latest revision of UCP is the sixth revision of the rules since they were first promulgated in 1933. It is the result of more than three years of work by the ICC's Commission on Banking Technique and Practice.

The UCP remain the most successful set of private rules for trade ever developed. A range of individuals and groups contributed to the current revision including: the UCP Drafting Group, which waded through more than 5000 individual comments before arriving at this final text; the UCP Consulting Group, consisting of members from more than 25 countries, which served as the advisory body; more than 400 members of the ICC Commission on Banking Technique and Practice who made pertinent suggestions for changes in the text; and 130 ICC National Committees worldwide played an active role in consolidating comments from their members.

The stated goal of the current revision has been identical to previous ones, that is, take into account the developments in banking, transportation and insurance—review the wording of the UCP to avoid differing interpretations and applications. In a note to its members and the national committees, the ICC itself labeled the new revision as "the most comprehensive in the entire history of the rules." Comprehensiveness however did not lead to substantive changes. The ICC has shortened the number of articles from 49 to 38. This change is mostly cosmetic however, since substantive changes are barely noticeable. An exception to the foregoing is the shortening of the time to examine documents from seven to five working days.

Parties to a Letter of Credit

The following persons are generally parties to a Letter of Credit:

1. *Beneficiary* The exporter of goods in whose favour the L/C has been established.

2. *Customer/importer* The person who intends to import the goods and instructs bank to establish the Letter of Credit.

3. *Issuing bank* The banker in the importer's country who opened the L/C.

4. *Correspondent bank or advising bank* The banker in the exporter's country, who is authorised by the issuing bank to advise the beneficiary of the credit and to effect such payment or to accept and pay such bills of exchange or to negotiate against stipulated documents and on compliance of stipulated terms and conditions specified by the importer on the exporter.

5. *Confirming bank* The banker in the exporter's (beneficiary) country, who at the desire of the beneficiary, adds confirmation to the letter of credit so that beneficiary can get payment without recourse from the confirming bank. The confirming bank may be a correspondent bank itself or some other bank.

Precautions to be Taken at the Time of Establishing Letter of Credit

A letter of credit (L/C) offers almost complete protection to the seller but the buyer is put to many disadvantages and has to make payments against documents only. The following precautions must be taken by the importer:

1. Before agreeing to open an L/C in favour of the seller, the opener must be satisfied with the creditworthiness and general reputation of the seller. Entire success of an L/C transaction depends on proper conduct of the seller.

2. Confidential report on the seller must be obtained at the time of first transaction with him.

3. Letter of credit also does not offer any protection for the quality/quantity of goods supplied under the L/C. It would, therefore be necessary to know the nature of goods and specify submission of quality reports/inspection reports from an independent agency to ensure receipt of goods of proper quality. This is particularly important in the case of import of chemicals and such other goods. The opener has to submit an L/C application to the opening bank.

4. The instructions contained in the L/C application are the mandate for the issuing bank and the letter of credit will be issued in accordance with this application. It is, therefore, necessary that complete and precise information must be given in the L/C application form specifying therein the description, unit rate and quantity of the goods covered under L/C and details of documents required in absolute, clear, and unambiguous terms. The reference to underlying sale contract must be avoided as far as possible. The L/C application must nevertheless contain all the required/information based on which L/C could be opened by the bank.

5. After the L/C has been issued by the bank, a copy thereof must be obtained immediately. The L/C must be scrutinised to ensure that it has been properly issued and is in conformity with L/C application. Discrepancy, if any, must be brought to the notice of opening bank immediately.

Import contract may be concluded either in terms of ₹ or in a foreign currency. Where the contracts are in ₹, the related documents are also prepared in ₹ and no conversion is involved. However, where the bill is drawn in a foreign currency, the payment is made in Indian rupees equivalent to the foreign currency. The equivalent rupee value is arrived at by applying suitable exchange rates. These rates are applied by banks to standardise the foreign exchange–rupee conversion process.

When the price of foreign currency is quoted in terms of home or local currency it is called direct quotation basis. This has been in application since 2 August, 1993.

However, there is a difference between inter-bank exchange rates and merchant rates.

    i. Merchant rates are the exchange rates applied by the bankers for transaction with their customers for various purposes, including imports and exports. These rates are calculated by the banks as per the guidelines issued by the Foreign Exchange Dealers Association of India (FEDAI).

ii.   Inter-bank rates are the rates for transactions amongst the authorised dealers in foreign exchange and depend on the market conditions. Since exchange rates are volatile, documents delivered by the bank at the time of a favourable exchange rate will enable the Indian purchaser to pay less of Indian rupees.

Forex rates are always quoted as two way price, that is, at a rate at which the bank is willing to sell foreign currency (buying rate) and at a rate at which the bank is willing to buy foreign currency (selling rate). There is always some difference in buying and selling rates. However, the maximum spread available to bank is restricted in terms of ceiling imposed by RBI. All exchange rates by authorised dealers are quoted in terms of their capacity as buyer or seller.

TT selling rate   This rate is applied for all clean remittances outside India. This rate is used for selling foreign currency to its customer by the bank such as for issuance of bank drafts, mail/telegraphic transfer, and so on.

TT buying rate   This rate is applied for purchase of foreign currency by banks when the banks in India have already obtained the cover in India. Thus all foreign inward remittances which are made payable in India are converted by applying this rate. A mail transfer issued by a bank, for instance, in Dubai, for US$ 10,000 drawn on any commercial bank having branch at the overseas destination will be converted into rupees at TT buying rate.

Reading rates   The rates announced by the banks every day morning are card rates.

Reputed importers can always bargain with the bank for improvement in the card rates for reducing their rupee liability on conversion of foreign currency into Indian rupees. Also a distinction is made between spot rates and forward rates. Spot rates are applicable on the day of transaction, whereas forward rates are fixed in advance for a transaction that will mature at a specified date or during a specified period in future imports.

Hedging against forex risk   Exchange risk arising on account of adverse movement of the exchange rates, can be avoided by

1.   requesting the supplier to invoice the goods in Indian rupees (possible only when the seller agrees to it); and

2.   entering into a forward exchange contract.

This involves booking of forward exchange contract with the bank of the importer.

For booking forward contract, the importer should approach his bank with which an L/C has been opened. The bank will book a forward contract only against genuine transaction. It will verify relevant documents to ensure the authenticity and the amount of permitted currency of the underlying transaction. The amount, date and number of the forward contract will be marked on such documents under the stamp and signature of the bank to ensure that more than one forward contract is not booked in respect of the same underlying transaction. A transaction may be covered either in parts or in whole.

The period and extent to which an exposure is to be covered is left to the choice of the customer. Ordinarily, the maturity of the forward contract matches with that of the underlying transaction. If the documents of import are not received within the agreed period of the contract, the contract needs to be cancelled (a fresh contract booked if desired) for which the bank will levy cancellation charges as per the FEDAI rules. In the case the documents are received before the stipulated date and the importer wants early delivery, the bank will again levy charges for early delivery, as per the FEDAI rules.

The importers should be careful in choosing the period of forward contract. Otherwise early delivery or cancellation of forward contract would lead to unnecessary charges. The RBI allows substitution of an import order on specific request, provided the bank is satisfied with the circumstance leading to the non-performance of the contract. Where the documents are under a contract (non-L/C case), the seller will submit the complete set of documents to his bankers with the request to either purchase/discount the documents to his banker with the request to either purchase/discount the documents or same on collection basis to the importer. In the former case, the seller's bank finances the seller whereas in the latter case, no financial facility is extended to the overseas seller. The seller's banker may advance some money against documents sent on collection basis while, treating the documents as collateral security. When the documents are under L/C, the documents are prepared strictly in conformity with the L/C.

After preparing the documents the overseas seller will tender the documents to his banker for negotiation. The bank, after receiving the documents, will examine them to ensure that they are strictly drawn as per the terms of the credit. Following this, the overseas banker will send the documents to the importer's banker in India. The importer's banker will advise the importer to collect the shipping documents either against payment or acceptance as per the terms of the contract. In case the documents are drawn under an L/C, the issuing banker (of the overseas supplier) will examine the documents and if found in order, it will hand over the same to the importer after debiting his account with the amount involved or against acceptance as per the terms of the credit.

If the documents are not in line with the terms of the credit, the overseas banker can either refuse to negotiate further and ask the seller to send them on collection basis only; or it can contact the importer's bank (in the buyer's country) for authorisation; or it can also make payment under the reserve against seller's indemnity.

Procedure for Grant of Import Licence

An application for grant of an import licence or CCP for import of the items mentioned as restricted for import in ITC (HS) Classification of Export and Import items may be made to the regional licencing authority concerned.

SCRUTINY OF DOCUMENTS

This is a very important function and this should be done with great care. After receiving the document from the overseas supplier's bank, the importer's bank will scrutinise them to verify the extent of correctness as per the terms of the L/C. For discrepancies in the documents, the following principles are adopted:

1. If the discrepancies are such which violate any of exchange control or import control regulations, the documents should straightaway be rejected.

2. If the discrepancies are of trivial nature not affecting the character of the transactions the documents may be accepted on merits.

3. If the documents are rejected, an immediate notice to that effect should be given to the bank to safeguard the importer's interests.

The documents prescribed by the beneficiary are carefully scrutinised by the issuing banker. The importer should also scrutinise the documents to ensure that

1. they were presented when the credit was in force and had not expired; the amendments and special instructions have been taken care of.

2. The amount of bill does not exceed the value of the L/C; all documents required in the L/C have been made available.

3. Documents carry required endorsements.

4. The documents do not contain discrepancies which violate any exchange control/ import control regulations.

5. The invoice is duly signed, and tallied with amount of draft, exact quantities are shown, and is drawn in appropriate currency of the origin of goods. Bill of lading is presented in full set of negotiable copies and is on board bill of lading and duly signed.

6. In the case the goods are imported on cash against documents (CAD), documents against payment (D/P) or documents against acceptance (D/A) basis, the importer needs to take delivery of documents from the banker before completion of the customs formalities. This process, known as retirement of documents, needs the importer to apply to authorised dealer/banker who is in possession of documents. This can be done by tendering the funds equivalent to the value of documents and the bank charges exchange control copy of import licence, where applicable, Form A-1 duly completed for remittance of foreign exchange.

The documents are released to the importers against payment in case of the DP bills and against acceptance in case of the DA bills. The payment in either case is accepted only from the bank account of importer. If the bank is out of funds, the interest is charged to the importer's account. For any overdue period a penal interest will be charged.

CHECKLIST FOR DOCUMENT (RECEIVED UNDER L/C) SCRUTINY

The following is a checklist for document (received under the L/C) scrutiny:

- General—check whether all documents in full sets as per the L/C terms have been received
- Documents had been presented before the expiry date
- All the documents are dated subsequent to the date of issue of the L/C
- Cancellation/overwriting in all the documents are authenticated
- Bills of Exchange—check whether drawn on the person indicated in the L/C and duly signed up by the beneficiary of the credit
- Drawing is within the L/C amount and in the same currency as per the L/C
- The amounts in words and figures are the same and identical with the amount stated in the invoice; superscription, regarding drawing under the L/C has been made and the bill must have been issued stamped
- Invoice—check whether invoice:
  - Is made out in the name of the person who opened the L/C
  - Quantity, unit price and value are quoted as per the L/C
  - Whether unit price and value are quoted as per the L/C
  - The description of the merchandise corresponds to the description in the L/C
  - The arithmetical calculations are correct
  - Import licence/OGL/Contract No./Order No./Indent No. mentioned as per the L/C
  - No charge other than stipulated in the L/C is included
- Additional copy for Exchange Control purposes is submitted
- The date and no. of the Licence/OGL indicated
- Bill of Lading is submitted within 21 days from the date of shipment, if no specific time is stipulated between the date of issue and expiry of the L/C
- The date of shipment is between the date of issue and the expiry date of the L/C
- Full quantity of goods is shipped, if part shipment is not allowed. Full set is submitted
- Freight is shown as prepaid/payable at destination, as per the L/C
- Bill of lading shows "on board shipment". Parties are notified as per the L/C terms
- Carrying vessel's name has been mentioned in the Bill of Lading
- The beneficiary's name is shown as consignor, unless the L/C terms permits third party bill of lading

- The consignee's name is as per the L/C. The B/L is manually signed
- The description of goods is consistent with the L/C
- The ports of loading/destination are mentioned as per the L/C
- Marks, numbers, quantity and weight agree with the invoice
- The carrying vessel belongs to any particular line as per the L/C
- Adequately stamped
- Properly endorsed
- If AWB, whether the flight number and the date of departure mentioned
- If freight has been added separately in invoice and no separate freight certificate of shipping company is submitted
- The B/L shows freight amount. Scrutiny for insurance documents—check whether the policy is taken out in the name of the shipper
- Certificate/policy is according to the Letter of Credit terms
- Risk commences w.e.f. date of the B/L.
- Amount of insurance as per the L/C terms
- Whether drawn in the same currency as the L/C
- Description of goods agrees with the B/L.
- Risks as per the L/C are covered
- The place where claims are payable is as per the L/C terms
- Details such as name of carrying vessel, ports of loading/destination, marks, agree with the B/L, certificate of analysis, and weighment
- The certificates are issued by the authority stipulated in the L/C
- Name of the shipper is properly shown
- The samples drawn relate to the goods actually shipped. The date of sample verification is within the date of shipment

DOCUMENTS ISSUED AND CHECKED

1. *Certificate of origin*   It is issued by the authority stipulated in the L/C. The description of goods agrees with that in the invoice.

2. *Checking other documents*   All other documents stipulated in the L/C are verified. They are issued by the authorities specified in the L/C. They contain the details as required by the L/C.

For matters relating to the documentary collections and commercial terms, the importers are likely to be conversant with the brochures issued by the International Chamber of Commerce (ICC), Paris.

TIME LIMIT FOR IMPORT REMITTANCE

The remittance against imports should be completed not later than 6 months from the date of shipment. Accordingly, deferred payment arrangements involving payments beyond 6 months are not permissible without approval of the RBI/GoI.

However, there is no objection to importers withholding a small part of the cost of the goods not exceeding 15 percent towards guarantee of performance, and so on. The authorised dealers may make remittances of amounts so withheld, provided the earlier remittance had been made through them. No interest payment should be allowed to be remitted on these withheld amounts.

Sometimes, settlement of import dues may be delayed due to disputes or financial difficulties. The authorised dealers are permitted by the RBI to make remittances in such cases even if the period of 6 months expires, provided they are satisfied about the bona fides of the circumstances leading to the delay in payment. No payment of interest is involved for the additional period. In the case where the overseas supplier insists on payment of interest, it may be allowed in accordance with the provisions contained in para 7A, 12 up to a maximum period of 60 days beyond 180 days from the date of shipment, provided the import bill is paid within that period. Remittances against import of text or other books may be allowed without restrictions as to time-limit, provided no interest payment is involved nor has the importer forgone any part of the discount/rebate normally allowed to importers towards compensation for delay in settlement of dues.

INTEREST REMITTANCE ON IMPORT BILLS

Interest accrued on usance bills under "normal interest clause" or of overdue interest paid on sight bills for a period not exceeding 6 months from the date of shipment in respect of imports may be remitted without prior approval of the RBI. In the case of pre-payment of usance import bills, remittances may be made only after reducing the proportionate interest for the unexpired portion of usance at the rate at which the interest has been claimed or the "prime" rate (or its equivalent) of the country in the currency of which the goods are invoiced, whichever is higher. Where interest is not separately claimed, remittances may be allowed after deducting the proportionate interest for the unexpired portion of usance at the prevailing prime rate. However, interest under normal interest clause would mean interest at the prime rate (or its equivalent) of the country, in the currency of which the goods are invoiced.

IMPORTER'S DOCUMENTS

The importer should comply with certain obligations, that is, he must submit the Exchange Control Copy of Bill of Entry for home consumption/postal wrappers to the authorised dealer. This will act as evidence that the goods for which the payment was made, have actually been imported into India.

The authorised dealers should ensure that in all the cases, including cases of advance remittances permitted (Vide para 7A, 10), these are submitted by their importer customers and are verified. In respect of imports made on D/A basis, since goods would normally be cleared before the due date of payment, authorised dealers should insist on production of documentary evidence of import, that is, Exchange Control Copy of Bill of Entry for home consumption/postal wrappers at the time of effecting remittance of import bill. The authorised dealers should also advise about this requirement to their importer customers in writing while delivering the documents against acceptance.

CUSTOMS CLEARANCE OF IMPORTED GOODS AT PORTS

The customs authorities and the clearing agents play the key role in the import of goods. All the goods imported into India have to pass through the procedure of customs clearance as they cross Indian border. The goods are examined, appraised, assessed, evaluated and then allowed to be taken out of charge of the customs for use by the importer. The entire process of customs clearance is complex and to carry out this procedure smoothly, the help of accredited customs clearing agents has to be sought.

The importers need to present a Bill of Entry on receipt of the advice of the arrival of the vessel. The B/E is noted in the Import Department, with corresponding endorsement made against the consignment entry in the IGM along with the date. The B/E will then be presented to the Appraising Department with all the relevant documents like invoice, Bill of Lading, Import Licence and catalogue literature. The appraising procedure may be of two types.

1. *The first check procedure*   It is applicable only when appraisers/assessing group finds it difficult to complete the assessment on the basis of the documents made available. The scrutinising appraiser in the group gives the examination order. The goods are then examined in the docks and the B/E returned to the scrutinising appraiser for completion and licence debit. In this case, the Customs "out of charge" is given by the accounts department soon after the recovery of duty.

2. *The second check procedure*   Under this 80 to 90% of the consignments are cleared.

If the documents are adequate for determining the classification, value, ITC licence, the form is completed by the appraiser and then countersigned by the assistant collector. It is then forwarded to the licence department for licensing debit and audit. Then it is returned to the importers for payment of duty in the accounts/cash department. After recovery of duty, the original B/E is retained in the accounts department and the duplicate and other copies are returned to the importer for getting the goods examined in the docks. In the docks, the shed appraiser/examiner shall examine the goods and if in order, shall give the out of charge for taking delivery from the custodian of the goods viz. port trust, after payment of port trust charges.

Irrespective of the procedure, the examination of cargo for assessment purpose is chiefly the function of the appraising department having special staff of examiners in the docks/air cargo shed. The records of the examination and weighment should be declared, attested and dated at the time of the examination. If the examination spreads over more than one day, the result on each day's progress should be disclosed.

These apart, some of the customs houses in India have introduced the simplified computer procedure for speedy clearance of consignment through B/E.

WAREHOUSING OF IMPORTED GOODS

An importer may not like to clear or may have certain problems in clearing the imported goods immediately on payment of duty for home consumption. In that case, the importer can deposit the goods in a public or private bonded warehouse, provided he is satisfied with the arrangement. Thus, the importer can avail the facility of deferring payment of duty on imported goods pending their actual clearance. Towards this the importer should file a set of yellow coloured B/E known as warehousing B/E.

POSTAL IMPORTS

Remittances against bills received for collection in respect of imports by post parcel may be made by authorised dealers, provided the goods imported are normally despatched by post-parcel. In these cases, the relative parcel receipts must be produced as evidence of dispatch through post, and on undertaking to submit importers should furnish post parcel wrappers within three months from the date of remittance. If the parcel has already been received in India, the parcel wrapper should be produced in support of the remittance application. Where goods to be imported are not of a kind normally imported by post parcel or where authorised dealer is not satisfied about the bona fides of the applications, the case should be referred to the RBI for prior approval with full particulars together with relative parcel receipts/or wrappers.

IMPORT THROUGH COURIER

As laid down by the current EXIM Policy, import of goods through courier is permitted in accordance with the Courier Imports and Exports (Clearance) Regulations, 1998. If the c.i.f. value of the consignment imported does not exceed ₹1,00,000, the relative Bill of Entry is required to be filed by the registered courier service. If the c.i.f. value is ₹1,00,000 or more, importers are to file separate B/E as in the case of other imports.

In the case of remittances for imports through courier services, the authorised dealers should ensure submission of Exchange Control Copy of Bill of Entry for home consumption in the case of imports valued at ₹1,00,000 or more.

This is not regarded as baggage for the purpose of assessment of duty and clearance thereof. The practice of charging a uniform duty on articles imported through courier has been discontinued. Imports by courier are now classified on merits in the respective customs tariff headings. The new system of assessment and clearance of goods imported by courier is now governed under the Courier Imports and Exports (Clearance) Regulations 1998.

Import Without Forex Remittances

Imports not involving foreign exchange remittance is allowed as in the following (vide Para 5.41 of the Handbook of Procedures):

- Import of items by United Nations Organisation and specialised agencies and its officials without payment of customs duty.

- Import of medical equipment by Indian doctors and professionals is allowed under the Baggage Rules, 1994.

- Goods as baggage by foreign mountaineering expedition teams and painting and other display articles, except consumables, are allowed.

- Foodstuffs and medicines by charitable organisations are also allowed.

- Import of food parcels, except alcohol and tobacco, subject to a limit of ₹1,00,000 per annum is allowed for personal consumption of foreign citizens.

- Import of free gifts and relief supplies by certain organisations/institutions, for example, Indian Red Cross Society, and National Defence Fund is allowed.

- Also import of equipments, raw-films, and the like by foreign publicists like radio, press, films, and television teams are allowed.

- Import of exhibits including construction and decorative materials required for the temporary stands of the foreign exhibitors at the exhibitions, fair or similar show or display for a period of 6 months on re-export basis is allowed provided these fairs are sponsored/approved by the Government of India in the Ministry of Commerce/ India Trade Promotion Organisation and is being held in public interest.

Import For Personal Use

Importers under this category do not need any IEC number. Import of goods by any person as passenger baggage is permitted to the extent admissible under the Baggage Rules 1994. However, quinine of more than 500 tablets or equivalent pounds powder or 100 ampules is not permissible. Also, for any tourist, articles of high value whose re-export is obligatory under the Baggage Rules shall be re-exported on his leaving India. Otherwise, those goods shall be deemed to be regarded as prohibited goods under the Customs Act, 1962.

Any type of goods for which the c.i.f. value shall not exceed ₹2,000 can also be imported through Post or otherwise for personal use, provided they are not vegetable seeds exceeding 1 pound in weight, bees, tea, books and periodicals, alcoholic beverages, consumer electronic items (save hearing aids and life-saving equipment) and items for which import is canalised under the EXIM Policy.

Nevertheless, the customs duty, as applicable, shall have to be paid. As regards the procedure for personal imports is concerned, the same may involve sending of advance remittance if required by the overseas supplier, opening of the L/C, retirement of documents and remittance of foreign exchange, customs clearance of the goods and payment of customs duty.

Import of Samples

Bona fide technical and trade samples of items, even those in the restricted in ITC (HS) Classifications of export and import items is allowed without a licence for a value not more than ₹1 lakh (c.i.f) in one consignment. Import of samples of vegetable seeds, tea, and new drugs may be made by any importer. Tea samples not above ₹2,000 (c.i.f) in one consignment is allowed without a licence by any person connected with the tea industry.

Prototype Import

This may be allowed on payment of duty without a licence to an actual user, the industry engaged in the production of or having industrial licence/LoI or research, as the case may be, provided the number of items imported does not exceed 10 in a year.

Import of Computer/Computer Software

Computers including personal computers, keyboards or monitor valued up to ₹1.50 lakh and ₹7000/- respectively can be imported freely without any licence. Computer software can also be imported freely without licence despite the fact that computer software is regarded as consumer goods.

SUMMARY

The economic needs of the country, effective use of foreign exchange, and industrial as well as consumer requirements are the basic factors which influence India's import policy. The policy of restricting import of consumer goods has been changing drastically. Unless regulated, exports and imports shall be free.

The important provisions of the import policy are related to the following:

* Exports and imports free
* Compliance of laws
* Restricted goods
* IEC Number
* Actual user conditions
* Second hand goods
* Import of samples and gifts
* Import on export basis
* Imports of goods used in projects abroad
* Clearance of goods for customs
* Private/public bonded warehouses for imports
* Registration-cum-membership certificate
* Grievance redressal mechanism
* EPCG scheme
* Export-oriented units

The procedure to be followed for importing goods from abroad are:

1. Selection of the product
2. Registration with the RA and obtaining the IEC Number.
3. Profile of the exporter/importer to be obtained in the specified format
4. Obtaining import licence
5. Obtaining importer's identity card
6. Selection of the overseas supplier
7. Finalising the terms of import

A check list is given for use by the importer for scrutiny. The import rules discussed in the chapter are:

1. Time limit for import remittance
2. Postal imports
3. Customs clearance of imported goods at ports
4. Warehousing for imported goods
5. Imports through courier
6. Imports without forex remittances
7. Imports for personal use
8. Import of samples
9. Prototype imports
10. Import of computer/computer software

REVIEW QUESTIONS (SHORT)

1. What are the import objectives of the Government?
2. List out the goods under the prohibited and restrictive lists.
3. "Exports and imports free."—What do you mean by this statement?
4. What is RCMC?
5. What is grievance redressal mechanism?
6. How would you select the commodity/product you wish to import?
7. What are the documents to be enclosed with the application for IEC No.?
8. Explain briefly the procedure followed for grant of import licence.
9. How would you select the overseas supplier?
10. Distinguish between Letter of Credit and Bank Guarantee.
11. Write short notes on the following:
    i. Warehousing of imported goods
    ii. Postal imports
    iii. Imports through Courier
    iv. Imports for personal use

Review Questions (Detailed)

1. Explain the important aspects of the import policy announced by the government in 2009.

2. Explain the procedure to be followed for import of goods in India.

3. Explain the process of finalising the terms of import.

4. Explain the significant aspects of the Letter of Credit.

5. Explain the role of customs authorities and clearing agents during clearance of imported goods at ports.

References

1. www.dgft.org

2. www.finance.indiamart.com/exports_imports/importing_india/

3. Handbook of Export–Import Procedures (Volumes I and II) 2009–2014.

4. www.iibf.org.in/scripts/pns1_ru_ucp.asp

7

INTERNATIONAL BUSINESS CONTRACTS

INTRODUCTION

International business contract is a tool for international business or international cooperation under the rule of law. However, in order to make a good or beneficial contract, the contracting parties must exert their best efforts in terms of understanding the legal culture, the legal terminologies involved, and the economic implication of the terms and conditions of the contract. In order to persuade the other contractual party to accept its own business plan, the party has to improve the skills of negotiation, sometimes making legal negotiations. It seems, therefore, necessary to understand the meaning of bargaining power, which the contractual party might or might not have.

The Latin words *Pact Sunt Servanda* meaning "the promise must be kept" have also been a maxim of international business contract. However, the business world has been rapidly changing, and this changing environment creates unfairness or unreasonableness in performing the business contract in a new or changed business environment. This implies that, whereas one party of the contract benefits under the changed environment, the other party suffers unreasonably. The question is whether such Latin norm shall still be kept or adjusted to fit the changed circumstances. Legal professionals say that the contract amendment or contract adjustment was originally implanted in keeping with the spirit of the meeting of minds between the contractual parties. However, most of the cases result in disputes rather than any harmonious contractual amendment.

When there is a successful performance of the contract by the contractual parties, the contract could be ended peacefully in a monumental tribute to international cooperation. However, the change in business environment where the contract was made might create a termination of the contract not because of a breach of trust, but because of business reasons held by the contractual parties. Sometimes the death of the contract does not necessarily mean a symbol of a sad thing or a failure of trust, because the contract had successfully fulfilled its destiny in the international business world.

TYPES OF INTERNATIONAL BUSINESS CONTRACTS

There are many types of international business contracts. Among them, the important are as follows:

1. International Sales Contracts
2. International Contracts for Distribution
3. International Contracts for Service Providers
4. International Contracts for Technology Transfer
5. International Contracts for Joint Ventures
6. International Contracts for Franchises

Let us now discuss these contracts briefly in the following sections.

INTERNATIONAL SALES CONTRACTS

These are very common forms of export contracts for goods. These contracts provide the formal written understanding between buyers and sellers in transactions for the sale and purchase of goods. In the last decade, proper international sales contracts became increasingly important, even in countries where business was traditionally done simply with a handshake. Understanding international sales contracts is vital to anyone involved in the cross-border sale or purchase of goods.

INTERNATIONAL CONTRACTS FOR DISTRIBUTION

A distributor not only possesses, but also owns title to the goods being sold, unlike a sales representative, who may possess the goods temporarily but does not own them. A distributor is usually not considered an agent of the manufacturer. He is acting on his own behalf, typically by purchasing the goods from the manufacturer, adding a profit margin, and reselling the goods. In comparison to a franchisee, a distributorship is less controlled by the manufacturer. A distributor is supplied with products, while a franchisee is supplied with an entire marketing package, business operation training, and the product line. The final contract should be reviewed by an attorney familiar with the laws of the country of both the manufacturer and the distributor because of the complexities of the relationship.

INTERNATIONAL CONTRACTS FOR SERVICE PROVIDERS

Contract management in this case is the active monitoring and control of all aspects of the relationship between the service provider/contractor and the client/customer. The aim of contract management is to ensure the delivery of a cost effective and reliable service at an agreed price and standard. It must be consistent with legal requirements and financial propriety. Effective monitoring of the contracts ensures that compliance is built-into the relationship between the contractor and the awarding body (the client/customer) at all stages of the contractual relationship.

INTERNATIONAL CONTRACTS FOR TECHNOLOGY TRANSFERS

Several major economic changes that took place worldwide have effected significant changes in the basic philosophy of international technology transfer policy, which was basically a change from "contract bargaining" to "sourcing". This, in turn, gave rise to new policy concerns in international technology transfer within a globalised economy.

Transfer of technology from its owner to other parties through licensing is an attractive alternative to exports, joint ventures and wholly-owned subsidiaries and is often a constituent of these structures. Several areas of technology may be involved such as: sale, leasing, operation and maintenance of machinery and equipment and blueprints; training and engineering assistance; supply of components and raw materials; marketing and promotion programmes; and management contracts.

International technology transfers often occur through patent and the knowhow or trade secret licensing. Patents may be obtained in all countries in which the owner anticipates that there will be parties interested in purchasing the technology.

Knowhow is the commercially valuable knowledge which may or may not constitute a trade secret and may or may not be patentable. Maintaining confidentiality of the owner's knowhow may be a critical strategy to protect the market position of the business. For example, Coca Cola has successfully protected its formula for several decades through a variety of methods. Legal protection of know-how varies from country to country. Protection of know-how involves contract, tort, and trade-secret law. Employees with access to important know-how should be bound by non-disclosure agreements. Certain industries, such as the chemical industry, rely upon trade-secret law due to the concerns over public disclosure and time limitations associated with patent rights.

INTERNATIONAL CONTRACTS FOR JOINT VENTURES

A foreign joint venture needs technical assistance and knowhow to commence operations. Licensing terms typically constitute a part of a joint venture agreement. A trade agreement may also be involved in which the licensor provides necessary supplies to the licencee or a joint venture. A form of transfer pricing may be used to mark up the price of goods to allocate revenues to preferred parties. If technology is transferred in a joint venture agreement, the agreement should specify the rights to access of the joint venture partner to sensitive technology.

In broad terms, international joint ventures can take two forms: i) contractual joint ventures (also known as unincorporated joint ventures, or consortium agreements), and ii) corporate (or, incorporated, or equity) joint ventures. The contractual joint venture is established through the direct contractual relationship of the parties and does not involve the formation of a corporate entity to operate the venture. The absence of corporate structure means that the contract documents can become very lengthy as they have to regulate the entire administration of the venture.

A corporate joint venture involves the creation of a separate corporate entity to own the assets and conduct the venture operations. The foundation documents for a corporate joint venture are of two types: the joint venture contract which expresses the intention of the parties to establish a joint venture in corporate form, and the constitutive documents (memorandum, articles of association, and so on) for incorporation required by the law with which the corporation is being established. The elements of the joint venture arrangements will be distributed between the types of documents as required by the law of incorporation.

INTERNATIONAL CONTRACTS FOR FRANCHISES

International franchising has been seriously hampered by laws and regulations which differ from country to country. In this context, the ICC Model International Franchising Contract provides franchisors and franchisees with a uniform framework for agreement within which their rights and responsibilities can be protected.

The International Chamber of Commerce Model Contract strikes a fair balance between the interests of the franchisor and franchisee and proposes to candidate franchisors and franchisees flexible drafting solutions that accurately respond to business needs, for legal certainty and compliance with common practice.

In doing so, the Contract:

1. takes into account the most commonly used clauses in franchise agreements;
2. suggests alternative clauses where no single solution is possible;
3. allows the parties to insert their own requirements on certain points;
4. provides annexes which the parties can modify without changing the basic text of the agreement;
5. provides a system to resolve disputes; and
6. includes a detailed commentary explaining the various provisions.

FORMATION OF INTERNATIONAL BUSINESS CONTRACT

Different stages of commercial negotiation can give rise to a certain number of documents which are neither offers nor contracts. Every time, it is necessary to enquire as to the legal value of these documents as they can have a legal impact. The documents can, more or less strongly, according to the legal system, on the one hand, show the intention of the parties to engage themselves and, on the other, explain to the judge, the intention of the parties in the contract which they enter into, following these negotiations.

These documents can be of a diverse nature. One can notably find the letter of intent. It is a document drawn up in long negotiations, carrying high sums. The finality of this document is generally to make known to the consignee the intention of contracting.

COMMERCIAL OFFER

At the start of every agreement, there is an offer which clearly manifests the contractor's willingness. Drafting an attractive and precise offer is therefore a key element of the sales process. Whether done under the initiative of the seller or in response to the demand of a foreign client, it comprises the first obligation of the company to supply a product or a service within defined conditions.

1. *The characteristics of the offer* The offer must be sufficiently precise, firm and without ambiguity so that its acceptance by its consignee is enough to form the contract. Its composition needs to observe a certain number of precautions as it is the basis of the sales contract.

2. *The Pro forma invoice* The most frequent support for the offer is the *pro forma invoice* which materialises the commercial offer. It is considered as an estimate which determines the large guidelines of sales. It formalises the seller's proposal and enables the potential purchaser to gain awareness of specifications relating to the offer (the amount, the terms of the order, and so on). It is also used by the purchaser to request authorisations such as import licences or the opening of documentary credit, when this payment technique is imposed by the seller. This type of document encompasses all the elements which appear in the commercial invoice: specifications relating to the product, price, methods of delivery, payment conditions. In short, this invoice binds the responsibilities and applies the seller's obligations.

3. *The acceptance of the offer* The acceptance of the offer constitutes the client's agreement and enables the sales contract to be concluded. The contract only materialises at the moment when the offer is followed by acceptance. As long as it is not in place, the offer can be retracted. An acceptance must be transmitted in written form in order for the seller to obtain a certain guarantee and provide evidence in the case of litigation. In this precise case, the acceptance takes the form of a purchase order or a contract.

Oral acceptance is not recommended in the absence of proof unless the contract is simple and will be carried out by trustworthy people and in good faith. In spite of everything, a written confirmation is always recommended. Be aware that in the case of litigation, acceptance by telex or fax does not always constitute sufficient proof. Companies can resort to standard contracts to formalise the agreement of the two parties. Standard contracts are the practical method, but they have the inconvenience of being non-negotiable. The most reliable method is to draw up contracts tailored to each client.

In some legislation, silence can be worth accepting. A prudent buyer will therefore refuse every offer carried out in negotiations in an explicit manner, or will formulate a counter-proposal.

GENERAL CONDITIONS OF EXPORT SALES

General conditions of export sales (GCES) enable companies to define their legal relations in a commercial context. They determine the rights of the seller and allow him to defend his interests towards the likely purchasers for his products. From then on, they are appropriate for each exporter. General conditions of sales are not the object of any specific regulation as such, and analyse themselves as part of the offer made to an undetermined person, to which it misses an acceptance so that a sale is definitely and satisfactorily concluded. They enable the legal framework to be defined in advance, applicable to each order which avoids having to draft contractual measures for each piece of business.

Characteristics of the GCES

They need to be drafted in a clear manner and be free of ambiguity either in the language of the buyer's country or in English. The exporter must go for the essentials and look into the most important elements such as conditions of payment, clauses connected with the regulation of disputes, extent of responsibility, and treatment of complaints.

To protect the financial interests of companies and to harmonise the commercial operations of professional organisations, international organisations (UNO in particular) have drawn up general conditions for export. The latter, which cannot be listed because they are too numerous, can be classified into three categories:

1. *From a territorial point of view*   Some of them are applied in the EU countries or in the whole of Europe, Asia, and Africa; others have a universal vocation.

2. *From a product point of view*   They are grouped according to whether they apply themselves to consumer goods, capital goods, technology transfer, and so on. They are often drawn up by professional organisations.

3. *From both territorial and sector point of view*   In this case, the GCES define the products concerned and the territorial field of their application at the same time.

Principles of Drawing up of the GCES

The following principles are to be followed while drafting international business contracts:

1. *Avoid excessive or improper clauses*   Many national legal systems forbid improper clauses which would deprive the client of all guarantee or resort in responsibility.

2. *Suiting the essentials*   General conditions must contain important arrangements relating to price, conditions of payment, the extent of the supplier's responsibility (time limit, guarantees) and to the methods of regulating disputes.

3. *Distinguishing the general from the particular*   General conditions must only normally present what is permanent and repetitive in space and time. The parameters which essentially depend on the nature of the envisaged operation must be grouped in "particular conditions".

4. *Do not hesitate to modify*   Sales conditions do not constitute an unchanging term and it can be necessary to put them in if once confronted by reality. They present weaknesses, if repetitive incidents produce themselves, notably on conditions of payment or also if modifications in the regulations have been noticed.

5. *Draw up general, legible conditions*   It is necessary to avoid very small characters or they may be subject to opposition. When general conditions are printed on the reverse of contractual documents, it is advisable to notify very apparently on the front, "see our general sales conditions on the reverse".

The GCES are subject to legal regime in the country to which you are exporting. Their interpretation therefore depends on the purchaser's country. One has to make enquiries on this subject in order to know the impact of the GCES in the purchaser's country.

ACCEPTANCE OF THE GCES

The GCES communicated from the stage of the offer enables the applicable legal system for the future contract to be defined at the earliest. If this is not the case, the seller must communicate the GCES before the contract is concluded, without what they would consider the contract as legally inefficient. Furthermore, the enumeration of general conditions on commercial invoices is legally inefficient since it intervenes after the contract has been concluded.

In law, general conditions are only applicable if the client or supplier has accepted them (expressly or tacitly). The conditions of this acceptance can vary from country to country. As long as you are the purchaser, you need to be vigilant, as in certain countries, the purchaser's silence can be seen as acceptance. For the seller, the ideal situation is where the client accepts the GCES in a formal manner, thus facilitating the proof of this acceptance. It is preferable to obtain the party's signature accompanied by the company stamp on the proforma invoice or the purchase order. Failing that, the seller can re-send an order confirmation stating the GCES.

If you are a purchaser and that you are confronted with the GCES at the time when you receive the invoice which you have not accepted, you have not even been kept informed, then you need to respond! For example, the GCES can determine a court which would not be in your interest.

GCES AND GENERAL SALES CONDITIONS

Certain countries impose general sales conditions. By nature, these conditions differ in nature, general sales conditions that protect the seller, and general purchase conditions that protect the purchaser. Furthermore, in the majority of cases, the two parties must negotiate and analyse the general conditions from the point of view of the law which governs the contract.

The problem posed here is extremely complicated. However, the following direct guidelines can be remembered:

1. General sales and purchase conditions which contradict, cancel out each other.

2. Particular clauses reserved for certain clients take precedence over general conditions.

3. Partial contradictions lead to the annulment of conflicting clauses.

4. When general purchase conditions are considered as partially acceptable, it is hoped for that the supplier sends his proposals for modifications by fixing a deadline for their acceptance in the shortest possible delay. The consignee's silence will be considered as a tacit acceptance of the recommended modifications.

5. A typed text takes precedence over a printed text as a hand-written comment takes precedence over a typed text by virtue of the principle according to which the particular conditions prevail over general conditions.

ELEMENTS OF AN INTERNATIONAL BUSINESS CONTRACT

The following items are the elements of a complete contract. While all items may not apply to every contract, referring to a checklist like this when considering a contract will help ensure that you have provided for as many contingencies as possible. Though you may not always be in a position to decide the terms of your contract, you must be aware of the key elements. You can be flexible regarding some contract terms, but there are terms that you should insist on to protect your interests.

1. Contract date

2. Identification of parties

3. Goods
    i. Description
    ii. Quantity
    iii. Price

4. Packaging arrangements

5. Transportation arrangements
    i. Carrier
    ii. Storage
    iii. Notice provisions
    iv. Shipping time

6. Costs and charges
    i. Duties and taxes
    ii. Insurance costs
    iii. Transport and handling
    iv. Terms defined

7. Insurance or risk of loss protection

8. Payment provisions

    i. Method of payment

    ii. Medium of exchange

    iii. Exchange rate

9. Import documentation

10. Inspection rights

11. Warranty provisions

12. Indemnity

13. Enforcement and remedies

    i. Time of enforcement

    ii. Modification

    iii. Cancellation

    iv. Contingencies

    v. Governing law

    vi. Choice of forum

    vii. Arbitration provisions

    viii. Severability

Legal Dimensions

In today's economy, every company is global—either operating internationally, or competing with others that do. The reality is that the legal and policy aspects of international trade and investment are critically important to every company that is serious about growth. The different stages of commercial negotiation can give rise to a certain number of documents which are neither offers nor contracts. Every time, it is necessary to enquire as to the legal value of these documents as they can have a legal impact. The documents can, more or less strongly, according to the legal system, on the one hand show the intention of the parties to engage themselves and on the other, explain to the judge the intention of the parties in the contract which they enter into following these negotiations.

Until quite recently, international sales were hardly "international" at all in legal terms: the party with the greater bargaining power, often the buyer, would generally impose its standard terms and its own national law. If the parties came from different legal cultures—for example, from civil law and common law countries—then understanding and negotiating contract terms were even more difficult. These factors did nothing to foster trust, and therefore hindered international trade development.

Fair Terms

In recent decades, however, much has been done to "level the playing field". This sporting metaphor is not entirely out of place, as it captures the effect of instruments that help contracting parties to obtain balanced and easily comprehensible contract terms.

The key initiative was the 1980 United Nations Convention on Contracts for the International Sale of Goods (CISG). The convention has been adopted by more than 50 countries (most of them in the North). For countries that have not yet adopted the convention, parties wishing to conduct international trade can still base their contract on the principles in the convention.

The CISG proposed a broadly worded standard set of rights and obligations for both buyer and seller, including the options open to them if there is a problem with the contract.

Since 1994, the CISG has been accompanied by the UNIDROIT Principles of International Contracts. This wide-ranging set of principles seeks to cover a much broader range of contracts than just sales. As with the CISG, it provides valuable assistance to a party trying to find internationally accepted wording for any given contract term.

Indeed, the CISG and the UNIDROIT are increasingly seen as tools that can be turned to at the negotiation stage when trying to counter oppressive terms proposed by the other side. Both texts can be found on the Juris International web site: http://www.jurisint.org

These instruments also help to harmonise international trade terms by reducing to a minimum the role to be played by a national system of law. In other words, if the parties use the CISG or the UNIDROIT Principles as the basis for their contract terms, then relatively little remains under the authority of national "governing law".

Box 7.1   The deal between a Belgian and a German

A Belgian made a German an irrevocable, albeit fixed-term, offer on conclusion of a licence agreement against payment of EUR 50,000. In order to save costs, the German didn't call in an attorney but simply took his specimen contract for cross-border purchase and sale of goods and modified it a bit. The contract stipulated, for example, that German law should apply to the entire business. Shortly before the deadline expired, the Belgian withdrew his contractual offer; the German, however, declared his acceptance of the offer within the deadline and now demanded payment of the contractual sum.

The German felt that he was on the safe side for he believed that he would be able to sue for the amount in a German court. To his great surprise, however, he received an official letter from Belgium a few days later. The letter read that the Belgian had filed a declaratory action against the German with the petition to have it declared that the Belgian was entitled to withdraw his offer and therefore did not owe the German EUR 50.000. It was only now that the German called in his attorney and was surprised to learn that it was already too late. Owing to an EU regulation, no action for payment of the licence sum can be filed in Germany. Since the Belgian had taken legal action in the same matter all German proceedings were on hold until the Belgian court approved of or disclaimed its jurisdiction. Meanwhile the Belgian court reviewed its jurisdiction and also noted that the licence agreement was to comply with German law. However, in this context German law also means that the international treaties shall apply that Germany signed. These treaties stipulate, among other things, where certain claims can be sued for. Since the German wanted to convince the court that the action had to be heard in a German court, he engaged the services of a Belgian attorney, whether he liked it or not, in order to argue his case in the Belgian court. In the end the Belgian court, however, came to the conclusion that the action could be filed in Belgium due to the agreement on German law.

As a result, the German could forget about his action for the recovery of money in Germany once and for all and he had to charge the Belgian attorney with his representation during the proceedings in a Belgian court. This outcome would certainly have been avoidable for the German if an attorney had been involved in the drawing up of the contract right from the start. An attorney would have told that the agreement on German law alone was not sufficient but that further restrictions would have been necessary. Besides, he would have been able to point out to the possibilities and consequences of a fast filing of an action.

The example in the Box 7.1 shows that it is not possible to adopt arrangements from other contracts, and use them to draw up a new contract. Considerable differences may arise depending on who the other party to the contract is and which type of contract it is (sale of goods, assignment of capital shares, etc.). The UN Convention on Contracts for the International Sale of Goods ("CISG"), for instance, has a limited scope of application so that it does not apply to all kinds of contracts. Moreover, the UN Convention on Contracts for the International Sale of Goods does not govern all contractual aspects so that it is necessary to fall back on national law. However, it is still unclear which national law has to be applied.

Besides, it has to be taken into account whether the other party to the contract is domiciled in an EU member state or not. In the case of non-European business partners, the respective EU regulations do, of course, not apply, unless indirectly via the respective national law. There are also dangers lurking for non-European business partners. When doing business with the EU citizens they should have it checked whether the EU law can "indirectly" be applied to the contract. This can only be checked by an attorney who works in the respective EU country for only he will know the relevant European regulations and the respective adjudication of the European Court of Justice on the interpretation of these regulations.

International business has increased and in step with it, legal problems and traps have also increased. Entrepreneurs are therefore well-advised to seek the advice of an attorney prior to international as well as national business transactions. If the attorney is well-versed, he will at the same time clarify the respective distinctive tax provisions, like for example the problems relating to turnover tax with business within or outside the European Union. Once contracts are signed or goods are delivered, it is too late to correct any mistakes made.

DISPUTE SETTLEMENT

Most international business contracts have a dispute resolution clause when the contract becomes sore or troubled because international lawyers have realised from experience that international contracts tend to produce disputes. There are two types of dispute resolution mechanisms: dispute resolution by the judiciary, and dispute resolution through mediation and arbitration. The concerned party seldom resorts to filing of suits in law courts as it is a tedious and time-consuming process.

As China achieves increasing prosperity against a background of accelerating globalisation, international trade friction is also changing. One of the most noticeable changes is that China has become one of the countries involved in frequent trade disputes along with the world's economic powers, such as the United States, Japan and the European Union. The disputes have several new features.

First, China is now subject to an increasing number of anti-dumping investigations, cases in which China is accused of selling goods at artificially low prices in order to corner a market. The number of anti-dumping investigations against China was 6.5 in each year in the 1980s. The number rose sharply to 37.6 each year in the latter half of the 1990s. It was 55,51 and 47 in 2001, 2002 and 2003 respectively. In the first nine months of 2004, Chinese commodities worth US$ 1.1 billion were involved in 46 investigations over alleged dumping and other accusations in twelve countries or regions. China suffered the most in anti-dumping investigations and anti-dumping measures of all World Trade Organization members.

Second, Chinese exports suffer from higher technological barriers. More countries are resorting to technological barriers to limit Chinese exports allegedly to protect local industries. Such barriers usually include quarantine standards, testing items, customs procedures, intellectual property rights and many other methods. According to official statistics, at least 60% of export-oriented enterprises in China have had trouble with their exports because of these technological barriers.

Third, more categories of commodities are involved in the trade conflicts. The volume of commodities involved in these investigations is swelling quickly. There is an opinion in international society that economic growth in China has changed the world's economy. Some governments even attribute the rise of unemployment in their countries to the growth of Chinese exports.

Fourth, more countries are now involved in trade disputes with China. Traditionally, trade disputes happened between China and major economic powers, especially developed countries. In recent years, China is seeing increasing conflicts with developing countries. Although these disputes involve a limited volume of commodities compared with conflict with developed countries, the number of cases is rising. The causes of this can be found in an analysis of the global trade situation. The fundamental reason for the worsening trade conflict between China and other countries is a deep-rooted preference towards trade protectionism.

It is true that most countries are following more open trade policies as a result of globalisation. But another trend is also a fact in many countries and regions: Governments are taking various measures to limit imports and encourage exports to protect their industries on the international market. Some developed countries even resort to protectionist trade policies to distract the public from their sluggish domestic economies. These tactics include technological barriers, anti-dumping investigations and special protection measures, all of which can trigger trade disputes. The second reason for this change is the concern in many countries about China's rocketing economic growth.

According to official statistics, China has seen an average growth of 14.5% of its import and export each year between 1980 and 2003. This growth rate is much higher than the country's GDP growth and the growth achieved in the world economy and international trade during the same period. Admittedly, the rocketing growth achieved by China has had an impact on the international trade pattern and the traditional export structure of some countries.

But this does not justify some countries' claims that China is the cause of problems in their own economies. Such opinions are often manipulated to benefit certain groups within the countries. Several facts have also contributed to the escalation of trade disputes. The difference between Chinese standards of quality products and those in other countries often obstructs the smooth entry of Chinese commodities into these places and even causes trade conflicts in some cases.

Another fact is that Chinese exports are usually products of industries that have comparative advantage or labour-intensive products with low added value, which often compete with many other similar products. At the same time, Chinese exports do not have diversified markets. More than three-quarters of Chinese exports are sold to the United States, Japan and EU countries. These trade disputes are expected to continue for quite some time, and are a major aspect of a world seeking to promote free trade. They will occur between developed and developing countries, as well as among developed countries themselves.

The escalation of trade disputes between China and other countries is a result of China's deepening integration into the world economy. But such disputes should be containable and should not influence the diplomatic ties China has with other countries. China is gaining more influence in regional and world economy because of its economic prosperity. Also, major economic powers, like the United States and Japan, have increasing stakes in China, which also serves to prevent disputes from becoming so severe as to destroy the ties between China and the rest of the world.

MEDIATION

In most jurisdictions, alternative dispute resolution is taken to mean only the non-adjudicative dispute resolution options, of which mediation is the most frequently used. In essence, mediation is a negotiated settlement, conducted and concluded with the assistance of a neutral third-party. The process is voluntary and does not lead to a binding decision, enforceable in its own right.

Most commercial disputes, in which it is not imperative that there should be a binding and enforceable decision, are amenable to mediation. Mediation may be particularly suitable where the parties in dispute hope to preserve, or to renew, their commercial relationships. As mediation is likely to be a shorter process than either litigation or arbitration, there may also be economic arguments for attempting a mediated settlement.

COMMENCING THE MEDIATION

Mediation is an entirely consensual process. There must be agreement to mediate, and agreement to continue to mediate once the process has begun. Parties will either have agreed to mediation in their contract, or they may agree to attempt a mediated settlement once a dispute has arisen, even when they have provided in their contract for some other form of dispute resolution, and even when they are in the course of litigation or arbitration.

THE PROCESS

Although the process should be as flexible as possible, parties often find it helpful to have the framework provided by a set of established procedures, like the London Court of International Arbitration (LCIA) mediation procedure, to bring shape and discipline to the process. The parties are free to select the mediator, though this will usually be somebody from the lists maintained by the recognised mediation organisations. All mediators must declare and maintain their independence and impartiality of the parties in dispute.

A representative of each of the parties will be confirmed as having the requisite authority to settle the dispute on behalf of that party. The representative must also have instructions as to the financial limit of his authority. The conduct of the mediation is in the hands of the parties and the mediator. However, most of the mediations take a similar form in a combination of joint sessions, with all parties and the mediator, and separate sessions, or caucuses, in which each side meets for private and confidential discussions with the mediator.

There is no set time limit for mediation, though most meetings take no more than one or two days. Parties should, however, set an overall time limit for the achievement of a mediated settlement, after which the dispute (if not settled) will be referred to an adjudicative tribunal. Unless they agree otherwise, parties are free to commence or to continue arbitration or judicial proceedings, despite having commenced, or being in the process of mediation.

However, parties may not introduce, or rely upon, anything arising out of the mediation for the purposes of any arbitration or litigation.

Concluding the Mediation

The mediation will be at an end when either a settlement or an agreement is signed by the parties, or the parties advise the mediator that it is their view that a settlement cannot be reached, or the mediator advises the parties that, in his or her judgment, the mediation process will not resolve the issues, or the agreed time limit for mediation has expired and the parties have not agreed to extend that time limit.

ARBITRATION

Arbitration is now the first-choice method of binding dispute resolution in the widest range of international commercial contracts. It is a private process requiring the agreement of the parties, which is usually given by way of an arbitration clause in the contract. If there is no contractual provision to arbitrate, a separate arbitration agreement may be entered into, once a dispute has arisen.

Arbitration offers parties the freedom to choose a method of dispute resolution tailored to their precise needs. That freedom extends to the choice of applicable law, the venue, the language, and the choice of arbitration procedures, whether under institutional rules, stand-alone procedures, like the UNCITRAL rules, or entirely ad hoc.

Parties may also choose their arbitrators, thus ensuring the constitution of a tribunal with precisely the right qualifications and experience.

It is this freedom of choice that reinforces the key elements of international arbitration: enforceability, procedural flexibility, party-control, neutrality, privacy and confidentiality, cost-effectiveness, and speed.

Let us discuss the key elements of international arbitration.

Enforcement of Awards

For the many parties for whom a final and binding settlement is paramount, the enforcement argument is, perhaps, the most persuasive and enduring. The rules of the major international arbitration institutions, including the LCIA, expressly provide that any award will be final and binding and will be complied with, without delay. By agreeing to be bound by such rules, the parties usually also exclude any right of appeal on the merits to a national court which may have jurisdiction to hear such an appeal.

In the event that a losing party, failing to comply with an award against it, enforcement may be considerably easier to achieve than would be the enforcement of the judgment of a national court in another jurisdiction. In a majority of the cases, the successful party will be able to rely on the provisions of the New York Convention, now ratified or acceded to by some 140 States.

Parties wishing to have the reassurance that an award will be enforceable must ensure that the arbitration takes place (and that the award is made) in a Convention State and that the enforcement is against assets of the losing party that are located in another Convention State.

Procedural Flexibility

Arbitration offers parties a great degree of control over the proceedings. It allows them to establish, from the outset, a method of resolving disputes which is not bound by the often rigid procedures and time-tables of the courts. Parties may agree to a wide range of procedural matters, including such key issues as the number of arbitrators and their qualifications, the venue and language of the arbitration, the time table, and the need, or otherwise, for oral hearings.

Such tailor-made dispute resolution provisions (both domestic and international) have been endorsed by the arbitration laws of many jurisdictions (in England, by the 1996 Arbitration Act) and are reflected in the rules of the major arbitral institutions.

Party-nominated arbitrators

In arbitration, parties may also choose the judges who will determine their dispute. Where they say so in their contracts, or subsequently agree, each side may nominate an arbitrator to be one of a panel of three. The third and presiding arbitrator may be nominated by the parties, or by the party-nominated arbitrators, or by the chosen arbitral institution.

Each side may satisfy itself that the arbitrator it nominates has the requisite experience and knowledge in the field relating to which the dispute has arisen. An arbitrator may also be nominated because of his or her knowledge of a particular national or state law and/or of a language pertinent to the dispute. Similarly, it may be expressly provided, or agreed by the parties, that the arbitrators should not be of the same nationality as the parties, and/or that, if two are, then the chairman will not be.

A party-nominated arbitrator is not, however, the representative of the party which nominates him. He or she must confirm and maintain his or her independence and impartiality. Where, in the interests, for example, of speed and cost saving, the parties agree on a sole arbitrator, an administering body will be able to select an arbitrator with the requisite neutrality and the relevant legal/commercial/linguistic expertise, if the parties are unable to do so.

Neutrality

Parties to international agreements may be concerned that the national courts of the party with which they are contracting may have an instinctive, or even a manifest, bias towards a party of the same nationality. Whether or not such concerns are well-founded, international tribunals and the administration of a recognised arbitral institution may be seen as offering greater neutrality than the courts.

ARBITRATION IN INDIA

The Arbitration process in India is based on the United Nations Commission on International Trade Law (UNCITRAL), the Model Law on International Commercial Arbitration. Indian law is largely based on English common law because of the long period of British colonial influence during the British rule.

The Applicable Arbitration Law

The Indian Arbitration and Conciliation Act, 1996 is the governing arbitration statute in India. It is based on the Model Law on International Commercial Arbitration adopted by the United Nations Commission on International Trade Law (UNCITRAL) in 1985. Previous statutory provisions on arbitration were contained in three different enactments, namely, the Arbitration Act, 1940, the Arbitration (Protocol and Convention) Act, 1937 and the Foreign Awards (Recognition and Enforcement) Act, 1961. The Arbitration and Conciliation Act, 1996 has repealed the Arbitration Act, 1940 and also the Acts of 1937 and 1961.

International Conventions on Arbitration

India is a party to the following conventions:

- The Geneva Protocol on Arbitration Clauses of 1923.
- The Geneva Convention on the Execution of Foreign Arbitral Awards, 1927.
- The New York Convention of 1958 on the Recognition and Enforcement of Foreign Arbitral Awards. It became a party to the 1958 Convention on 10th June, 1958 and ratified it on 13th July, 1961.

There are no bilateral Conventions between India and any other country concerning arbitration.

The Types of Arbitration

The Indian Arbitration and Conciliation Act, 1996 applies to both domestic arbitration in India and to international arbitration. Section 2(1)(f) of the Act defines "International Commercial Arbitration" as arbitration relating to disputes arising out of legal relationships, whether contractual or not, considered as commercial under the law in force in India where at least one of the parties is:

1. An individual who is a national of, or habitually resident in any country other than India; or

2. A body corporate which is incorporated in any country other than India; or

3. A company or an association or a body of individuals whose central management and control is exercised in any country other than India; or

4. The Government of a foreign country.

REQUIREMENTS OF AN ARBITRATION AGREEMENT

The law requires the following for an arbitration agreement:

1. Section 7(3) of the Act requires that the arbitration agreement must be in writing.

2. Section 7(2) provides that it may be in the form of an arbitration clause in a contract or it may be in the form of a separate agreement.

3. Under Section 7(4), an arbitration agreement is in writing, if it is contained in: (a) a document signed by the parties, (b) an exchange of letters, telex, telegrams or other means of telecommunication, providing a record of agreement, (c) or an exchange of claims and defense in which the existence of the agreement is alleged by one party and not denied by the other.

4. In section 7(5), it is provided that a document containing an arbitration clause may be adopted by "reference", by a contract in writing.

VALIDITY OF AN ARBITRATION AGREEMENT

Section 16 of the Act empowers the arbitral tribunal to rule on its jurisdiction. Under the Act, the arbitration tribunal can rule on its own jurisdiction, including ruling on any objections with respect to the existence or validity of the arbitration agreement, and for this purpose:

1. An arbitration clause which forms part of a contract will be treated as an agreement independent of the other terms of the contract.

2. A decision by the arbitral tribunal that the contract is null and void will not entail, *ipso jure*, the invalidity of the arbitration clause.

A plea that the arbitral tribunal does not have jurisdiction will, however, have to be raised not later than the submission of the statement of defense. However, a party shall not be precluded from raising such a plea merely because he has appointed, or participated in the appointment of an arbitrator. A plea that the arbitral tribunal is exceeding the scope of its authority has to be raised as soon as the matter alleged to be beyond the scope of its authority is raised during the arbitral proceedings. The arbitral tribunal may, in either of the cases referred to above, admit later a plea if it considers that the delay is justified. The arbitral tribunal has to decide on a plea about that lack of jurisdiction or about the tribunal exceeding the scope of its authority and where the arbitral tribunal takes a decision rejecting the plea, it shall continue with the arbitral proceedings and make the arbitral award. A party aggrieved by such an arbitral award is free to make an application for setting aside the award under section 34 of the Act. Section 34(2)(a) inter alia permits a challenge to an award on the above grounds.

THE LONDON COURT OF INTERNATIONAL ARBITRATION (LCIA)

The LCIA is one of the longest-established international institutions for commercial dispute resolution. It is also one of the most modern and forward-looking international courts of arbitration. Although based in London, the LCIA is a thoroughly international institution, providing efficient, flexible and impartial administration of dispute resolution proceedings for all parties, regardless of their location, and under any system of law. Its operation and outlook are geared to ensuring that the parties may have complete confidence in its international credentials and in its impartiality. The details about the LCIA may be traced here briefly.

The organisation   The LCIA operates under a three-tier structure comprising the Company, the Arbitration Court and the Secretariat. The LCIA is a non-profit company limited by guarantee. The LCIA Board of Directors (made up largely of prominent London-based arbitration practitioners) is concerned with the operation and development of the LCIA's business and with its compliance with applicable company law.

The Board does not have an active role in the administration of dispute resolution procedures, though it does maintain a proper interest in the conduct of the LCIA's administrative function.

The arbitration court   The LCIA Court is the final authority for the proper application of the LCIA Rules. Its key functions are appointing tribunals, determining challenges to arbitrators, and controlling costs. Although the LCIA Court meets regularly in plenary session, most of the functions to be performed by it under LCIA rules and procedures are performed, on its behalf, by the President, by a Vice-President or by a Division of the Court. The Court is made up of up to thirty-five members, selected to provide and maintain a balance of leading practitioners in commercial arbitration, from the major trading areas of the world, and of whom no more than six may be of UK nationality.

The secretariat   Headed by the Registrar, the LCIA Secretariat is based at the International Dispute Resolution Centre in London and is responsible for the day-to-day administration of all disputes referred to the LCIA.

The LCIA case administration is highly flexible. Computer and hard-copy files and computerised account ledgers are allotted to each case. Every case is computer-monitored, but the level of administrative support adapts to the needs and wishes of the parties and the tribunal (or ADR neutral), and to the circumstances of each case.

Casework   Many major international businesses entrust their disputes to the LCIA. Many cases are technically and legally complex and sums in issue can run into US$ billions. Parties come from a very large number of jurisdictions, of both civil law and common law traditions.

The subject matter of contracts in dispute is wide and varied, and includes all aspects of international commerce, including telecommunications, insurance, oil and gas exploration, construction, shipping, aviation, pharmaceuticals, shareholders agreements, IT, finance and banking.

LCIA dispute resolution services   The LCIA provides an extensive administration service, which is not confined to the conduct of arbitration and ADR under its own rules and procedures. It also acts as appointing authority and administrator in UNCITRAL-Rules cases and will act as fundholder for deposits filed on account of the costs in otherwise entirely ad hoc proceedings.

LCIA arbitration   The LCIA arbitration rules are universally applicable. They offer a combination of the best features of the civil and common law systems, including in particular:

- Maximum flexibility for parties and tribunals to agree on procedural matters
- Speed and efficiency in the appointment of arbitrators, including expedited procedures
- Means of reducing delays and counteracting delaying tactics
- Tribunals' power to decide on their own jurisdiction
- A range of interim and conservatory measures
- Tribunals' power to order security for claims and for costs
- Fast-track option
- Waiver of right of appeal
- Costs computed without regard to the amounts in dispute
- Staged deposits—parties are not required to pay for the whole arbitration in advance

Seat of arbitration   Although the LCIA is headquartered in London, the choice of seat, or legal place, is entirely up to the parties to decide. Parties wishing to provide for a seat elsewhere than London should not, therefore, be deterred from adopting the LCIA rules.

Parties adopting, or adapting, the LCIA's recommended clauses will, anyway, specify the seat in their contract. If they do not follow the standard wording, and cannot subsequently agree the seat, Article 16.1 of the LCIA rules provides the safety net of a London default seat, although, if the parties argue for an alternative seat, the LCIA Court will determine the issue.

Arbitrators

The LCIA has a unique database of arbitrators with the widest range of professional qualifications and expertise (legal and non-legal), guaranteeing a tribunal of the highest calibre. The database is not, however, a closed list and parties are free to nominate arbitrators who are not on the database. Similarly, the LCIA will look outside its own database when necessary.

In all cases, the LCIA Court alone may appoint arbitrators, whether or not the arbitrators are nominated by the parties, and in accordance with the following procedure:

1. The LCIA Secretariat reviews the request for arbitration and accompanying contractual documents, and the response (if any).

2. A résumé of the case is prepared for the LCIA Court. Key criteria for the qualifications of the arbitrator(s) are established and recorded.

3. The criteria are entered into the database, from which an initial list is drawn; if necessary, other institutions are consulted for further recommendations.

4. The résumé, the relevant documentation, and the names and CVs of the potential arbitrators are forwarded to the LCIA Court.

5. The LCIA Court advises which arbitrator(s) the Secretariat should contact to ascertain their readiness; the Registrar sends to those candidates an outline of the dispute.

6. When the candidate(s) indicate(s) their availability, confirm their independence and impartiality, and agree to fee rates within the LCIA's bands, the form of appointment is drafted.

7. The LCIA Court formally appoints the tribunal and the parties are notified.

THE INTERNATIONAL CHAMBER OF COMMERCE (ICC)

The Commission on Arbitration aims to create a forum for experts to pool ideas and impact new policy on practical issues relating to international arbitration, the settlement of international business disputes and the legal and procedural aspects of arbitration. The Commission also aims to examine the International Chamber of Commerce (ICC) dispute settlement services in view of current developments, including new technologies. The ICC Commission on Arbitration handles more than 500 cases each year.

The ICC Commission on Arbitration and its task forces and groups boast over 500 members from 90 countries, including partners in international law firms, in-house counsel, law professors, experts in different dispute resolution services, and trade executives in member companies and international organisations.

TASK FORCE ON GUIDELINES FOR ICC EXPERTISE PROCEEDINGS

Following the adoption by the ICC Commission on Arbitration of the revised ICC Rules for Expertise in 2003, and in an effort to try to overcome the lack of awareness surrounding the existence, techniques and requirements of expertise proceedings in the business and legal communities, the Commission on Arbitration voted to create a Task Force whose mandate is to examine this issue in detail and to produce a set of guidelines for ICC expertise proceedings.

The Guide to the ICC Rules for Expertise having been adopted by the Commission in 2004, the Task Force is presently working on the elaboration of explanatory notes for the use of experts.

The Co-Chairs have prepared an outline for the Notes entitled "Practice of Expertise in ICC Expertise Dispute Resolution". This report, which is presently being drafted by the members of the Task Force, will cover topics such as:

- Using experts in ICC Arbitration
- Using experts under the ICC Rules for Expertise as fact finders
- Neutral experts as facilitators under the ICC ADR and Dispute Board Rules.

The Task Force is composed of over 35 registered members from 14 different countries.

How does it work?

ICC, as the foremost business rule-maker for international trade, sets voluntary rules that companies from all parts of the world apply to millions of transactions every year. The rules created by the Commission on Arbitration, such as the Rules of Arbitration, the ADR Rules, the Expertise Rules and the Dispute Board Rules, have become part of the legal fabric of international commerce.

A detailed discussion of the arbitration procedures in international trade is available given in Chapter 20.

SUMMARY

- The international business contract is a tool for international business or international cooperation under the rule of law. However, in order to make a good or beneficial contract, the contracting parties must exert their best efforts in terms of understanding the legal culture, legal terminology, and the economic implications of the terms and conditions of the contract.

- There are many types of international business contracts. Among them, the important ones are:

  1. International Sales Contracts,
  2. International Contracts for Distribution,
  3. International Contracts for Service Providers,
  4. International Contracts for Technology Transfers,
  5. International Contracts for Joint Ventures, and
  6. International Contracts for Franchises.

❀ The different stages of commercial negotiation can give rise to a certain number of documents which are neither offers nor contracts. Every time, it is necessary to enquire as to the legal value of these documents as they can have a legal impact. The two important steps in the formation of the contract are: 1. Commercial Offer, and 2. Acceptance of General Conditions of Export Sales (GCES).

❀ In today's economy, every company is going global—either operating internationally, or competing with others that do. The reality is that the legal and policy aspects of international trade and investment are critically important to every company that is serious about growth.

❀ Most international business contracts have a dispute resolution clause when the contract becomes sore or troubled because international lawyers have found from experience that international contracts tend to produce disputes.

❀ There are two types of dispute resolution mechanisms: dispute resolution by the judiciary and dispute resolution through mediation and arbitration. The concerned party seldom resorts to filing of suits in law courts as it is a tedious and time-consuming process.

❀ The arbitration process in India is based on the UNCITRAL Model Law on International Commercial Arbitration. The Indian Arbitration and Conciliation Act, 1996 is the governing arbitration statute in India. It is based on the Model Law on International Commercial Arbitration adopted by the United Nations Commission on International Trade Law (UNCITRAL) in 1985.

❀ The London Court of International Arbitration (LCIA), and International Chamber of Commerce (ICC) are the other important agencies for arbitration between the aggrieved parties.

Review Questions (Short)

1. Explain briefly an international contract for distribution.

2. Explain briefly an international contract for service providers.

3. Explain briefly an international contract for technology transfer.

4. Explain briefly an international contract for joint ventures.

5. Explain briefly an international contract for franchising.

6. Explain briefly the elements of a commercial offer.

7. What do you mean by GCES?

8. What is mediation?

9. What is arbitration?

10. Explain briefly the functioning of the International Chamber of Commerce.

Review Questions (Detailed)

1. Explain briefly the different types of international business contracts.

2. Explain in detail the procedure of formation of an international business contract.

3. Explain the General Conditions of Export Sales (GCES).

4. Explain the elements of an international business contract.

5. Explain the legal dimensions of an international business contract.

6. Explain the functioning of the London Court of International Arbitration.

7. What are the key elements of international arbitration?

References

1. www.kimkimlaw.com/Contract.pdf

2. www.fukudalaw.com/International_Licensing_Transactions.html

3. www.iccwbo.org/policy/law/id275/index.html

4. www.eur-export.com/anglais/apptheo/.../formcontventea.htm

5. www.tradeforum.org/news/fullstory.php/aid/508/

6. www.kimkimlaw.com/Contract.pdf

MARKETING RESEARCH OVERSEAS

INTRODUCTION

Indian consumers today are enjoying all kinds of hi-tech and other products available across the globe. It was not the case before a few decades as far as India is concerned. The government under the leadership of Rajiv Gandhi introduced measures significantly reducing the *License Raj*, allowing businesses and individuals to purchase capital, consumer goods and import without bureaucratic restrictions. In 1986, he announced a National Policy on Education to modernise and expand higher education programmes across India. The Narasimha Rao government continued the policies of Rajiv Gandhi and decided to embark upon globalisation policy in India upon the rising capability of China due its economic liberalisation. Many people were skeptical over the government's historic decision to go ahead with economic liberalisation. The country was opened up for foreign goods and the industrialists were asked to stand on their own legs. The policy of protectionism was withdrawn and companies were asked to compete with foreign multinationals. Initially there was a big suspicion in the minds of all the stakeholders of the economy. But today, we find enormous growth in spite of the fears in the minds of the people in the initial stages of the new economic policy.

It was also partly because of the massive growth sustained by the Chinese economy which deviated from its sworn policy of communism. At that time we were all watching and wondering on Chinese development which made our political leaders think on the lines of Chinese development. Leaders began to think that when it was possible for China, why not for India. When the Chinese reforms started way back in 1978, India was slow to follow suit. Only after watching the speedy growth of the Chinese economy for more than 10 years, our leaders decided to introduce the same kind of reforms in our country. Then came the liberalisation of the economy. Today, we are enjoying the fruits of these policies. But the growth has been slow compared to China for the fact that China is a controlled economy. A controlled economy can make decisions quicker than a free economy.

Indian industries are able to successfully overcome the threats posed by their foreign counterparts and they are on the threshold of even becoming among the top twenty corporations of the world. Indian business tycoons, whether within or outside the country, are creating histories in the global business.

Unemployment among educated and qualified youth has come down sharply. In fact, employers find it difficult to find people for their factories. The recent economic melt down experienced by the G–20 nations, of course, had its spill-over effects on the Indian economy. The captains of the country believe that the effect of the global slow-down has been very less in our country. The problem in the US and other developed countries became worse and they were actually afraid whether they would be able to recover from the setback by turning the tide. However, they were able to overcome it with lot of government initiatives of hitherto unheard size.

In such a background, Indian industries have to chalk out their strategies in such a way that, what they reaped will not be lost. Perhaps the fall of industrial empires of the developed world may be said to be due to the awakening of Asian powers like India, China, South Korea and Singapore. The emerging economies of China and India have made the developed nations to revise their strategies. Economies like China and India have started wielding their economic power which was hitherto hidden like pearls. Therefore Indian industries have to be doubly cautious while framing their growth strategies. They cannot sit idle and watch the show. In fact, they must take extra care in whatever they do. Marketing research across the globe plays an important role in determining who is in need of what. The Indian Government as well as the business people must assess the market potentials beyond our frontiers and win orders from across. At the same time, they should not forget the huge Indian market while concentrating on the foreign markets.

IDENTIFYING PROSPECTIVE GLOBAL CUSTOMERS

The first thing you must do is to identify the prospective global buyers. It is necessary to find out the global trends in customer attitudes. You can collect addresses of the prospective buyers of the commodity from the following sources:

- Enquiries from friends and relatives or other acquaintances residing in foreign countries.

- Visiting/participating in International Trade Fairs and Exhibitions in India and abroad.

- Contact with the Export Promotion Councils, Commodity Boards and other Government Agencies.

- Consulting International Yellow Pages (A Publication from New York by Dun and Bradstreet, USA or other Yellow Pages of different countries like Japan, Dubai, and the like).

- Collecting addresses from various Private Indian Publications Directories.

- Collecting information from the International Trade Directories/Journals/periodicals available in the libraries of Directorate General of Commercial Intelligence and Statistics, IIFT, EPCs, ITPO etc.

- Making contacts with Trade Representatives of Overseas Government in India and Indian Trade and Other Representatives/International Trade Development Authorities abroad.

- Reading biweekly, fortnightly, monthly bulletins such as Indian Trade Journal, Export Service Bulletin, bulletins and magazines issued and published by Federation of Indian Exporters' Organisations, ITPO, EPCs, Commodity Boards and other allied agencies. A list of Indian Trade Periodicals containing names and addresses of importers is given in Embassies, Consulates, and so on of other countries and taking note of addresses of importers for products proposed to be exported.

- Advertising in newspapers having overseas editions and other foreign newspapers and magazines.

- Consulting ITPO, IIFT, and other similar organisations.

- Contacting authorised dealers in foreign exchange with whom exporter is maintaining bank account.

THE RELEVANT QUESTIONS

Why should we probe the world market? And, how should we do it? What are the hurdles we will have to face in the process? What strategies should we follow to counter them? How reliable are our market information? These are all very relevant questions that persist in the minds of the export executives. The global executive shoulders the responsibility of finding the market for his product.

Firstly, the global executive should possess the latest information on world markets. He must have the right contacts and look for valuable information from whatever source it may come from. He should keep himself abreast of changes that are taking place in the world economy.

Secondly, he should approach his problem systematically. He must, first, identify the problem. Then he must gather relevant facts. He must analyse the facts in order to find out the source of the problem. He should further move to understand the environment of the problem. A systematic approach will give him the necessary direction toward the solution to the problem.

Thirdly, the global executive must see to it that his mind is calm while dealing the matter. He should not confuse himself with several issues in mind, must take one problem at a time. This will help him to reach the point where he wanted to be. Like the rays of sun are able to make fire on a piece of paper while they pass through a lens, the global executive also can do wonders by his focussed attention to one problem.

Fourthly, the global marketing executive should turn to the advices of his superiors whenever he thinks that he is unable to spot the problem or a remedy to it. The delay in this may sometimes cost the organisation heavily. Decisions have to be timely. Belated decisions serve no purpose. Ego has no place in the minds of winning people. He goes here and there seeking clues on the problem. However, he must not become restless on any account.

Fifthly, the global marketing executive should not become panicky and try to become hateful toward his work. This will lead him nowhere. As already said, he must calm his mind by doing relaxation exercises to his body and mind. Many organisations conduct programmes to teach how to calm the body and mind. These techniques will be greatly useful to a tired manager. A few minutes in the course of his work may be spent for this. And he will see that his mind is refreshed with new energy.

WHY SHOULD WE PROBE THE WORLD MARKET?

The answer is simple. It is to attain sustainable growth of the organisation. When your organisation is a global player, you ought to see what is going on in the international environment. Therefore, it is necessary to study the global scene through an environmental scanning. No executive can afford to spend his hours wastefully when opportunities are knocking his door. He must keep things well under his control and that must be his objective. When he is unable to keep things under his control, he must go along with it up to a certain distance and his thinking faculty should be in full gear, finding the right point to deviate and succeed.

How Should We do It?

Researching to attain our objective is a task that nobody can ignore. An alert executive must chalk out his strategy to go further into the problem. Experts offer so many conventional ways of researching the market. In the modern world of information technology, many modern tools have become handy to the researcher. The point is he must conduct his research in an orderly way so that any looking back becomes unnecessary. What you find out through your research must be proportionate to the effort you put in it. Sometimes the contrary can also happen. An effective researcher restricts his area of operation and still he reveals many good findings through his research. The success lies in the way we approach the problem on hand and how we seek solutions to the problem. The problem may sometimes divert you to a wrong destination. An alert researcher finds this out cleverly and sets his path correctly. In today's knowledge-centred life, knowledge is everything. When you must delay a particular action in order to get the desired result, you have to necessarily delay it. There is no point in hurrying.

Impending Hurdles and the Strategies to Follow

Research, especially while it is world-wide, is a tough task. To an outsider, it may look to be simple and a work involving some papers, some communication, and travelling. But it is not that simple a job. The researcher in the course of his work has to face many hurdles which he can not ignore.

Firstly, the researcher must place trust in his abilities. Self distrust is the biggest enemy of the researcher and it spoils the whole thing. If the researcher is knowledgeable and caring, he can overcome this threat. Once he understands the problem in its right perspective, half of the problem is solved.

Secondly, he may ignore small things because he had already made up his mind that the problem should be a big one. Therefore when the problem appears before him from a wrong corner, he ignores it. Small things lead to big achievements.

Thirdly, the researcher disbelieves himself, when he is nearing the right solution. This disbelief is a fatal mistake committed by even talented executives. When suspicion appears before him about the solution, he must calm his mind with mind-relaxation exercises and then he must consider the merit of the solution. Now he will come to the right conclusion.

Fourthly, information may not be forthcoming. Lack of sufficient information will distort the findings. The researcher should satisfy himself about the quality and quantity of information. And, there may be many more hurdles. A researcher who knows to apply his mind will certainly identify the hurdles and win the race.

How Reliable are Our Market Information?

We may be right in every step of our approach. We might have followed the best methods for our survey. We might have employed able men to collect information. These men may be a well-motivated lot. Apart from all these things, we may have that one per cent in our mind. Even though we are ninety-nine per cent certain about an outcome, that one per cent always disturbs us. When we have adopted total quality in our process, why should we be afraid of the outcome? Given these things, the result must be highly reliable and deserves appreciation.

GLOBAL MARKETING RESEARCH

Basically, there is no difference in approach between domestic and global marketing research. Global marketing research process is same as what we follow for the domestic research. But the difference lies in the scale of operations and the expenses incurred. In the case of marketing research overseas, government assistance is sizeable. Government has several schemes for the exporters in this connection. It has its own machinery to identify markets for our products in the foreign soil. Most of the government predictions and findings are reasonably good and many manufacturers rely on government sources for market information. Export promotion councils, commodity boards, institutes like IIFT, our embassies, newspaper reports and analysis, and so on offer a good wealth of information on overseas markets. In addition to all these sources the information revolution of today has offered a very good source of market research information. The number of Internet users is constantly growing. Therefore, it is necessary that global marketers should make use of this new source.

Techniques Used

1. Qualitative research techniques offer a number of advantages in international marketing research insofar as they are unstructured and do not entail the imposition of the researcher's pre-specified conceptual model or terminology on the respondent. As a consequence, qualitative techniques are especially helpful in probing the contextual embedding of attitudes and behaviour, providing deep understanding of situational and contextual factors, and providing inputs into interpreting observed differences between countries and cultures. In addition, as qualitative techniques are often observational or unstructured, they require minimal cognitive skills, and are particularly suited to research in emerging markets. They

can also provide insights into underlying or hidden motivations as well as probing future trends and scenarios.

2. Videotaping of consumers in purchase or consumption situations can provide a rich source of information relating to the role of contextual and situational factors on consumer behaviour and response patterns in different cultures and contexts. Videotaping of consumers in an in-store environment provides a wealth of information about visual cues and their role in product evaluation not easily obtained from other forms of data collection. In some cases, in-store videotaping can be used to prompt or elicit responses from consumers. In emerging markets, videotaping of consumer usage and consumption behaviour often provides deeper understanding of how consumers use products and how these are embedded in the cultural fabric of society, as well as perceptions and associations of foreign products and brands.

3. Projective and elicitation techniques such as collages, picture completion, analogies and metaphors, psycho-drawing and personalisation can be used to encourage respondents to project their private and unconscious beliefs and personal and subjective associations. Collages were, for example, used in a study of teenagers, worldwide to explore their feelings about the future. This revealed significant differences between countries especially in terms of the degree of pessimism and hedonism. Equally, brand perceptions can be explored through personalisation, association techniques or analogies, to probe culturally embedded images and associations that vary across cultures.

At the same time, international marketing researchers will need to incorporate the latest technological developments in data collection and dissemination into the research design. These enable researchers to dramatically reduce the time required to collect data across geographic distances as well as substantially enhancing and enriching the type of stimuli that can be used in collecting data from international markets. It is, however, important to recognise that use of sophisticated technological techniques is subject to certain limitations in international markets, due either to the development of the technological infrastructure or the technological sophistication of respondents.

Advances in computer technology such as scanners, CATI (Computer Assisted Telephone Interviewing), and CAPI (Computer Assisted Personal Interviewing) are well established in the developed countries and are beginning to be used elsewhere. They provide faster, more accurate methods of data collection, providing direct input of response and facilitating steering of data collection based on response. Techniques such as CATI and CAPI can also be used to centrally administer and organise data collection from international samples, subject to telephone and computer penetration in different countries as well as use of a common language or availability of software to automatically translate questionnaires.

Overseas Marketing Research via Internet

The internet offers many advantages not only to the common man but also to large businesses. The benefits of Internet are innumerable. Manufacturers can advertise their products on the Internet and receive orders online. Many customers come to know of a product online and they make their purchase offline. Table 8.1 shows the growth statistics in India.

Table 8.1   Internet Usage and Population Statistics in India

Year	Users	Population	% Population	Usage source
1998	1,400,000	1,094,870,677	0.1%	ITU
1999	2,800,000	1,094,870,677	0.3%	ITU
2000	5,500,000	1,094,870,677	0.5%	ITU
2001	7,000,000	1,094,870,677	0.7%	ITU
2002	16,500,000	1,094,870,677	1.6%	ITU
2003	22,500,000	1,094,870,677	2.1%	ITU
2004	39,200,000	1,094,870,677	3.6%	C.I. Almanac
2005	50,600,000	1,112,225,812	4.5%	C.I. Almanac
2006	40,000,000	1,112,225,812	3.6%	IAMAI
2007	42,000,000	1,129,667,528	3.7%	IWS
2008	60,840,000	1,147,995,904	5.3%	ITU
2009	81,000,000	1,156,897,766	7.0%	ITU
2010	81,000,000	1,173,108,018	6.9%	ITU

Source: Internet Usage Statistics and Telecommunications Market Report.

India continues to be one of the fastest growing major telecom markets in the world. Sweeping reforms introduced by successive Indian governments over the last decade have dramatically changed the nature of telecommunications in the country. The mobile sector has grown more than hundred fold from 2001 to around 545 million subscribers in April 2010. Whilst GSM technology still dominates, CDMA has quickly grabbed 23% of this market. The mobile industry should continue to boom. Fixed-lines, although not as spectacular as mobiles, is growing solidly. This report presents the key measures of this dynamic market and takes a general look at the development and direction of the market. Broadband policy and other initiatives by the IT and Telecom Ministry encourage increased adoption.

Marketing Research and the Internet

Even though some people argue that Internet is not an effective tool for marketing research, it can be used effectively by a prudent researcher. The Internet has its merits as well as demerits. Internet is slow in collecting information from the prospective buyers. Response rate is low. Information is not reliable. These demerits very well apply to other marketing tools also. What we should do as researchers is to minimise the ill effects of these demerits and make the tool sensible and workable. Internet is characterised by dynamic technological developments which in turn influence the information search process.

Internet and Primary Research

E-mails are a very good source of collecting information through Internet. These mails reach the respondents in no time. It is interesting to note that e-mail users are very much concerned about the mails received by them and they open their inboxes daily to see whether they have any new mail. The Internet has an in-built system of conveying the user about new mails instantly. The Internet users are very responsible persons and we can expect that response rate as well as the accuracy of information so collected will be compared to the other traditional methods.

It must be admitted that information on the Internet, in spite of its security systems, are less secure compared to the traditional methods. It is impossible to guarantee the anonymity of e-mail responses because every e-mail includes the respondent's name and network address. Therefore, the researcher who gathers data through the internet should include a statement in the survey that explains this shortcoming to the participants. One of the limitations of online research is that the result cannot be projected to the general population because not everyone has access to a computer, modem, and online service.

Internet and Secondary Research

The internet is a wonderful source to collect secondary data with greater ease and comfort. Many researchers today opt for Internet to collect their secondary information. Internet helps to find out the activities of competitors. The internet is a prime tool for this task, as it reduces the time spent and may increase substantially the quality of information collected. Both product and financial information are probably suited best for competitive tracking. Especially larger organisations display this information most often in their websites. Information about products and companies can be obtained using search engines on the web. However, these search engines have certain limitations and hence do not guarantee that all relevant information is obtained.

How to Search Information on the Web

In order to search the Web more effectively, there are a few basic skills that you need to learn to make your searches less frustrating and more successful. Here are the top ten basic Web search skills that you need to have.

1. *Looking for a specific phrase? Use quotation marks*   Putting the search item in quotes will save time. When you use quotation marks around a phrase, you are telling the search engine to only bring forth pages that include these search terms exactly how you typed them in-order, proximity, and the like.

2. *Site search with Google*   You can use Google or any other search engine to search within a site.

3. *How to use the Inurl Syntax*   The inurl search syntax allows you to search for words within the Uniform Resource Locator (URL). This is just another interesting way to search the web and find Web sites that you might not have found by just entering in a query word or a phrase.

4. *How to search a specific domain*   If you would like to limit your searches to a specific domain, such as .edu, .org, .gov, and more, you can use the site: command to accomplish this.

5. *Search the web with toolbars*   Many people save a lot of time in their web searches by using a toolbar, which is basically a software application which gives searches the ability to perform searches and other functions quickly.

SUMMARY

* Today's consumers are enjoying all products manufactured across the globe in view of the new policies of globalisation of successive governments.

* The country was opened up for foreign manufacturers and Indian business men were asked to be ready to compete with foreign brands in the Indian market. The policy of protectionism was wholly withdrawn. However Indian industries have been able to manage the new situation in the country.

* The global marketing executive shoulders the responsibility of finding market for his products. The relevant questions that arise are: Why should we probe the world market? How should we do it? What are the impending hurdles in the process? What strategies should we follow to counter them? How reliable are the market information? All these questions have been answered in this chapter.

* There is no difference basically between domestic and global marketing research. The only difference is the scale of research and the money involved. However, most of the market information are available with government agencies like export promotion councils.

* Emphasis was given to qualitative research techniques that offer a number of advantages in international marketing research. Videotaping of consumers in purchase or consumption situations can provide a rich source of market information. International marketing researchers will need to incorporate the latest technological developments in data collection and dissemination into the research design.

* Internet offers a good opportunity to undertake global marketing research. A brief discussion is made on internet and global marketing research, internet and primary research, internet and secondary research, the method of searching information on the web, intranets, and the future of Internet.

REVIEW QUESTIONS (SHORT)

1. Discuss briefly the background of Indian entry into the global market.
2. Discuss the process of identifying the global customers.
3. Why should we probe the world market and how should we do it?
4. What are the hurdles in the process of probing world market?
5. Discuss briefly the reliability of global market information.
6. What is Internet?
7. How does Internet help in primary research?
8. How does Internet help in secondary research?

REVIEW QUESTIONS (DETAILED)

1. Discuss in detail the relevant questions in connection with marketing research overseas.
2. Discuss researching overseas market via Internet.
3. Explain the techniques used in global marketing research.

REFERENCES

1. www.indiandata.com/trade_policy/export_procedures.html
2. Barnard, P. (1997). "Global developments and future directions in marketing research," *Globalization and the Millennium: Opportunities and Imperatives, Marketing Science Institute*, June 16–17, Brussels, Belgium.
3. Craig, C.S. and Douglas, S.P. (2000). *International Marketing Research*, 2nd Edition. John Wiley and Sons, Chichester, UK.
4. www.iamai.in
5. www.internetworldstats.com/asia/in.htm
6. www.windows.microsoft.com/en-IN/windows-vista/Tips-for-searching-the-Internet

EXPORT-CENTRED GOVERNMENT INSTITUTIONS

LEARNING OBJECTIVES

To know about the functioning of the various export-centred institutions of the government. These institutions are:

* Agricultural and Processed Food Products Export Development Authority (APEDA)

* Marine Products Export Development Authority (MPEDA)

* Export Promotion Councils (EPCs)

* Federation of Indian Exporters' Organisations (FIEO)

* India Trade Promotion Organisation (ITPO)

* Board of Trade (BoT)

* Export Promotion Board (EPB)

* Commodity Boards

* Indian Institute of Foreign Trade

KEY TERMS

* APEDA
* MPEDA
* DFIA Scheme
* Standard Input and Output Norms (SION)
* Focus Market Scheme
* KALEEN
* FIEO
* Total Quality Management
* Market Development Assistance
* ITPO
* TIDCO
* EPCs
* Commodity Boards
* Prabhu Committee
* IIFT

INTRODUCTION

The significance of exports for a country is very well recognised by all the stakeholders of the nation. Nobody can question the wisdom of the government to export the surplus commodities available in the country. Exports are the basic source of goods and services that make life comfortable and meaningful. It is evident from the fact that whenever the country faces shortages of essential commodities, foreign trade comes to the rescue of the people. It must also be recognised that we must export commodities in order to import from the foreign soil. This is a kind of barter system which was prevalent before the introduction of the currency system in the world. Therefore foreign trade, in particular exports, becomes very essential for the country's development in the global arena. In inducing exports, the government plays a pivotal role. This is evident from the fact that it has established a number of organisations to boost trade with foreign countries. This section of the book studies about various export-centred government organisations which have been rendering yeoman service for developing exports from the Indian soil and enable the country to possess sufficient foreign reserves so that the country can tide over all kinds of crises the country might encounter due to shortage of commodities in the domestic market.

AGRICULTURAL AND PROCESSED FOOD PRODUCTS EXPORT DEVELOPMENT AUTHORITY (APEDA)

Agricultural and Processed Food Products Export Development Authority (APEDA) was established by the Government of India under the Agricultural and Processed Food Products Export Development Authority Act passed by the Parliament in December, 1985. The Act (2 of 1986) came into effect from 13 February, 1986 by a notification issued in the Gazette of India: Extraordinary: Part-II [Sec. 3(ii): 13.2.1986). The authority replaced the Processed Food Export Promotion Council.

FUNCTIONS

In accordance with the Agricultural and Processed Food Products Export Development Authority Act, 1985, (2 of 1986) the following functions have been assigned to the authority:

- Development of industries relating to the scheduled products for export by way of providing financial assistance or otherwise for undertaking surveys and feasibility studies, participation in equity capital through joint ventures and other reliefs and subsidy schemes.

- Registration of persons as exporters of the scheduled products on payment of such fees as may be prescribed.

- Fixing of standards and specifications for the scheduled products for the purpose of exports.

- Carrying out inspection of meat and meat products in slaughter houses, processing plants, storage premises, conveyances or other places where such products are kept or handled for the purpose of ensuring the quality of such products.

- Improving of packaging of the scheduled products.

- Improving of marketing of the scheduled products outside India.

- Promotion of export-oriented production and development of the scheduled products.

- Collection of statistics from the owners of factories or establishments engaged in the production, processing, packaging, marketing or export of the scheduled products or from such other persons as may be prescribed on any matter relating to the scheduled products and publication of the statistics so collected or of any portions thereof or extracts therefrom.

- Training in various aspects of the industries connected with the scheduled products.

- Such other matters as may be prescribed.

The APEDA is mandated with the responsibility of export promotion and development of the following scheduled products:

- Fruits, vegetables and their products

- Meat and meat products

- Poultry and poultry products

- Dairy products

- Confectionery, biscuits and bakery products

- Honey, jaggery and sugar products

- Cocoa and its products, chocolates of all kinds

- Alcoholic and non-alcoholic beverages

- Cereal, and cereal products

- Groundnuts, peanuts and walnuts

- Pickles, papads and chutneys

- Guar gum

- Floriculture and floriculture products

- Herbal and medicinal plants

- Rice (non-Basmati)

In addition to this, the APEDA has been entrusted with the responsibility to monitor exports of some non-scheduled items such as basmati rice, wheat, coarse grains and also import of sugar.

Composition of the APEDA Authority

As prescribed by the statute, the APEDA authority consists of the following members namely:

- A chairman, appointed by the Central Government.

- The agricultural marketing advisor to the Government of India, ex-officio.

- One member appointed by the Central Government representing the planning commission.

- Three members of Parliament of whom two are elected by the House of People and one by the Council of States.

- Eight members appointed by the Central Government representing respectively the Ministries of the Central Government dealing with:

  - Agriculture and rural development

  - Commerce

  - Finance

  - Industry

  - Food

  - Civil supplies

  - Civil aviation

  - Shipping and transport

- Five members appointed by the Central Government by rotation in the alphabetical order to represent the States and the Union Territories

- Seven members appointed by the Central Government representing

  - Indian Council of Agricultural Research

  - National Horticultural Board

  - National Agricultural Cooperative Marketing Federation

  - Central Food Technological Research Institute

  - Indian Institute of Packaging

  - Spices Export Promotion Council

  - Cashew Export Promotion Council.

- Twelve members appointed by the Central Government representing

  - Fruit and vegetable products industries

  - Meat, poultry and dairy products industries

- Other scheduled products industries
- Packaging industry

Two members appointed by the Central Government from amongst specialists and scientists in the fields of agriculture, economics, and marketing of the scheduled products.

The APEDA has marked its presence in almost all agro potential states of India and has been providing services to agri-export community through its head office, five regional offices and 13 virtual offices. The virtual offices have been established in association with respective State Governments/agencies. Basic information about the APEDA, its functions, registration and financial assistance schemes, and the like is being made available to entrepreneurs/prospective exporters by these virtual offices.

Appendix 12 gives the list of regional offices of APEDA. Appendix 13 gives the form of application for registration-cum-membership certificate.Appendix 14 gives registration-cum-membership certificate.

MARINE PRODUCTS EXPORT DEVELOPMENT AUTHORITY (MPEDA)

The role envisaged for the MPEDA under the statute is comprehensive—covering fisheries of all kinds, increasing exports, specifying standards, processing, marketing, extension and training in various aspects of the industry.

STRUCTURE, ACTIVITIES AND NETWORK

The MPEDA functions under the Ministry of Commerce, Government of India and acts as a coordinating agency with different Central and State Government establishments engaged in fishery production and allied activities.

Standing committees of the MPEDA are:

- Executive committee
- Technical committee
- Export promotion committee

The plan schemes of the authority are implemented under seven major heads:

- Market promotion
- Capture fisheries
- Culture fisheries
- Processing infrastructure and value addition
- Quality control
- Research and development
- Viability gap funding

Work Programme of the MPEDA

The following are the work programmes of the MPEDA

1. Registration of infrastructure facilities for seafood export trade.

2. Collection and dissemination of trade information.

3. Projection of Indian marine products in overseas markets by participation in overseas fairs and organising international seafood fairs in India.

4. Implementation of development measures vital to the industry like distribution of insulated fish boxes, putting up fish landing platforms, improvement of peeling sheds, modernisation of industry such as upgrading of plate freezers, installation of IQF machinery, generator sets, ice making machineries, quality control laboratory, and so on.

5. Promotion of aquaculture for production of shrimp and prawn for export.

6. Promotion of value added seafoods.

7. Promotion of Tuna fishery.

8. Implementation of organic farming.

9. Conservation management.

Foreign Policy regarding Marine Products

Let us now briefly study the foreign policy regarding marine products.

1. *Items permitted*

    i. No quantitative restrictions on export.

    ii. Licence under Foreign Trade Policy not required for import of 125 species/groups of fish, crustaceans, molluscus and other aquatic invertibrates covered under FREE policy in Chapter 3 of ITC (HS) classification of export and import items under the EXIM policy.

    iii. Import of five groups of live fish permitted under restricted policy (EXIM Code 0301).

    iv. Import of whale shark (*Rhincodon typus*) and parts and products of the species is restricted.

2. *Promotional measures*

    i. Central assistance to states for development of critical infrastructure for export such as roads, inland container depots, container freight stations, export promotion industrial parks and for equity participation in infrastructure projects.

    ii. Encouragement to State Governments for setting up export zones.

iii. Declaration of towns of export excellence to encourage setting up of critical infrastructure for export production, encourage common service providers and facilitate availability of better technological services and integrate benefits under the other schemes of EXIM Policy for the units in such towns.

iv. Market access initiative schemes for encouraging increased marketing efforts by exporters/brand promotion.

v. Schemes to promote the concept of total quality management.

3. *Import for export production*   Advance authorisation for duty-free import of inputs for export production.

i. Duty-free import authorisation (DFIA) scheme

a. Scheme DFIA is issued to allow duty-free import of inputs, fuel, oil, energy sources, catalyst which are required for production of export product. The DGFT, by means of public notice, may exclude any product(s) from purview of the DFIA. This scheme is in force from 1st May, 2006.

b. Entitlement provisions of paragraph 4.1.3 (FTP) shall be applicable in case of DFIA. However, these authorisations shall be issued only for products for which Standard Input and Output Norms (SION) have been notified.

ii. Pre-export authorisation shall be issued with actual user condition and shall be exempted from payment of basic custom duty, additional customs duty, education cess, anti-dumping duty and safeguard duty, if any. A minimum 20% value addition shall be required for issuance of such authorisation.

iii. Manufacturer exporters, merchant exporters tied to supporting manufacturers and service providers eligible for import of capital goods at 5% Customs duty linked to fulfilment of export obligation in 8 to12 years under EPCG Scheme.

4. *EOU/EPZ/SEZ*   The scheme of 100% EOU/Export Processing Zone/Special Economic Zone for export production continues. No trading units are permitted under the scheme.

5. *Package for marine sector*

i. Duty-free import of specified specialised inputs/chemicals and flavouring oils as per a defined list shall be allowed to the extent of 1% of FOB value of preceding financial year's export. Use of these special ingredients for seafood processing will enable us to achieve a higher value addition and enter new export markets.

ii. To encourage the existing mechanised vessels and deep sea trawlers to adopt modern technology for scientific exploitation of our marine resources in an eco-friendly manner and boost marine sector exports, it is proposed to allow import of monofilament long line system for tuna fishing at a concessional rate of duty.

iii. The present system of disposal of waste of perishable commodities like seafood after inspection by a customs official is very cumbersome and leads to development of unhygienic conditions. To overcome this, a self removal procedure for clearance of waste shall be applicable, subject to prescribed wastage norms.

Focus Market Scheme (FMS)

The objective is to offset high freight cost and other externalities to selected international markets with a view to enhance India's export competitiveness in these countries. Entitlement exporters of all products through EDI enabled ports to notified countries (as in Appendix 37C of HBP volume 1) shall be entitled for duty credit scrip equivalent to 2.5% of FOB value of exports for each licensing year commencing from 1 April, 2006. However additional Markets notified in Appendix 37C of HBP volume 1 shall be entitled for Duty Credit scrip on exports w.e.f 1 April, 2007.

Focus Product Scheme (FPS)

The objective is to sanction incentives for export of such products, which have high employment intensity in rural and semi urban areas, so as to offset infrastructure inefficiencies and other associated costs involved in marketing of these products. Entitlement exports of notified products (as in Appendix 37D of HBP volume 1) through EDI enabled ports to all countries shall be entitled for duty credit scrip equivalent to 1.25% of FOB value of exports for each licensing year commencing from 1 April, 2006. However, additional products notified/clarified in Appendix 37D of HBP volume 1 shall be entitled for duty credit scrip on exports w.e.f 1 April, 2007.

Export Trends

The export of marine products from India set an ever time record of 612641 tonnes of value ₹8363.53 crore and US$ 1852.93 million during 2006–07. During 2006–07, a total of 475 items were exported to as many as 90 countries.

Item-Wise Exports

In terms of export earnings, frozen shrimp continued to be the largest export item (54% in value), followed by frozen fish (17%), cuttlefish (10%), squid (7%), and dried items (2%).

Country-Wise Exports

Exports were effected to 90 countries during the year. Except the US, all the other countries increased their import of marine products from India.

International Shows

The MPEDA organises three international shows in association with the trade. It has been organising seafood trade fairs like India International Seafood Show (IISS) every alternate year within India. Over the years, these biennial fairs have achieved a distinct position among international trade fairs. In order to popularise the concept of aquaculture and to exploit the resources in the sector, the MPEDA organises IND-AQUA every alternate years.

The MPEDA organises IND-AQUARIA, the international ornamental aquatic event, every year. This is envisioned to showcase the infinite promise and potential of the Indian ornamental fish industry. Indaquaria provides a platform for annual get-together of ornamental fish producers, accessory suppliers, exporters and traders from all over India as well as importers from different countries. It also provides an exciting platform for joint venture and business tie-ups.

EXPORT PROMOTION COUNCILS

There are at present eleven Export Promotion Councils under the administrative control of the department of commerce and nine Export Promotion Councils related to textile sector under the administrative control of Ministry of Textiles. These Councils are registered as nonprofit organisations under the Companies Act/Societies Registration Act. The Export Promotion Councils perform both advisory and executive functions. These Councils are also the registering authorities under the Export Import Policy, 1997–2002. These Councils have been assigned the role and functions under the said Policy.

The committee constituted to look into the aspects of rationalisation of election procedure of the Export Promotion Councils (EPCs) and the criteria to be adopted for their restructuring so that they retain their relevance to the national export effort in the context of globlisation and economic liberalisation, and also has made recommendations to streamline and strengthen the functioning of the EPCs. The government has since accepted the recommendations of the committee and issued model bye-laws and guidelines to all EPCs for adoption.

The EPCs are required to send their detailed annual action plan and estimated funds required for reimbursement to individual exporters to the Export and Market Development Assistance (E and MDA) Division three months in advance. The activities approved in the annual meetings with each EPC well before the start of the financial year shall only be financed from the MDA funds. The EPCs shall have to utilise the MDA funds in a financial year for purposes for which these are sanctioned. 50% of the MDA budget approved for both the code activities as well as for reimbursement to individual exporters shall be released to the EPCs in the beginning of the financial year. The EPCs shall indicate their further requirement of funds latest by 30 November of the year. Funds for reimbursement to individual exporters shall be released only when 90% of the first instalment has been utilised, and a utilisation certificate to this effect has been submitted by the concerned organisation. The earmarked grant for the financial year not claimed within the year or wherein complete information has not been provided to facilitate its release, would lapse and shall not be carried over to the next financial year.

Let us study about a few EPCs.

Handloom Export Promotion Council (HEPC)

It is the driving force to magnify the elegance of handloom varieties with exquisite excellence. It is sponsored by the Ministry of Textiles, Government of India. Handloom Export Promotion Council (HEPC) functions as a non-profit making company under section 25 of the Companies Act. The Memorandum and Articles of Association framed by the Council govern the company. It is a statutory body constituted under The Ministry of Textiles, Government of India to promote the exports of all handloom products like fabrics, home furnishings, carpets, and floor coverings. Constituted in the year of 1965 with 65 members, today it has a membership around 2000 spread all over the country.

The Handloom industry mainly exports fabrics, bed linen, table linen, toilet and kitchen linen, towels, curtains, cushions and pads, tapestries and upholsteries, carpets and floor coverings, etc. The HEPC functions with the main objective to provide all kinds of support and guidance to the Indian handloom exporters and the international buyers for trade promotion and international marketing. With its headquarter at Chennai and regional offices at Mumbai and New Delhi, it is administered by an executive committee consisting of elected representatives from the export trade, ex-officio members and nominated government officials. The committee is headed by chairman, who holds his office for a period of two years along with the vice-chairman. The secretary (executive director) of the council assists the council to run the administration. One of the primary objectives of the HEPC is organising participation in the fairs, exhibitions and buyer-seller meets in India and abroad.

It aims to provide guidance, consultation and support to the handloom exporters in view to promote handloom exports, and lays down standards of quality and packaging in respect of Indian handlooms for export. It approves agents, representatives or correspondence in foreign markets for continuous reporting of prices, market preferences and reception accorded to Indian handloom products.

Coir Board of India

The Coir Board of India performs effective functions to promote the coir industry. It is a statutory body established by the Government of India under a legislation enacted by the Parliament namely Coir Industry Act 1953 (45 of 1953) to promote coir industry in India as a whole. The main functions of the board as laid down in Section 10 of the Coir Industry Act are:

1. Promoting exports of coir yarn and coir products and carrying on propaganda for that purpose.

2. Regulating the production of husks, coir yarn and coir products under the supervision of the Central Government by registering coir spindles and looms for manufacturing coir products.

3. Undertaking, assisting or encouraging scientific, technological and economic researches to maintain one or more research institutes.

4. Collecting statistics from manufacturers of and dealers in coir products. It can also obtain such information from the other persons related to the coir industry. The publication of statistics so collected or portions thereof or extracts therefrom.

5. Fixing grade standards and necessary inspection of coir fibre, coir yarn and coir products.

6. Improving the marketing of coconut husk, coir fibre, coir yarn and coir products in India, preventing unfair competition.

7. Setting up or assisting in the setting up of factories for the producers of coir products with the aid of power.

8. Promoting cooperative organisation among producers of husks, coir fibre and coir yarn and manufacturers of coir products.

9. Ensuring remunerative returns to producers of husks, coir fibre and coir yarn and manufacturers of coir products.

10. Licensing of renting places and warehouses and otherwise regulating the stocking and sale of coir fibre, coir yarn and coir products both for the internal market and for exports; and

11. Advising on all matters relating to the development of the coir industry.

THE CARPET EXPORT PROMOTION COUNCIL OF INDIA

The Carpet Export Promotion Council of India (CEPC) was set up by the Government of India in 1982 with a view to promote the exports of hand knotted carpets and other floor coverings. It is a responsible authority to enhance the utility of carpet industry. The council advises the government on export promotion measures and helps the exporter's community in bringing their problems and requirements to the notice of the government. It provides expertise in many spheres, both for the Indian exporters and foreign buyers.

The council is a high profile body consisting of senior trade representatives and government officials. It provides necessary assistance to the Indian exporters. It identifies the markets, provides financial assistance, sponsors participation in fairs and exhibitions and also conducts publicity abroad. Regarding overseas buyers/importers, the CEPC locates the estimate suppliers and provides credibility reports on Indian exporters. It also arranges buyer–seller meets and assists in trade disputes. To eradicate the incidence of child labour from the carpet industry, the CEPC has been adopting a label "KALEEN". This KALEEN label on carpets ensures that no child labour has been used for the production of the carpet. The exporters are required to fulfil certain prerequisites to obtain this label. They have to contribute a certain percentage of the FOB value of their exports to the child welfare fund. The main objectives of adopting this label are:

1. Total eradication of child labour,
2. Welfare of the weaver community,
3. Education for the children with mid-day meal,
4. Medicare of the weaver families, and
5. Vocational training for the children with assured stipend.

APPAREL EXPORT PROMOTION COUNCIL (AEPC)

The Apparel Export Promotion Council (AEPC) was incorporated under section 25 of the Companies Act, 1956 on 22 February, 1978. The council carries out its function as a nodal agency sponsored by the Ministry of Textiles, Government of India. It holds the dual responsibility of monitoring garment exports quotas and promotion of exports of readymade garments from India. The AEPC acts as a catalyst for the Indian Garment Exports. It organises the buyer–seller meets, garment shows with the sponsoring of the Trade Delegations and offers technical advice, market briefs, and so on. It also provides service to its more than 35,000 registered exporter members in a specialised manner through its committees and various sub-committees. The AEPC's Executive Committee Functioned through its various sub-committees including, Quota Advisory Committee, Export Promotion Committee, Exhibition Advisory Committee, and Finance and Budget Sub-Committee.

The AEPC organises a variety of fairs including India and International Garment Fair twice a year at Delhi, India Knit Fair at Tirupur, the knitwear capital of India, and Men's Fashion Fair at Mumbai, the commercial capital of India. The AEPC runs Apparel Training and Design Centres at places like Delhi, Mumbai, Tirupur, Bangalore, Chennai, Jaipur and Hyderabad. These centres impart training and thereafter even help the trained to get placed in various industries at shop-floor level to improve the efficiency and productivity of the Garment Industry. The AEPC also provides rich library to its members as well as research scholars. Its grandiose project of a world class Trade Mart cum Exhibition Complex in Delhi is in the anvil. It will house exclusive showrooms of exporters as much as hundred and an auditorium, plus a permanent "Exhibition Complex". The council administers the Export Entitlement Policy of the Government of India. It has also been authorised to allot quotas to exporters and issue certificates.

EXPORT PROMOTION COUNCIL FOR HANDICRAFTS

The Export Promotion Council for Handicrafts (EPCH) has been established under the EXIM Policy of Government of India in 1986–87 and is a non-profit organisation. The organisation works under the administrative control of the office of the Development Commissioner (Handicrafts), Ministry of Textiles, Government of India and governed by the policies of Ministry of Textiles. It is an apex body which projects India's image abroad as a reliable supplier of high quality of handicraft goods and services. It also insures various measures keeping in view of observance of international standards and specifications.

The Council has created necessary infrastructure as well as marketing and information facilities, which are availed both by the member exporters and importers. The membership of the council rose from 35 in year 1985–86 to 6873 in 2002–03. It is run and managed by a team of professionals headed by the executive director. The Committee of Administration consists of eminent exporters, professionals and senior Government officials. The Export Promotion Council for Handicrafts has the rarest distinction of being considered as Model Council which is self-sustaining and where all the promotional activities are self financed. Today, Indian Handicrafts and gifts fair has become a show window of Indian handicrafts among all the leading overseas buyers.

The Federation of Indian Export Organisations (FIEO)

The Federation of Indian Export Organisations represents the Indian entrepreneurs' spirit of enterprise in the global market. Set up in October, 1965, the Federation, popularly known as "FIEO", has kept pace with the country's evolving economic and trade policies, and provided the content, direction and thrust to India's expanding international trade. As the apex body of all Indian export promotion organisations, the FIEO works as a partner of the Government of the India to promote Indian exports.

Today, the FIEO expresses all the dynamism and resurgence that are the hallmark of India's open, liberal and progressively market-friendly economic and trade regime, representing the Indian export promotion efforts entirely. Its membership, largely comprising professional exporting firms or long experience called Government-recognised Export Houses, Trading Houses, Star Trading Houses and Super Star Trading Houses and consultancy exporting firms, contributes 72% of the total exports of India.

In essence, the FIEO represents directly or indirectly, over 1,00,000 exporters across India. Exports by the FIEO members comprise a wide spectrum of products including gems and jewellery, textiles, garments, engineering goods, leather and leather products, handicrafts, chemicals and allied products, cosmetics, drugs and pharmaceuticals, and the like as well as a wide range of Consultancy Services covering infrastructure, engineering industries, cement, leather, paper and rubber industries, agro-based industries, small scale industries, and so on. The activities of the members also include manufacturing, international trading, investment and joint ventures, etc. To any foreign investor, user or seller, the FIEO is the one-stop organisation which will put him in touch with a trade partner or high repute, backed by its own credentials as an organisation of excellence in India.

The FIEO has forged strong links with counterpart organisations in several countries as well as international agencies to enable direct communication and interaction between India and world businessmen. It is registered with the UNCTAD as a national non-government organisation, and has direct access to information/data originating from the UN bodies and world agencies like the IMF, ADB, ESCAP, World Bank, FAO, UNIDO and others. In addition, it has bilateral arrangements for exchange of information as well as for liasioning with several overseas chambers of commerce, and trade and industry associations.

How FIEO Developed

Today, the Federation is proud of the fact that its members account for an estimated exports of US$ 24.3 billion out of the total India's export of US$ 33.0 billion. It shows for itself an achievement which notes that approximately 73.6% of the total exports from India emanate from the FIEO members. This enviable position has been reached rapidly in a very short span, albeit with a long legacy behind it. It was in the year 1965 that this Federation came into being with the support of Ministry of Commerce, Government of India and private trade and Industry. It has now graduated to a level of organisation providing global links to exporters and working as a "nerve centre" of Indian exports.

FIEO Activities

What does the FIEO specifically achieve? The Federation keeps its members posted with the latest developments in the field of export/import by organising seminars and workshops, inviting delegations, organising buyer-seller meets in India and abroad, organising trade fairs, providing advisory and consultative services and bringing about constant interaction between member exporters and various government departments. The end result of such activity is discussion of issues in depth, evolving of suitable action plans to promote Indian exports, formulation and dissemination of government policies pertaining to all sectors in manufacturing and merchant exporting and apprising Government on problems and suggesting remedial measures.

What FIEO does?

When the Federation was constituted in 1965, certain economic realities had taken shape in India. There was greater industrialisation, centralised planning and government controls. Side by side, there existed a buoyant and thriving private sector. Thus there was an urgent need for

1. Wider exchange of views between allied industries in public as well as the private sectors.

2. Apprising all concerned bodies of status of exports.

3. Monitoring the effects of the Government policies on Exports and Imports.

4. Interacting with the Government on behalf of the exporting community.

Basically, the Federation fulfils the above needs in these three ways:

1. Sending representations on policy matters to the Central and State Governments.

2. Providing a wide range of services designed to help member companies.

3. Creating and setting up contracts between the Government and commercial bodies both in India and overseas.

These needs are achieved through the following departments:

1. *Total quality management (TQM) department* The TQM department is dedicated to help industries to launch quality initiatives. It organises workshops/seminars on TQM, ISO, and so on.

2. *FIEO information centre* It has a well established database and provides useful information on India's Export sector both at the company and industry level, Indian city-wise, state-wise, etc. India's Imports commodity-wise, port-wise etc. is also made available. Assistance to buyers abroad in sourcing the right product from India is also provided.

3. *Electronic data interchange and EDP department* The Government of India has implemented EDI with all the departments engaged in international trade. The task of this department has thus increased manifold in its effort to provide awareness and education on EDI to India's private trade and industry. Training, consultancy and host of other services on EDI is also provided. As a part of the awareness and educational programme, the FIEO has launched an electronic network, viz. FIEONET for the India's private trade and industry. It facilitates fast and low-cost communication facilities. Non-members can also avail of the facility.

4. *Market development assistance (MDA) department* The Ministry of Commerce, Government of India, through FIEO, reimburses to a certain percentage, expenses incurred by the recognised exporters, viz. Super Star Trading Houses/Star Trading Houses/Trading Houses/Export Houses on account of Sale-cum-Study Tour, participation in exhibitions/fairs abroad, bringing out publications for use abroad, and advertising in foreign media (brand publicity). The Market Development Assistance Department takes care of the grant disbursement.

5. *EXIM policy, customs and excise department* The department offers advisory services on India's Export–Import Policy, Customs and Excise rules and regulations. It takes up the problems of the exporters on these areas with the appropriate authorities. It also monitors and suggests the Government of India on the various policies, laws, rules and regulations.

6. *Market research and development department* The Market Research Department as a part of its business facilitation effort offers the exporting community:

    i. meetings with diplomats, incoming delegations and buying missions,

    ii. inviting delegations,

    iii. organising trade fairs abroad to project Indian products (recently organised fairs in Morocco, Moscow, St. Petersburg, Tunisia),

iv. opening of foreign offices and warehouses,

v. organising seminars for promotion of international trade,

vi. preparing of country notes/studies,

vii. opening of new FIEO Chapters/Offices abroad, and

viii. signing Memorandums of Understanding (MOU) with International Chambers and Institutions for trade promotion.

7. Banking and direct taxes division   The Banking and Direct Taxes Division offers advisory services to exporters on matters related to exchange Control and Foreign Exchange Dealers Association of India (FEDAI). It also provides information to exporters regarding benefits available under Income-tax Act, 1961 such as section 80 HHC for merchandise exports 80 HHC for software, and the like and 80 HHB for projects.

It also takes up problems of exporters regarding exports finance, and issue related to Exchange Control and the FEDAI. It organises open houses/workshops with the concerned Government officials of the RBI, and commercial banks for the exporters to have a face to face interaction to resolve their problems on the spot.

INDIA TRADE PROMOTION ORGANISATION (ITPO)

The Indian Trade Promotion Organisation (ITPO), New Delhi, is the premier trade promotion agency of India and provides a broad spectrum of services to trade and industry so as to promote export. With headquarters at Pragati Maidan, a modern exhibition complex spread over 150 acres in New Delhi and regional offices at Bangalore, Chennai, Kolkata and Mumbai, the ITPO ensures a representative participation of trade and industry from different regions of the country at its events in India and abroad.

Various promotional tools used by the ITPO are organising of fairs and exhibitions in India and abroad, buyer–seller meets, contact promotion programmes, product promotion programmes, promotion through overseas department stores, market surveys and information dissemination. In India, it has its offices in Mumbai, Bangalore, Kolkata, and Chennai. On international front, its offices are in Germany, Russia, USA, Japan, and Brazil.

The state-of-the art exhibition halls have enhanced the appeal of Pragati Maidan as the ideal centre for an increasing number of fair organisers and business visitors from different parts of the world. The ITPO has an extensive infrastructure as well as marketing and information facilities that are availed both by exporters and importers. The ITPO's overseas offices assist buyers seeking information relating to sourcing products from India.

The ITPO's overseas offices at New York, Frankfurt, Tokyo, Moscow and Sao Paulo are pursuing opportunities for enhancement of India's trade and investment. Similarly, India Trade Promotion Organisation's regional offices at Bangalore, Chennai, Kolkata, and Mumbai, through their respective profile of activities, ensure a well-attenuated trade promotion drive throughout the country.

Significantly, the ITPO has successfully completed the first phase of setting up of a modern exhibition facility outside Delhi following the commissioning of the state-of-the-art Chennai Trade Centre (CTC) on 31 January, 2001. Managed by Tamil Nadu Trade Promotion Organisation (TNTPO), a subsidiary of the ITPO jointly set up with the Tamil Nadu Industrial Development Corporation (TIDCO), the CTC addresses a long-felt need for a permanent and modern exhibition venue in the State which has emerged as a hub of trade-related activities.

The establishment of the Trade Centre, Bangalore, a joint initiative of ITPO and the Karnataka State Industrial Area Development Board, is expected to confer a major impetus to trade promotion through fairs, exhibitions and associated activities in the state. Yet another initiative has been taken up jointly with West Bengal Industrial Development Corporation (WBIDC) and the Kolkata Municipal Corporation (KMC), at Kolkata, near ITC Sonar Bangla, a super luxury hotel, where the foundation stone of the Kolkata Trade Centre (KTC) has recently been unveiled.

Various Activities and Services of the ITPO

Let us briefly discuss the activities and services of the ITPO to the exporters.

1. Management of the trade fair complex, that is, Pragati Maidan.

2. Proper organisation of varied trade fairs and exhibitions in Pragati Maidan and in other centres of India.

3. Ensuring timely and effective services for international buyers in vendor identification, drawing itineraries, fixing appointments and various other steps.

4. Maintaining viable relations between Indian suppliers and international buyers. Aiding Indian companies in product development and easily adapting for meeting with various buyers needs.

5. Effective organisation of promotions with department stores and mail order houses on global map.

6. Getting participation into various international trade fairs and exhibitions.

7. Timely organisation of various seminars, conferences and workshops for covering trade related subjects.

8. Enlisting the Indian state governments' participation for promoting nation's foreign trade.

9. Imparting trade information services with the electronic accessibility at Business Information Centres.

BOARD OF TRADE (BOT)

The Board of Trade was set up on 5 May, 1989 with a view to providing an effective mechanism to maintain continuous dialogue with trade and industry in respect of major developments in the field of International Trade. Its role is to, inter-alia, advise the government on measures connected with the foreign trade policy and how to achieve the desired objective of boosting India's exports. The terms of reference of the board are:

1. Advise the government on policy measures for preparation and implementation of both short and long term plans for increasing exports in the light of emerging national and international economic scenario;

2. Review export performance of various sectors, identify constraints and suggest industry specific measures to optimise export earnings;

3. Examine the existing institutional framework for imports and exports and suggest practical measures for further streamlining to achieve the desired objectives;

4. Review the policy instruments and procedures for imports and exports and suggest steps to rationalise and channelise such schemes for optimum use;

5. Examine issues which are considered relevant for promotion of India's foreign trade, and to strengthen the international competitiveness of Indian goods and services; and

6. Commission studies for furtherance of the above objectives.

The board is required to meet at least once every quarter and make recommendations to the government on issues pertaining to its terms of reference. The board has the power to set up sub-committees and to co-opt experts to these and to make recommendations on specific sectors and objectives.

EXPORT PROMOTION BOARD (EPB)

The Export Promotion Board functions under the chairmanship of the Cabinet Secretary to provide policy and infrastructural support through greater coordination amongst concerned Ministries for boosting exports. All ministries directly connected with facilitating foreign trade are represented on the Board by their Secretaries. This, inter-alia, includes Secretaries of Department of Commerce, Ministry of Finance, Department of Revenue, Department of Industrial Policy and Promotion, Ministry of Textiles, Department of Agriculture and Cooperation, Ministry of Civil Aviation, and Ministry of Surface Transport.

COMMODITY BOARDS

A commodity board is a registered agency designated by the Ministry of Commerce, Government of India for purposes of export promotion and has offices in India and abroad. There are five statutory Commodity Boards, which are responsible for production, development and export of tea, coffee, rubber, spices and tobacco. India continues to operate commodity boards, under its department of commerce, for tea, coffee, spices, and tobacco. These Boards are responsible for production, development, and export promotion activities.

RUBBER BOARD

The Rubber Board of India is responsible for supporting, developing and maintaining all activities in India's rubber industry. This not only includes production of natural rubber, but uniquely in the world, production of synthetic rubber and subsequent processing of all types of elastomer. In addition, the Rubber Board advises the government on policy and collects the cess (tax) on exports of rubber. The Rubber Board also limits the imports of rubber to the country.

It is a quasi-government organisation, set up under India's Rubber (Production and Marketing) Act, 1947, to help and support the development of the rubber industry in the country. It is headquartered in Kottayam, in Kerala State, as Kerala is the home of rubber production in India.

COFFEE BOARD

The Coffee Board of India is an autonomous body, functioning under the Ministry of Commerce and Industry, Government of India. The Board serves as a friend, philosopher and guide of the coffee industry in India. Set up under an Act of the Parliament of India in the year 1942, the Board focuses on research, development, extension, quality upgradation, market information, and the domestic and external promotion of Coffees of India.

Till 1995, the Coffee Board had a pool (controlled) marketing system of coffee in India. However, the winds of liberalisation swept the Indian coffee industry and since 1995, marketing of coffee is strictly a private sector activity. In fact the Coffee Board went through a massive downsizing and two-thirds of its employees were retired under a voluntary retirement scheme.

The Coffee Board conducts basic and applied research on coffee and can boast of 75 glorious years in coffee research. The Central Coffee Research Institute in the Chikmagalur District, Karnataka State has been in the forefront of coffee research over the years and continues to remain one of the premier institutes of the world as far as coffee research is concerned.

TEA BOARD

The Tea Board of India, a commodity board under the administrative control of the Ministry of Commerce, Government of India, was established by the enactment of the Tea Act, 1953. The constitution of the Board is represented by various interest groups of the tea industry such as owners of tea estates and producers of tea, consumers of tea, government representatives from the tea growing states of India viz. Assam, West Bengal, Tripura, Tamil Nadu, Kerala and Himachal Pradesh, members of parliament, exporters and internal traders of tea, persons employed in tea estates/gardens, and persons representing other interests.

The functions of the Board are defined by the provisions of the Tea Act. It is primarily concerned with the development of the tea industry and trade of tea, extension of area under tea cultivation, research activities concerned with improvement in the quality of tea production and cultivation methods, promotion of exports, other licensing activities aimed at containing adulteration and other undesirable activities, interception on behalf of workers for adoption of welfare measures and so on.

TOBACCO BOARD

The Government of India established the Tobacco Board under an Act of Parliament in the year 1975 and opened its head quarters at Guntur, Andhra Pradesh with a view to bring about an all-round development to the tobacco industry. Tobacco and tobacco products earn a whopping annual sum of about ₹0271 crore to the national exchequer by way of excise revenue, and ₹2022 crore (2006–07) by way of foreign exchange. Furthermore, tobacco is a source of gainful employment. Several lakhs of people thrive on this weed crop.

SPICES BOARD

The Spices Board of India was established by the Government of India under Ministry of Commerce. The board was constituted on February 26, 1986 under the Spices Board Act 1986. Spices Board of India was founded as a result of the merging of Cardamom Board and Spices Export Promotion Council. The board is one of the five Commodity boards working under the Ministry of Commerce and Industry.

Spices Board is the flagship organisation for the development and worldwide promotion of Indian spices. The Board is an international link between the Indian exporters and the importers abroad. The Board has been spearheading activities for excellence of Indian spices, involving every segment of the industry. The Board has made quality and hygiene the corner stones for its development and promotional strategies.

The Board is a link between the Indian exporters and the importers abroad. Its broad-based activities include formulation and implementation of quality improvement systems, research and development programmes, education and training of farmers, processors, packers and exporters on post harvest handling and registration and licensing of traders and exporters.

COIR BOARD

Coir Board is a statutory body established by the Government of India under a legislation enacted by the Parliament namely Coir Industry Act 1953 (45 of 1953) for the promotion and development of Coir Industry in India as a whole. It is based in Kochi (Cochin), and works for the promotion, research, education and training of the coir industry. The board functions under the Ministry of Micro, Small and Medium Enterprises. The Coir Board has worked actively to support the International Year of Natural Fibres 2009.

The details of these Boards are given below:

1. RUBBER BOARD

Chairman

Sub-Jail Road, P.B.No.1122, Kottayam, Kerala-686002

Tel.   :   (91) 481-571231, 571232, 571235, 571236, 571361

Fax   :   (91) 481-571380

e-mail   :   rbktm@ker.nic.in, rrii@vsnl.com

Website   :   http://rubberboard.org.in/

2. COFFEE BOARD

Chairman

1-Dr.Ambedkar Veedhi, Bangalore-560001

Tel.   :   (91) 80-257890

Fax   :   (91) 80-2255557

Website   :   http://www.indiacoffee.org/

3. TEA BOARD

Chairman

14, BTM Sarani, Brabourne Road, P.B.No.2172, Kolkata-700001

Tel.   :   (91)33-2251411

Fax   :   (91)33-2251417

Website   :   http://www.indiateaportal.com

4. TOBACCO BOARD

Chairman

P.B.No.322, G.T.Road, Guntur-522004

Tel.   :   (91) 0863-2358399, 2358499, 2327550, 2358531, 2358532, 2327555, 2327554, 2327556

Fax   :   (91) 0863-2354232

e-mail   :   info@indiantobacco.com

Website   :   http://www.indiantobacco.com/

5. SPICES BOARD

Chairman

Sugandha Bhavan, P.B.No.2277, Palarivattom.P.O., Cochin-682025

Tel.   :   (91)484-2333610 to 2333616 (7 Lines) and 2348417, (91)484-2331429/2334429

e-mail   :   spicesboard@vsnl.com, mail@indianspices.com

Website   :   http://www.indianspices.com

6. COIR BOARD

Chairman

M.G. Road, Kochi, Kerala

Tel.   :   (91) 484-351807, 351954, 354397

Fax   :   (91) 484-370034

Website   :   http://coir-india.com

THE P.P. PRABHU COMMITTEE ON COMMODITY BOARDS

The P.P. Prabhu Committee report on the functioning of the Commodity Boards as also to conceptualise a price stabilisation fund for the commodities has not come a day too soon as the EXIM Policy has laid primacy of importance to promoting agricultural product exports. Though prices of farm products have not been on any roller-coaster rides abroad to give the comfort of higher export earnings at this juncture, there is increasing realisation that India should have a consistent agri-export policy without letting short-term domestic factors come in the way of evolving a long-term durable farm export policy.

The one-man Committee, which studied the statutory Commodity Boards such as tea, coffee, rubber as also the Marine Products Export Development Authority (MPEDA) and the Agricultural and Processed Food Products Export Development Authority (APEDA), contended that the growth of production in the last three decades (100% increase in the case of tea to six times increase in the case of natural rubber) as well as the comparatively satisfactory achievement in productivity levels "speaks for the performance of the Boards." A point to ponder is the admission by the committee that the expenditure on the bureaucracy of the Boards has not been "high" and the resources requirements have also been mostly generated from the industry itself by way of cess.

The Committee said the boards have been able to develop a sense of belonging and establish credibility with the growers who desire the Boards' continuance. This ought to be a riposte to the numerous critics of quasi-governmental export promotional bodies because over a million growers are engaged in the cultivation of plantation commodities with this sector providing direct employment to nearly two million and earning substantial foreign exchange earnings for the country.

The Committee's suggestion for effective representation for small growers in the boards and hence 50% of the small grower nominees might be selected from among those growers owning less than four hectares deserve implementation. The significance of small growers of plantation industry needs to be viewed against the QR-free regime India has ushered in since 1 April, 2001 with the potential threat of 100% Foreign Direct Investment (FDI) in plantation sector hanging like Damocles' sword over its fortune and future. As a cost-cutting measure, the committee found scant or no justification to continue domestic promotion outlets being managed by these Boards which could be progressively privatised. Rightly, the Committee noted that the Boards are not equipped to undertake any market intervention operations as the minimum and maximum prices are difficult to implement. Instead, the Boards do well to focus on processing, post-harvest management and quality assurance. In the evolving standards-conscious export markets, the Boards might accredit private labs on the basis of transparent criteria for issue of quality certification so that plantation products from India found the going smooth without being smitten by bogey of sanitary and phytosanitary standards.

On the important issue of safeguarding growers and exporters from wild swings in prices of plantation products, the Committee said that there were few worthwhile global attempts to help developing countries to cope with the problems of price volatility. It said that the World Bank had convened an International Task Force (ITF) on commodity risk management in developing countries. The ITF's suggestion was for the creation of an international Intermediation which would bridge the gap between the providers of the risk management instruments and the entities in the developing world. The proposal favoured a price insurance scheme under which a guaranteed price based on the quotations of futures exchange could be ensured against payment of premium. But this would still fall short of growers' expectations as the premium payout might be a sticky issue. The Prabhu Committee, however, felt that a price insurance scheme, which would guarantee deficiency payments to growers if there were to be a fall in prices below a threshold level, might be acceptable. But the price threshold ought to be attractive and the scheme should be simple to administer for commodities prone to large-scale gyrations in prices like coffee, cardamom, even cotton or chilli.

The Committee suggested a Price Stabilisation Fund for commodities which must be commodity-specific and built up through transfer of a portion of cess amount and any export-tax proceeds and such other amounts generated from the industry. But this required coordinated management from various levels involving administrative cost and attendant hassles that might leave the growers still groping for a lasting solution to the vagaries of markets.

INDIAN INSTITUTE OF FOREIGN TRADE

The Indian Institute of Foreign Trade (IIFT) was set up in 1963 by the Government of India as an autonomous organisation to help professionalise the country's foreign trade management and increase exports by developing human resources; generating, analysing and disseminating data, and conducting research. The IIFT, today, is a deemed university. Initially, the IIFT concentrated in imparting quality education and training in foreign trade only. But today its outlook has changed drastically. It has become one of the premier institutions offering high quality management education. Its role has expanded considerably to suit the modern day needs of the world.

The IIFT acts as a catalyst for new ideas, concepts and skills for the internationalisation of the Indian economy. It is the primary provider of training and research-based consultancy in the areas of international business, both for the corporate sector, government and the student community. The Institute is an organisation with proven capability to continuously upgrade its knowledge-base with a view to servicing the requirements of the government, trade and industry through both sponsored and non-sponsored research and consultancy assignments.

The Institute has national and international linkages. It is a member of the International Association of Trade Training Organisations (IATIO), the UK Academy of International Business (AIB), and the USA Association of Training Institutions for Foreign Trade in Asia and the Pacific (ATIFTAP), Manila, Philippines. The Institute has also entered into a MOU with Korean Institute for Industrial Economics and Trade for collaborative research. The ESCAP has recognised the Institute as a Centre of Maritime Education and Training which offers a specialised part-time programme for the benefit of shippers and others involved in this area. The Institute has so far offered its training services to thousands of professionals from 30 developing countries. As a part of technical cooperation among the developing countries, the Institute has conducted training programmes in Mongolia and Vietnam. It also organises inter-regional seminars/workshops in association with International Trade Centre, UNCTAD/WTO. Within the country, the IIFT has institutional linkages with major trade and industry associations, such as Confederation of Indian Industries (CII), and the Federation of Indian Export Organisations (FIEO). Joint Seminars on important national issues are the primary outcomes of these linkages.

The IIFT's portfolio of long-term programmes is as follows:

1.   Two-year residential MBA (International Business), New Delhi, Dar-es-Salaam (Tanzania) and Kolkata. This is the flagship course, offering specialisation in Marketing, Finance, Systems and Trading.

2.   Three-year MBA (International Business) (Weekends), New Delhi and Kolkata.

3.   Executive Master's in International Business, New Delhi, Dubai, and Dar-es-Salaam.

4.   Certificate Course in Export Management, New Delhi, Guwahati (Assam).

Since its inception, the Institute has focused on facilitating executives in Indian and multinational companies, to explore new frontiers of knowledge, sharpen their tools and help their organizations to achieve commanding heights. Besides management programmes, the Institute also provides training and research based consultancy to the government and the corporate sector. IIFT's portfolio of educational programmes is diverse and caters to the requirements of aspiring business executives and mid-career professionals.

With the objective of harnessing best practices in management education from leading B-schools the world over and providing capacity building inputs to developing countries, the IIFT has entered into academic collaborations with more than 30 Business Schools/ Universities across Europe, North America, Africa and South East Asia. These collaborations give the IIFT participants the opportunity to interact with faculty and participants from different parts of the world through exchange programmes and study tours.

SUMMARY

This chapter discussed briefly the functioning of the following organisations that are supporting Indian exporters:

* Agricultural and Processed Food Products Export Development Authority
* Marine Products Export Development Authority
* Export Promotion Councils
* Federation of Indian Export Organisations
* India Trade Promotion Organisation
* Board of Trade
* Export Promotion Board
* Commodity Boards
* Indian Institute of Foreign Trade

These and many other organisations are rendering great service to Indian exporters by guiding, assisting, and supporting them in a big way. The Government of India has been consistently taking steps to support and help the exporters through all possible novel ideas. No doubt, India will soon reach a good spot in the world map of international trade.

Review Questions (Short)

1. What are the functions of APEDA?

2. What are the products dealt with by APEDA?

3. Explain briefly the foreign trade policy regarding marine products.

4. What are the promotional measures undertaken by MPEDA?

5. What is Focus Market Scheme?

6. What is Product Market Scheme?

7. What are Export Promotion Councils?

8. Explain briefly the functioning of Handloom Export Promotion Council.

9. Explain briefly the functioning of Coir Board of India.

10. Explain briefly the functioning of Apparel Export Promotion Council.

11. Explain briefly the functioning of FIEO.

12. Explain briefly the functioning of ITPO.

13. What is BoT?

14. What are Commodity Boards?

15. Explain the working of the IIFT.

Review Questions (Detailed)

1. Expain in detail the functioning of APEDA.

2. Explain in detail the functioning of MPEDA.

3. Write an essay on the EPCs.

4. Discuss the organisation and activities of FIEO.

REFERENCES

1. www.export.gov›International Logistics
2. www.unzco.com/basicguide/c10.html
3. www.businesslink.gov.uk/bdotg/action/detail?
4. www.businesslink.gov.uk/bdotg/action/detail?
5. www.msamb.com/english/faq/ex_faq.htm
6. www.hse.gov.uk/cdg/manual/regenvirnment.htm
7. www.vca.gov.uk›Dangerous Goods
8. Export Packaging Note No. 20 International Trade Centre UNCTAD/WTO on *The Arrival Condition of Export Packages from Developing Countries*
9. www.productpolicy.org/.../Green-Design-White-Paper_Stitzhal_OR-PSWorkgroup.pdf
10. www.packagingconsultancy.com/packaging-regulations.html
11. www.deq.state.or.us/lq/pubs/docs/sw/.../intlpkgregulations.pdf
12. www.packagingconsultancy.com/design-requirements.html
13. www.deq.state.or.us/lq/pubs/docs/.../packaging/intlpkgregulations.pdf
14. www.iip-in.com/Aboutus.htm

10

FOREIGN EXCHANGE MANAGEMENT IN INDIA

LEARNING OBJECTIVES

After reading this chapter, you will

* know about the background of Foreign Exchange Management Act 2000

* become knowledgeable about the objectives and scope of FEMA

* know about the important provisions of FEMA

* know about the amendments to FEMA made up to July 2009

* understand the role of Reserve Bank of India in enforcing FEMA.

KEY TERMS

* Current account
* Capital account
* Authorised person
* Contravention
* Penalty
* Adjudicating authority
* Enforcement
* Appellate tribunal
* Foreign direct investment (FDI)
* Foreign portfolio investment
* Authorised dealer
* Non-resident Indian (NRI)
* Foreign Venture Capital Investors
* External commercial borrowings
* Approval route

INTRODUCTION

During the World War II, the then Government of India introduced the Exchange Control Act to regulate and control the flow of foreign exchange into and out of India. As soon as India became independent in the year 1947, the Government brought in temporarily the Foreign Exchange Regulations Act to suit the needs of an independent country and to frame policies for the economic and industrial development in a fast pace.

As the conditions changed with the time, the country required a more effective Act for regulating the flow of foreign exchange in the country. Therefore, a new Foreign Exchange Regulations Act was passed by the Parliament of India in 1973. In the year 1973, the country was facing foreign exchange problems in the form of deficit and the government found it difficult to manage with the old Act on foreign exchange. The new Act's aim was to consolidate and preserve foreign exchange in India so that the industrial development of the country will take a jump from the prevailing slow pace of industrial development by allowing foreign investment in the country. The initiative to pass a new Act for regulating foreign exchange was taken by the then Prime Minister of India, Shrimathi Indira Gandhi.

Under the FERA guidelines, the Reserve Bank of India (RBI) permitted only authorised dealers to guarantee debt in favour of an Indian resident on behalf of nonresident Indians (NRIs) or provide guarantees to foreign buyers of Indian exports. Companies in India had to offer guarantees to income tax authorities for taxes due from foreign-national employees. Also, Indian companies had to obtain RBI approval to hire overseas consultants. Foreign companies (except high technology, and export firms) operating in India could own only up to 40% of the equity in their business. Shipping agents were permitted to guarantee the debt of foreign shipping principals only under specific laws.

Transactions that were not mentioned in the Act were not permitted. The FERA regulations were enforced by the office of the Enforcement Directorate under the Department of Revenue, and supervised by the Ministry of Finance. The directorate consisted of the head office, seven zonal offices, nine sub-zonal offices and a field unit. The Act permitted 813 officers to scrutinise transgressions by businesses and individuals. Violations of the Act could result in imprisonment.

The IBM and Coca-Cola closed their Indian operations because of the FERA's equity regulations. Naunihal Singh wrote in his book "India and the United States", "The Finance Minister George Fernandes, claimed the soft drink company was making excessively large profits—15 million rupees annually—on initial investment of only ₹6,00,000." At that time the multinational companies were repatriating large profits.

FEMA IN THE PLACE OF FERA

The Indian economy was significantly altered in 1991, and the FERA regulations were found to be incompatible with globalisation. Consequently, the FERA was replaced by the Foreign Exchange Management Act (FEMA) in 1999, which eased restrictions on foreign exchange and overseas investment in India.

The Foreign Exchange Regulation Act of 1973 (FERA) in India was repealed on 1 June, 2000. It was replaced by the Foreign Exchange Management Act (FEMA). Enacted in 1973, in the backdrop of acute shortage of foreign exchange in the country, the FERA had a controversial 27-year stint during which many bosses of the Indian corporate world found themselves at the mercy of the Enforcement Directorate (ED). Any offence under the FERA was a criminal offence liable to imprisonment, whereas the FEMA seeks to make offences relating to foreign exchange civil offences.

The FEMA, which replaced the FERA, had become the need of the hour since the FERA had become incompatible with the pro-liberalisation policies of the Government of India. The FEMA has brought a new management regime of Foreign Exchange consistent with the emerging framework of the World Trade Organisation (WTO). It is another matter that the enactment of the FEMA also brought with it Prevention of Money Laundering Act, 2002 (PMLA) which came into effect from 1 July, 2005.

Unlike other laws where everything is permitted unless specifically prohibited, under the FERA nothing was permitted unless specifically permitted. Hence the tenor and tone of the Act was very drastic. It provided for imprisonment of even a very minor offence. Under the FERA, a person was presumed guilty unless he proved himself innocent whereas under other laws, a person is presumed innocent unless he is proven guilty.

OBJECTIVES AND SCOPE OF FEMA

The objective of the Act is to consolidate and amend the law relating to foreign exchange with the objective of facilitating external trade and payments and for promoting the orderly development and maintenance of foreign exchange market in India.

The FEMA extends to the whole of India. It applies to all branches, offices and agencies outside India owned or controlled by a person who is a resident of India and also to any contravention there under, committed outside India by any person to whom this Act applies.

Except with the general or special permission of the Reserve Bank of India, no person can:

1. deal in or transfer any foreign exchange or foreign security to any person not being an authorised person;

2. make any payment to or for the credit of any person resident outside India in any manner;

3. receive otherwise through an authorised person, any payment by order or on behalf of any person resident outside India in any manner;

4. reasonable restrictions for current account transactions as may be prescribed.

Any person may sell or draw foreign exchange to or from an authorised person for a capital account transaction. The Reserve Bank may, in consultation with the Central Government, specify

1. any class or classes of capital account transactions which are permissible;

2. the limit up to which foreign exchange shall be admissible for such transactions.

However, the Reserve Bank cannot impose any restriction on the drawing of foreign exchange for payments due on account of amortisation of loans or for depreciation of direct investments in the ordinary course of business.

POWERS OF THE RESERVE BANK OF INDIA UNDER THE FEMA

The Reserve Bank can, by regulations, prohibit, restrict or regulate the following:

1. transfer or issue of any foreign security by a person resident in India;

2. transfer or issue of any security by a person resident outside India;

3. transfer or issue of any security or foreign security by any branch, office or agency in India of a person resident outside India;

4. any borrowing or lending in foreign exchange in whatever form or by whatever name called;

5. any borrowing or lending in rupees in whatever form or by whatever name called between a person resident in India and a person resident outside India;

6. deposits between persons resident in India and persons resident outside India;

7. export, import or holding of currency or currency notes;

8. transfer of immovable property outside India, other than a lease not exceeding five years, by a person resident in India;

9. acquisition or transfer of immovable property in India, other than a lease not exceeding five years, by a person resident outside India; and

10. giving of a guarantee or surety in respect of any debt, obligation or other liability incurred

    i. by a person resident in India and owed to a person resident outside India, or

    ii. by a person resident outside India.

A person, who is a resident of India may hold, own, transfer or invest in foreign currency, foreign security or any immovable property situated outside India if such currency, security or property was acquired, held or owned by such a person when he was resident outside India or inherited from a person who was resident outside India.

A person resident outside India may hold, own, transfer or invest in Indian currency, security or any immovable property situated in India if such currency, security or property was acquired, held or owned by such a person when he was resident in India or inherited from a person who was resident in India.

The Reserve Bank may, by regulation, prohibit, restrict, or regulate establishment in India of a branch, office or other place of business by a person resident outside India, for carrying on any activity relating to such branch, office or other place of business. Every exporter of goods and services must:

1. furnish to the Reserve Bank or to such other authority, a declaration in such form and in such manner as may be specified, containing true and correct material particulars, including the amount representing the full export value or, if the full export value of the goods is not ascertainable at the time of export, the value which the exporter, having regard to the prevailing market conditions, expects to receive on the sale of the goods in a market outside India; and

2. furnish to the Reserve Bank such other information as may be required by the Reserve Bank for the purpose of ensuring the realisation of the export proceeds by such exporter. The Reserve Bank may, for the purpose of ensuring that the full export value of the goods or such reduced value of the goods as the Reserve Bank determines is received without any delay, and direct any exporter to comply with such requirements as it deems fit.

Where any amount of foreign exchange is due or has accrued to any person resident in India, such person shall take all reasonable steps to realise and repatriate to India such foreign exchange within such period and in such manner, as may be specified by the Reserve Bank.

Except as provided in the FEMA Act, rules and RBI permission, no person shall:

1. deal in/transfer any forex to any person not being an authorised person,

2. make any payment to or for the credit of any nonresident,

3. receive otherwise through an authorised person, any payment by order or on behalf of any nonresident, and

4. enter into any financial transaction in India as consideration for or in association with acquisition or creation or transfer of a right to acquire, any asset outside India by any person.

IMPORTANT PROVISIONS OF THE FOREIGN EXCHANGE MANAGEMENT ACT

Let us now study the important provisions of the Foreign Exchange Management Act of India.

Definiton of "person" The meaning of a "person" includes

- An individual
- A Hindu undivided family
- A company
- A firm
- An association of persons or a body of individuals, whether incorporated or not
- Every artificial juridical person, not falling within any of the preceding sub-clauses
- Any agency, office or branch owned or controlled by such person

A "person resident in India" means

1. A person residing in India for more than one hundred and eighty-two days during the course of the preceding financial year but does not include
   i. a person who has gone out of India or who stays outside India, in either case
      (a) for or on taking up employment, or
      (b) for carrying on outside India a business or vocation outside India, or
      (c) for any other purpose, in such circumstances as would indicate his intention to stay outside India for an uncertain period;
   ii. a person who has come to or stays in India, in either case, otherwise than
      (a) for or on taking up employment in India, or
      (b) for carrying on in India a business or vocation in India, or
      (c) for any other purpose, in such circumstances as would indicate his intention to stay in India for an uncertain period;
2. Any person or body corporate registered or incorporated in India,
3. An office, branch or agency in India owned or controlled by a person resident outside India,
4. An office, branch or agency outside India owned or controlled by a person resident in India;

A "person resident outside India" means a person who is not resident in India.

"Repatriate to India" means bringing into India the realised foreign exchange.

Dealing in foreign exchange Except as otherwise provided in this Act, rules or regulations made there under, or with the general or special permission of the Reserve Bank, no person shall

1. deal in or transfer any foreign exchange or foreign security to any person not being an authorised person;

2. make any payment to or for the credit of any person resident outside India in any manner;

3. receive otherwise through an authorised person, any payment by order or on behalf of any person resident outside India in any manner; and

4. enter into any financial transaction in India as consideration for or in association with acquisition or creation or transfer of a right to acquire, any asset outside India by any person.

Except as otherwise provided in this Act, no person resident in India shall acquire, hold, own, possess or transfer any foreign exchange, foreign security or any immovable property situated outside India.

Current account transactions Any person may sell or draw foreign exchange to or from an authorised person if such sale or withdrawal is a current account transaction: Provided that the Central Government may, in public interest and in consultation with the Reserve Bank, impose such reasonable restrictions for current account transactions as may be prescribed.

Capital account transactions

1 Subject to the provisions of this Act, any person may sell or draw foreign exchange to or from an authorised person for a capital account transaction.

2. The Reserve Bank may specify

    i. any class or classes of capital account transactions which are permissible;

    ii. the limit up to which foreign exchange shall be admissible for such transactions.

3. Without prejudice to the generality of the provisions of this Act, the Reserve Bank may, prohibit, restrict or regulate the following:

    i. transfer or issue of any foreign security by a person resident in India;

    ii. transfer or issue of any security by a person resident outside India;

    iii. transfer or issue of any security or foreign security by any branch, office or agency in India of a person resident outside India;

    iv. any borrowing or lending in rupees in whatever form or by whatever name called;

    v. any borrowing or lending in rupees in whatever form or by whatever name called between a person resident in India and a person resident outside India;

    vi. deposits between persons resident in India and persons resident outside India;

   vii. export, import or holding of currency or currency notes;

  viii. transfer of immovable property outside India, other than a lease not exceeding five years, by a person resident in India;

   ix. acquisition or transfer of immovable property in India, other than a lease not exceeding five years, by a person resident outside India;

    x. giving of a guarantee in respect of any debt, obligation or other liability incurred

      (a) by a person resident in India and owed to a person resident outside India; or

      (b) by a person resident outside India.

4. A person resident in India may hold, own, transfer or invest in foreign currency, foreign security or any immovable property situated outside India if such currency, security or property was acquired, held or owned by such person when he was resident outside India or inherited from a person who was resident outside India.

5. A person resident outside India may hold, own, transfer or invest in Indian currency, security or any immovable property situated in India if such currency, security or property was acquired, held or owned by such person when he was resident in India or inherited from a person who was resident in India.

6. Without prejudice to the provisions of this section, the Reserve Bank may, by regulation, prohibit, restrict, or regulate establishment in India of a branch, office or other place of business by a person resident outside India, for carrying on any activity relating to such branch, office or other place of business.

EXPORT OF GOODS AND SERVICES

1. Every exporter of goods shall

    i. furnish to the Reserve Bank or to such other authority a declaration containing true and correct material particulars, including the amount representing the full export value; and

   ii. furnish to the Reserve Bank such other information as may be required by the Reserve Bank for the purpose of ensuring the realisation of the export proceeds by such exporter.

2. The Reserve Bank may, for the purpose of ensuring that the full export value of the goods or such reduced value of the goods as the Reserve Bank determines, direct any exporter to comply with such requirements as it deems fit.

3. Every exporter of services shall furnish to the Reserve Bank or to such other authorities a declaration in such form and in such manner as may be specified, containing the true and correct material particulars in relation to payment for such services.

REALISATION AND REPATRIATION OF FOREIGN EXCHANGE

Except as otherwise provided in this Act, where any amount of foreign exchange is due or has accrued to any person resident in India, such person shall take all reasonable steps to realise and repatriate to India such foreign exchange within such period and in such manner as may be specified by the Reserve Bank.

EXEMPTION FROM REALISATION AND REPATRIATION IN CERTAIN CASES

The provisions of sections 4 and 8 shall not apply to the following, namely,

1. possession of foreign currency or foreign coins by any person up to such limit as the Reserve Bank may specify;

2. foreign currency account held or operated by such person or class of persons and the limit up to which the Reserve Bank may specify;

3. foreign exchange acquired or received before the 8th day of July, 1947 or any income arising or accruing thereon which is held outside India by any person in pursuance of a general or special permission granted by the Reserve Bank;

4. foreign exchange held by a person resident in India up to such limit as the Reserve Bank may specify, if such foreign exchange was acquired by way of gift or inheritance from a person referred to in clause (c), including any income arising therefrom;

5. foreign exchange acquired from employment, business, trade, vocation, services, honorarium, gifts, inheritance or any other; and legitimate means up to such limit as the Reserve Bank may specify;

6. such other receipts in foreign exchange as the Reserve Bank may specify.

AUTHORISED PERSON

1. The Reserve Bank may authorise any person to be known as authorised person to deal in foreign exchange or in foreign securities, as an authorised dealer, money changer or off-shore banking unit or in any other manner as it deems fit.

2. An authorisation granted may be revoked by the Reserve Bank at any time if the Reserve Bank if the situation requires so.

3. An authorised person shall comply with such general or special directions or orders as the Reserve Bank may think fit to give. An authorised person shall engage in any transaction involving any foreign exchange or foreign security only with the permission of the RBI.

An authorised person shall, before undertaking any transaction in foreign exchange on behalf of any person, require that person to make such declaration and to give such information as will reasonably satisfy him that the transaction will not involve and is not designed for the purpose of any contravention or evasion of the provisions of this Act.

Reserve Bank's Powers to Issue Directions to Authorised Person

1. The Reserve Bank may give to the authorised persons any direction in regard to making of payment or the doing or desist from doing any act relating to foreign exchange or foreign security.

2. The Reserve Bank may direct any authorised person to furnish such information, in such manner, as it deems fit.

3. Where any authorised person contravenes any direction given by the Reserve Bank or fails to file any return as directed by the Reserve Bank, the Reserve Bank may impose on the authorised person, a penalty which may extend to ten thousand rupees and in the case of continuing contravention with an additional penalty, may extend to two thousand rupees per day till such contravention remains.

Power of the Reserve Bank to Inspect the Authorised Person

1. The Reserve Bank may, at any time, cause an inspection to be made, by any officer of the Reserve Bank specially authorised in writing by the Reserve Bank in this behalf, of the business of any authorised person as may appear to it to be necessary or expedient for the purpose of

    i. verifying the correctness of any statement, information or particulars furnished to the Reserve Bank;

    ii. obtaining any information or particulars which such authorised person has failed to furnish on being called upon to do so;

    iii. securing compliance with the provisions of this Act or of any rules, regulations, directions or orders made thereunder.

2. It shall be the duty of every authorised person, and where such person is a company or a firm, every director, partner or other officer of such company or firm, as the case may be, to produce to any officer making an inspection of such books, accounts and other documents in his custody or power and to furnish any statement or information relating to the affairs of such person, company or firm as the said officer may require within such time and in such manner as the said officer may direct.

Contravention and Penalties

Let us now study the penalties in the case of contravention of rules.

Penalties

1. If any person contravenes any provision of the Act, he shall be liable to a penalty up to thrice the sum involved in such contravention where such amount is quantifiable, or up to two lakh rupees where the amount is not quantifiable. Where such contravention is a

continuing one, a further penalty up to five thousand rupees for every day after the first day during which the contravention continues may be imposed.

2. Any Adjudicating Authority adjudging any contravention may direct that any currency, security or any other money or property in respect of which the contravention has taken place shall be confiscated to the Central Government.

Enforcement of the orders of adjudicating authority

1. If any person fails to make full payment of the penalty imposed on him under this Act, within a period of ninety days from the date on which the notice for payment of such penalty is served on him, he shall be liable to civil imprisonment.

2. No order for the arrest and detention in civil prison of a defaulter shall be made unless the Adjudication Authority has issued and served a notice upon the defaulter calling upon him to appear before him on the date specified in the notice and to show cause why he should not be committed to the civil prison.

3. A warrant for the arrest of the defaulter may be issued by the Adjudicating Authority if the Adjudicating Authority is satisfied that with the object or effect of delaying the execution of the certificate, the defaulter is likely to abscond or leave the local limits of the jurisdiction of the Adjudicating Authority.

4. A warrant of arrest issued by the Adjudicating Authority may also be executed by any other Adjudicating Authority within whose jurisdiction the defaulter may, for the time being, be found.

5. When a defaulter appears before the Adjudicating Authority pursuant to a notice to show cause or is brought before the Adjudicating Authority, the Adjudicating Authority shall give the defaulter an opportunity to show the cause why he should not be committed to the civil prison.

6. Pending the conclusion of the inquiry, the Adjudicating Authority may, in his discretion, order the defaulter to be detained in the custody of such officer as the Adjudicating Authority may think fit or release him on his furnishing the security to the satisfaction of the Adjudicating Authority for his appearance as and when required.

7. Upon the conclusion of the inquiry, the Adjudicating authority may make an order for the detention of the defaulter in the civil prison and shall in that event cause him to be arrested if he is not already under arrest.

8. When the Adjudicating Authority does not make an order of detention, he shall direct his release.

9. A defaulter released from detention under this section shall not, merely by reason of his release, be discharged from his liability for the arrears, but he shall not be liable to be arrested under the certificate in execution of which he was detained in the civil prison.

Appeal to appellate tribunal

The central government or any aggrieved person may file an appeal with the appellate authority and the relevant provisions are as follows:

1. The Central Government or any person aggrieved by an order made by an Adjudicating Authority may file an appeal petition before the appellate tribunal.

2. Every appeal shall be filed within a period of forty-five days from the date on which a copy of the order made by the Adjudicating Authority or the Special Director (Appeals) is received by the aggrieved person.

3. On receipt of an appeal, the Appellate Tribunal may, after giving the parties to the appeal an opportunity of being heard, pass such orders thereon as it thinks fit, confirming, modifying or setting aside the order appealed against.

4. The Appellate Tribunal shall send a copy of every order made by it to the parties, to the appeal and to the concerned Adjudicating Authority or the Special Director (Appeals), as the case may be.

Appeal to high court   Any person aggrieved by any decision or order of the Appellate Tribunal may file an appeal to the High Court within sixty days from the date of communication of the decision or order of the Appellate Tribunal to him on any question of law arising out of such order.

DIRECTORATE OF ENFORCEMENT

The Central Government is empowered by the Act to establish a Directorate of Enforcement with a Director and such other officers or class of officers as it thinks fit. These officers shall be called officers of Enforcement, for the purposes of this Act.

The Director of Enforcement and other officers of Enforcement, not below the rank of an Assistant Director, shall take up for investigation the contravention referred to it as per regulations. The Central Government may also, by notification, authorise any officer or class of officers in the Central Government, State Government or the Reserve Bank, not below the rank of an Under Secretary to the Government of India to investigate any contravention referred to it.

The Central Government may, by order and subject to such conditions and limitations as it thinks fit to impose, authorise any officer of customs or any central excise officer or any police officer or any other officer of the Central Government or a State Government to exercise such powers and discharge such duties of the Director of Enforcement.

SUSPENSION OF OPERATION OF THE FEMA

If the Central Government is satisfied that circumstances have arisen rendering it necessary that any permission granted or restriction imposed by this Act should cease to be granted or imposed, or if it considers necessary or expedient so to do in public interest, the Central Government may by notification, suspend or relax to such extent either indefinitely or for such period as may be notified, the operation of all or any of the provisions of this Act.

Every notification issued in this regard shall be laid before each House of Parliament, while it is in session, for a total period of thirty days which may be comprised in one session or in two or more successive sessions. If, before the expiry of the session immediately following the session or the successive sessions aforesaid, both Houses agree in making any modification in the notification or both Houses agree that the notification should not be issued, the notification shall thereafter have effect only in such modified form or be of no effect, as the case may be. However, any such modification or annulment shall be without prejudice to the validity of anything previously done under that notification.

POWER OF THE CENTRAL GOVERNMENT TO GIVE DIRECTIONS

For the purposes of this Act, the Central Government may, from time to time, issue to the Reserve Bank such general or special directions as it thinks fit, and the Reserve Bank shall, in the discharge of its functions under this Act, comply with any such directions.

RECENT MEASURES TO MANAGE FOREIGN INVESTMENTS

Some of the important and recent measures taken by Indian government to manage foreign investments in India are discussed in detail.

FOREIGN DIRECT INVESTMENT

The Foreign Direct Investment (FDI) is permitted under the Automatic Route in items/ activities in all sectors up to the sectoral caps except in certain sectors where investment is prohibited. Investments not permitted under the automatic route, require approval from Foreign Investment Promotion Board (FIPB). The receipt of remittance has to be reported to the RBI within 30 days from the date of receipt of funds and the issue of shares has to be reported to the RBI within 30 days from the date of issue by the investee company.

Advance against equity   An Indian company issuing shares to a person resident outside India can receive such amount in advance. The amount received has to be reported within 30 days from the date of receipt of funds. There is no provision on allotment of shares within a specified time. The banks can refund the amount received as advance, provided they are satisfied with the bonafides of the applicant and they are satisfied that no part of remittance represents interest on the funds received.

FOREIGN PORTFOLIO INVESTMENT

FIIs   Investment by non-residents is permitted under the Portfolio Investment scheme to entities registered as FIIs and their sub-accounts under SEBI (FII) regulations. Investment by individual FIIs is subject to a ceiling of 10% of the Pollution under Control (PUC) of the company and limit for aggregate FII investment is subject to limit of 24% of PUC of the company. This limit can be increased by the company, subject to the sectoral limit permitted under the FDI policy. The transactions are subject to daily reporting by designated ADs (Authorised Dealers) to the RBI for the purpose of monitoring the adherence to the ceiling for aggregate investments.

NRIs   The investment by NRIs under the Portfolio Investment Scheme is restricted to 5% by individual NRIs/OCBs (not incorporated in Bangladesh and Pakistan) and 10% in aggregate (which can be increased to 24% by the company concerned).

ADR/GDR   Indian companies are allowed to raise resources through issue of ADR/GDR and the eligibility of the issuer company is aligned with the requirements under the FDI policy. The issues of sponsored ADR/GDR require prior approval of ministry of finance.

Foreign venture capital investors   Foreign Venture Capital Investors (FVCIs) registered with the SEBI are allowed to invest in units of venture capital funds any limit. FVCI investment in equity of Indian venture capital undertakings is also allowed. The limit for such investments would be based on the sectoral limits under the FDI policy. FVCIs are also allowed to invest in debt instruments floated by the India Venture Capital Undertakings (IVCUs). There is no separate limit stipulated for investment in such instruments by FVCIs.

External Commercial Borrowings (ECB)

Under the Automatic Route, ECB up to US$ 500 million per borrowing company per financial year is permitted only for foreign currency expenditure for permissible end-uses of ECB. Borrowers in infrastructure sector may avail ECB up to US$ 100 million for rupee expenditure for permissible end-uses under the Approval Route. In the case of other borrowers, the limit for Rupee expenditure for permissible end-uses under the Approval Route has been enhanced to US$ 50 million from earlier limit of US$ 20 million. Entities in the services sector, namely, hotels, hospitals and software companies have been allowed to avail ECB up to US$ 100 million, per financial year, for the purpose of import of capital goods under the Approval Route. The all-in-cost interest ceiling for borrowings with maturity of 3–5 years has been increased from 150 basis points over 6-month LIBOR (London Inter-bank Offered Rate) to 200 basis points over 6-month LIBOR. Similarly, the interest ceiling for loans maturing after 5 years period has been raised to 350 basis points over 6-month LIBOR from 250 basis points over 6-month LIBOR.

Investment by NRIs in Immovable Properties

The NRIs are permitted to freely acquire immovable property (other than agricultural land, plantations and farmhouses). There are no restrictions regarding the number of such properties to be acquired. The only restriction is that where the property is acquired out of inward remittances, the repatriation is restricted to principal amount for two residential properties.

There is no such restriction in respect of commercial property. The NRIs are also permitted to avail of housing loans for acquiring property in India and repayment of such loans by close relatives is also permitted. Added to the above-mentioned developments in the regulatory framework, recently the Government of India has decided to restrict the entry of foreign investors (effective from 31 March, 2009) in some sectors like multi-brand retail, atomic energy, lottery, gambling and betting. Added to this, the government has also decided to restrict the entry of foreign investors up to a specified level.

AMENDMENTS TO FOREIGN EXCHANGE REGULATIONS

The Reserve Bank of India makes necessary amendments to the Foreign Exchange Management Act as and when necessary under different heads such as

1. Export of goods and services
2. Acquisition and transfer of immovable properties
3. Adjudication proceedings and appeal
4. Borrowing and lending in rupees
5. Borrowing and lending in foreign exchange
6. Current Account transactions
7. Deposit
8. Encashment of draft, cheque, instruments, and so on
9. Establishment in India of branch or office
10. Export and import of currency
11. Foreign currency accounts by a person
12. Foreign exchange derivatives contracts
13. Guarantees
14. Insurance
15. Investment in firm or proprietary concern
16. Issue of security in India by a branch, office in India
17. Manner of receipt and payments
18. Offshore banking unit
19. Permissible Capital Account transactions
20. Possession and retention of foreign currency

The Reserve Bank of India has, so far, made a number of amendments to foreign exchange regulations. This has become necessary to cope with changing international economic conditions as well as domestic compulsions. The following are the amendments made to the provisions of the FEMA up to July, 28 in 2009:

NOTIFICATION NO. FEMA 196/2009-RB DATED JULY 28, 2009

"Subject to the Regulations in Part I, an Indian party engaged in financial services sector in India may make investment in an entity outside India: provided that the Indian party has earned net profit during the preceding three financial years from the financial services activities; is registered with the regulatory authority in India for conducting the financial services activities; has obtained approval from the concerned regulatory authorities both in India and abroad, for venturing into such financial sector activity; and has fulfilled the prudential norms relating to capital adequacy as prescribed by the concerned regulatory authority in India."

NOTIFICATION NO.FEMA193/2009-RB DATED JUNE 2, 2009

In the Foreign Exchange Management (Deposit) Regulations, 2000 (Notification No. FEMA 5/2000-RB dated May 3, 2000), in Regulation 4, in sub-regulation (3), for clause (a), the following shall be substituted, namely, "(a) credits to the account shall be only by way of (i) proceeds of inward remittances received from outside India through normal banking channels; and (ii) transfer of funds, from the rupee account of the diplomatic mission in India, which are collected in India as visa fees and credited to such account."

NOTIFICATION NO. FEMA 191/2009-RB DATED MAY 20, 2009

In the Foreign Exchange Management (Foreign Exchange Derivative Contracts) Regulations, 2000 (Notification No. FEMA 25/RB-2000 dated May 3, 2000), after Regulation 6, the following new regulation shall be inserted namely, "Freight" hedge.

6A

i. The Reserve Bank may, on an application made in accordance with such procedure as may be directed by the Reserve Bank, permit a person resident in India, subject to such terms and conditions as may be considered necessary, to enter in to a freight derivative contract in an exchange or a market out side India to hedge the freight-risk such person is exposed to.

ii. Notwithstanding anything contained in sub regulation

- an authorised dealer in India specially authorised by the Reserve Bank under sub-regulation

- Regulation 6 may permit an oil refining company or a shipping company, resident in India, to enter in to freight derivative contracts in an exchange or market outside India, to hedge the freight risk which the company is exposed to, subject to such terms and conditions as may be stipulated by the Reserve Bank from time to time.

Provided that such authorised dealer category-I bank shall exercise the authority subject to directions and guidelines issued to them by the Reserve Bank in that behalf.

Notification No. FEMA 188/2009-RB Dated February 3, 2009

3. *Amendment to Section 2*—In the Foreign Exchange Management (Transfer or Issue of any Foreign Security) Regulations, 2004 (Notification No. FEMA 120/RB-2004 dated July 7, 2004) (hereinafter referred to as "the principal regulations"), in regulation 2,

(i) after clause (r), the following shall be inserted and shall be deemed to have been inserted with effect from September 23, 2008, namely, "(s) "Foreign Currency Exchangeable Bond" means a bond expressed in foreign currency, the principal and interest in respect of which is payable in foreign currency, issued by an issuing company and subscribed to by a person who is a resident outside India in foreign currency and exchangeable into equity share of offered company, in any manner, either wholly, or partly or on the basis of any equity related warrants attached to debt instruments. (t) "issuing company" means a company registered under the Companies Act, 1956 (1 of 1956) and eligible to issue Foreign Currency Exchangeable Bond under these regulations. (u) "offered company" means a company registered under the Companies Act, 1956 (1 of 1956) and whose equity share/s is/are offered in exchange of the Foreign Currency Exchangeable Bond. (v) "promoter group" has the same meaning as defined in the Securities and Exchange Board of India (Disclosure and Investor Protection) Guidelines, 2000". (ii) clause (s) shall be renumbered as "(w)".

4. *Amendment to Regulation 21* In Part III, in regulation 21 of the principal regulations, after clause (ii) of sub-regulation (2), the following clause shall be inserted and shall be deemed to have been inserted with effect from September 23, 2008, namely, (iii) "may issue Foreign Currency Exchangeable Bonds to a person resident outside India in accordance with and subject to the conditions specified in Schedule IV with the specific approval of the Reserve Bank."

5. *Insertion of new schedule* After schedule III of the principal regulations, the following new schedule shall be inserted and shall be deemed to have been inserted with effect from September 23, 2008, namely,

"Schedule IV [see Regulation 21(2)]
Foreign Currency Exchangable Bonds (FCEBs)

1. *Currency* The FCEB may be denominated in any freely convertible foreign currency.

2. *Eligible issuer* The issuing company shall be part of the promoter group of the offered company and shall hold the equity share/s being offered at the time of issuance of FCEB.

3. *The offered company* The offered company shall be a listed company which is engaged in a sector eligible to receive Foreign Direct Investment and eligible to issue or avail FCCB or External Commercial Borrowings (ECB).

4. *Entities not eligible to issue the FCEB*   An Indian company, which is not eligible to raise funds from the Indian securities market including a company which has been restrained from accessing the securities market by the SEBI, shall not be eligible to issue the FCEB.

5. *Eligible subscriber*   Entities complying with the Foreign Direct Investment policy and adhering to the sectoral caps at the time of issue of the FCEB can subscribe to the FCEB. Prior approval of Foreign Investment Promotion Board, wherever required under the Foreign Direct Investment policy, should be obtained.

6. *Entities not eligible to subscribe to the FCEB*   Entities prohibited to buy, sell or deal in securities by the SEBI will not be eligible to subscribe to the FCEB.

7. *End-use of FCEB proceeds*

Issuing company

i.   The proceeds of the FCEB may be invested by the issuing company outside India by way of direct investment including in Joint Ventures or Wholly Owned Subsidiaries abroad, subject to the existing guidelines on Overseas Investment in Joint Ventures or Wholly Owned Subsidiaries (abroad).

ii.   The proceeds of the FCEB may be invested by the issuing company in the promoter group companies.

Promoter group companies   Promoter Group Companies receiving investments out of the FCEB proceeds may utilise the FCEB proceeds in accordance with end-uses prescribed under the External Commercial Borrowings policy.

8. *End-uses not permitted*   The promoter group companies receiving such investments will not be permitted to utilise the proceeds for investments in the capital market or in real estate in India.

9. *All-in-cost*   The rate of interest payable on the FCEB and the issue expenses incurred in foreign currency shall be within the all-in-cost ceiling as provided in the Foreign Exchange Management (Borrowing or Lending in Foreign Exchange) Regulations, 2000, (Notification No.FEMA 3/2000-RB, dated May 3, 2000) and the directions issued in that behalf by the Reserve Bank of India.

10. *Pricing of the FCEB*   At the time of issuance of the FCEB, the exchange price of the offered listed equity shares shall not be less than the higher of the following two:

i.   The average of the weekly high and low of the closing prices of the shares of the offered company quoted on the stock exchange during the six months preceding the relevant date; and

ii.   The average of the weekly high and low of the closing prices of the shares of the offered company quoted on a stock exchange during the two week preceding the relevant date.

Explanation to clause (i) and (ii): "Relevant date" means the date on which the board of directors of the issuing company passes the resolution authorising the issue of the FCEB.

11. *Average Maturity* Minimum maturity of the FCEB shall be five years. The exchange option can be exercised at any time before redemption. While exercising the exchange option, the holder of the FCEB shall take delivery of the offered shares. Cash (Net) settlement of the FCEB shall not be permissible.

The proceeds of the FCEB shall be retained and/or deployed overseas by the issuing/group companies in accordance with the Foreign Exchange Management (borrowing or lending in foreign exchange) Regulations, 2000, (FEMA 3/2000-RB, dated May 3, 2000) and the directions issued in that behalf by the Reserve Bank from time to time.

12. *Parking of the FCEB proceeds abroad* The proceeds of the FCEB shall be retained and/or deployed overseas by the issuing/promoter group companies in accordance with the policy for the ECB. It shall be the responsibility of the issuing company to ensure that the proceeds of the FCEB are used by the promoter group company only for the permitted end-uses prescribed under the ECB policy. The issuing company should also submit audit trail of the end-use of the proceeds by the issuing company/promoter group companies to the Reserve Bank duly certified by the designated Authorised Dealer bank.

13. *Operational Procedure* Issuance of the FCEB shall require prior approval of the Reserve Bank of India as specified in the Foreign Exchange Management (Borrowing or Lending in Foreign Exchange) Regulations, 2000, (Notification No FEMA 3/2000-RB, dated May 3, 2000).

14. *Reporting* The provisions of the Foreign Exchange Management (Borrowing or Lending in Foreign Exchange) Regulations, 2000, (Notification No FEMA 3/2000-RB, dated May 3, 2000) with regard to reporting of external commercial borrowings shall apply to the FCEB.

NOTIFICATION NO. FEMA 187/2009-RB DATED FEBRUARY 3, 2009

Amendment of regulation 5—In the Foreign Exchange Management (Guarantees) Regulations, 2000 (Notification No. FEMA 8/2000-RB) dated 3 May, 2000, in regulation 5, after clause (c), the following new clause shall be inserted and shall be deemed to have been inserted with effect from the 11th July, 2008, namely,

"(d) a bank which is an authorised dealer may, subject to the directions issued by the Reserve Bank in this behalf, permit a person resident in India or on behalf such a person to issue guarantee in favour of an overseas lender or security trustee to secure an external commercial borrowing availed under the provisions of the Foreign Exchange Management (Borrowing or Lending in Foreign Exchange) Regulations, 2000 (Notification No FEMA 3/2000-RB, dated 3 may, 2000)."

Notification No. FEMA 186/2009-RB Dated February 3, 2009

3. *Amendment of regulation 6*   In the Foreign Exchange Management (Acquisition and Transfer of Immovable Property in India) Regulations, 2000 (Notification No. FEMA 21/2000-RB dated 3 May, 2000 (hereinafter referred to as the "principal regulations") in regulation 6, in clause (b) after sub clause (iii), the following clause shall be inserted and shall be deemed to have been inserted with effect from the 11th July, 2008, namely, "(c) In the event of failure in repayment of external commercial borrowing availed by a person resident in India under the provisions of the Foreign Exchange Management (borrowing or lending in foreign exchange) Regulations, 2000, (Notification No. FEMA 3/2000-RB, dated 3 May, 2000) a bank which is an authorised dealer may permit the overseas lender or the security trustee (in whose favour the charge on immovable property has been created to secure the ECB) to sell the immovable property on which the said loan has been secured only to a (by the) person resident in India and to repatriate the sale proceeds towards outstanding dues in respect of the said loan and not any other loan."

4. *Amendment to regulation 8*   In the principal regulations, in regulation 8, after the proviso, the following new proviso shall be inserted and shall be deemed to have been inserted with effect from the 11th day of July, 2008, namely, "Provided further that a bank which is an authorised dealer may, subject to the directions issued by the Reserve Bank in this behalf, permit a person resident in India or on behalf of such person to create charge on his immovable property in India in favour an overseas lender or security trustee, to secure an external commercial borrowing availed under the provisions of the Foreign Exchange Management (Borrowing or Lending in Foreign Exchange) Regulations, 2000 (Notification No. FEMA 3/2000-RB, dated 3 May, 2000)."

Notification No. FEMA 183/2009-RB Dated 20 January, 2009

In the Foreign Exchange Management (borrowing and lending in rupees) Regulations, 2000 (Notification No. FEMA 4/2000-RB dated 3rd May, 2000), in Regulation 5, after sub-regulation (3) the following new sub-regulation (4) shall be inserted, namely, "(4) The borrowing by way of issue of preference shares on or after 30th day of April 2007 other than those which are fully and mandatorily convertible into equity within a specified time and issue of convertible debentures on or after 7th day of June 2007, other than those which are fully and mandatorily convertible into equity within a specified time, to a person resident outside India, shall be considered as debt and shall accordingly conform to Regulation 6 of the Foreign Exchange Management (Borrowing or Lending in Foreign Exchange) Regulations 2000 (Notification No. FEMA 3/2000-RB dated 3rd May, 2000) including the limits to such Borrowings as specified in the said regulations."

Notification No. FEMA184/2009-RB Dated 20 January, 2009

Insertion of new regulation 27: In the Foreign Exchange Management (Transfer or Issue of Any Foreign Security) Regulations, 2004 (Notification No. FEMA.120/2004-RB dated 7 July, 2004, after regulation 26, the following regulation shall be inserted, namely, *"27: Opening of Demat Accounts by Clearing Corporations of Stock Exchanges and Clearing Members* A Person resident in India being a Securities and Exchange Board of India approved clearing corporation of stock exchanges and their clearing members may, subject to the guidelines issued by the SEBI from time to time;

i. open and maintain demat accounts with foreign depositories and acquire, hold, pledge and transfer the foreign sovereign securities, offered as collateral by FIIs;

ii. remit the proceeds arising from corporate action, if any, on such foreign sovereign securities; and

iii. liquidate such foreign sovereign securities and repatriate the proceeds thereof to India."

SUMMARY

❈ The Foreign Exchange Regulation Act of 1973 (FERA) in India was repealed on 1 June, 2000. It was replaced by the Foreign Exchange Management Act (FEMA), 1999.

❈ The FEMA, which replaced the FERA, had become the need of the hour since the FERA had become incompatible with the pro-liberalisation policies of the Government of India.

❈ The objective of the FEMA is to consolidate and amend the law relating to foreign exchange with the objective of facilitating external trade and payments and for promoting the orderly development and maintenance of foreign exchange market in India.

❈ The Reserve Bank of India has enormous powers in the management of foreign exchange matters in India.

❈ There are several important provisions of the FEMA which the exporters and importers must be aware.

❈ Amendments are being made to it as and when the government feels necessary.

Review Questions (Short)

1. Discuss briefly the history of the FEMA.

2. Discuss briefly the nature of the FERA provisions.

3. State the objectives and scope of the FEMA.

4. What are the powers of the Reserve Bank of India in regulating foreign exchange in India?

5. What are the duties of the exporters under the FEMA?

6. Who is an authorised person?

7. Explain the provisions of the FEMA regarding penalties.

8. Who can appeal to Appellate Tribunal? Explain the provisions of the FEMA in relation to appeals.

9. Explain the functions of the Directorate of Enforcement.

Review Questions (Detailed)

1. Explain in detail the powers of the Reserve Bank of India in managing foreign exchange in India.

2. Explain the provisions of the FEMA in connection with the dealing in foreign exchange.

3. Discuss the provisions of the FEMA regarding realisation and repatriation of foreign exchange.

4. Explain the provisions of the FEMA in relation to enforcement of the orders of the Adjudicating Authority.

5. Explain about the recent measures taken by the Government of India to manage foreign investments in India.

References

1. www.cybex.in/…/Agricultural-Processed-Food-Products-Export-Development-Authority.aspx

2. www.mpeda.com/Overview/about.htm

3. www.indembassysuriname.com/export_promotion_councils.html

4. www.giftsnaccessories.com/indian-handicrafts/138.htm

5. www.articlesnatch.com/Article/India-Export-Promotion.../

6. www.biztradeshows.com/.../carpet-expo-promotions.html

7. www.aepcindia.com/faq.asp

8. www.maharashtradirectory.com/industrialresources/fieo.htm

9. www.indembassysuriname.com/india_trade_promotions_organisation_itpo.html

10. www.commerce.nic.in/aboutus/aboutus_advisorybodies.asp

11. www.infodriveindia.com › Exim › HOW-TO-EXPORT

12. www.planningcommission.nic.in/aboutus/committee/wrkgrp11/wg11_heasys.pdf

13. www.iift.edu/

11

ROLE OF FINANCIAL INSTITUTIONS

LEARNING OBJECTIVES

To understand the role of the following financial institutions in the promotion of foreign trade in India:

* Reserve Bank of India

* EXIM Bank of India

* Export Credit Guarantee Corporation of India, and

* Commercial Banks.

KEY TERMS

* Working Group
* Gold Card Scheme
* On-line credit
* Fast track clearance
* Customer education
* Export Credit Performance Indicator
* Global economic slowdown
* Export services group
* Supplier's group
* Forfeiting
* Standard policy
* Packing credit guarantee
* Exchange fluctuation cover
* Policies for SME sector
* Specific shipment policy
* Export turnover policy
* Buyer exposure policy
* Consignment exports policy
* Service policy
* Software project policy
* Construction works policy
* Line of credit
* Rupee export credit
* Export bill rediscounting
* Bank guarantees

INTRODUCTION

In today's world, a country must export and earn foreign exchange for its survival. Or, the country must have a good number of gold mines, if it wants to remain aloof from exporting. But India has neither gold mines nor sufficient petroleum resources to remain indifferent with regard to exports. It is a compulsory requirement for our country to export. The slogan "Export or Perish" would suit best to India. To feed India's masses, to offer employment to them, and to become free of foreign debts, India must export its surplus commodities and services to foreign countries. But the irony is India's masses consume most of the commodities produced domestically. Only in a few cases, the country is in possession of surplus goods. So the problem is to produce surplus commodities locally. The government has been making an all-out effort to do it. But in every month, we find imports exceeding the exports thereby leaving no room to build up its foreign reserves. If our nationals residing abroad do not send their hard earned money to India, the already debt-trapped country cannot make its journey towards development.

The government, finally, decided to embark upon globalisation in 1991 through its new economic policy. The new economic policy and the measures taken by the government alongside have resulted in a surge of exports. But the quantum of imports also jumped like an angry leopard. The position on the other side has, however, changed due to globalisation of the economy. Employment generation has been on expected lines. The country has been receiving lot of FDI. The country has been improving its infrastructure in an unbelievable pace.

The present scenario has reinforced the country's resolve to export more. The government has been taking a number of steps to encourage exporters and others as well to earn more foreign exchange. It too has been working for providing relief and assistance to the exporters in the form of providing finance through government-owned and other financial institutions. It is important to note that to promote exports of the country, the RBI has a policy stance that 10% of the total credit should comprise loans to exporters in case of private and public sector banks. Unlike PSU and private banks, for foreign banks, export credit is part of its priority sector lending. Let us study in this chapter how the Indian financial system and its components are supporting the exporters in their task to increase their exports.

THE RESERVE BANK OF INDIA

Exports play an important role in accelerating the economic growth of developing countries like India. In view of the important role played by exporters, several initiatives have been taken by the Reserve Bank of India and Government of India. These initiatives have contributed to an impressive increase in our exports. Of the several factors influencing export growth, credit is a very important factor which enables exporters in efficiently executing their export orders. The commercial banks provide short-term export finance, mainly by way of pre- and post-shipment credit. Export finance is granted in rupees as well as in foreign currency.

In view of the importance of export credit in maintaining the pace of export growth, the RBI has initiated several measures in the recent years to ensure timely and hassle free flow of credit to the export sector. These measures, inter alia, include rationalisation and liberalisation of export credit interest rates, flexibility in repayment/prepayment of pre-shipment credit, special financial package for large value exporters, export finance for agricultural exports, Gold Card Scheme for exporters, and so on. Further, the banks have been granted freedom by the RBI to source funds from abroad without any limit, exclusively for the purpose of granting export credit in foreign currency, and this has enabled banks to increase their lending under export credit in foreign currency substantially during the last three years.

The RBI introduced the Export Financing scheme in 1968. The policy behind the scheme was to make short-term export finance available to exporters at internationally competitive interest rates, while at the same time ensuring that the rates are well above the financing banks' cost of finance for short-term loans of the same duration in the relevant currency. Under the scheme, banks extend working capital loans to exporters at pre- and post-shipment stages. The credit limits sanctioned to exporters is based upon the financing banks' perception of the exporter's creditworthiness and past performance.

Export Financing may be denominated either in Indian rupees or in a foreign currency. For both types of pre-shipment financing, the RBI set a ceiling on the interest rate that banks may charge to borrowers under the scheme. Since the RBI fixes only the ceiling rate of interest for export credit, the banks are free to fix lower rates of interest for exporters on the basis of their actual cost of funds, operating expenses and taking into account the track record and the risk perception of the borrower/exporter.

Working Group to Review the Scheme of Export Credit

The RBI desired that a Working Group consisting of Department of Banking Operations and Development (DBOD) and Monetary Policy Department (MPD) of the RBI, the banks, and the export organisations may be set up to quickly review the scheme of export credit and that the report of the Group should be placed in public domain for feedback.

The terms of reference of the Working Group which was constituted in 2005 were the review of

1. Existing procedures for export credit,

2. Action taken on exporters' satisfaction survey,

3. Gold Card Scheme,

4. Export credit for non-star exporters and

5. Current interest rate regulations in export credit

Accordingly, a Working Group was constituted under the Chairmanship of Shri Anand Sinha, Chief General Manager, in charge of Department of Banking Operations and Development, (DBOD) Central Office, Reserve Bank of India. The other Members of the Group consisted of Senior Officials from Monetary Policy Department of Reserve Bank of India RBI), State Bank of India, Canara Bank, Federal Bank Limited, Federation of Indian Exporters' Organisations (FIEO), Engineering Export Promotion Council (EEPC) and All India Association of Industries (AIAI).

The Group reviewed the existing procedures for export credit, after which members opined that existing procedures in place were adequate to take care of the interest of the exporters. The Export Promotion Organisations represented that they have been receiving complaints that the timeframe prescribed by the RBI for disposal of the applications for export credit is not complied with by many banks, especially in the case of small and medium exporters and exporters in smaller centres. Piecemeal queries were raised, which resulted in delays in sanctioning/rejecting the loan applications from exporters. Non-adherence to the set procedures and systems was more pronounced in the case of small and medium exporters who are expected to play a bigger role in the promotion of exports in the coming years.

RECOMMENDATIONS

The Working Group made the following recommendations on export credit to Indian exporters.

1. There is a need for attitudinal change in the approach of banks' officials. While posting officials, banks may keep in view the attitude of officials to exporters' credit requirements, especially the small and medium exporters.

2. The banks should put in place, a control and reporting mechanism to ensure that the applications for export credit especially from small and medium exporters are disposed of within the prescribed timeframe. They should ensure that this recommendation is implemented in letter and spirit. The Internal/Concurrent audit in banks should comment on whether or not the prescribed timeframe for disposal of export credit applications are being adhered to by the banks. The regional managers of banks, during their branch visits, should also look into this aspect.

3. The banks should raise all queries in one shot and should avoid piecemeal queries, in order to avoid delays in sanctioning credit.

4. The SMEs especially in the upcountry centres should be properly trained by the SSI/ export organisations with technical assistance from banks regarding correct filling up of forms and furnishing all required information to banks to avoid delay.

5. The IBA may take initiative to devise a simplified loan application form in consultation with the FIEO and other export promotion organisations which should serve a model for all banks.

6. Alternatives to collateral security should be found and fully made use of.

7. State Level Export Promotion Committees which have been reconstituted as sub-committees of the SLBCs should play a greater role in promoting coordination between the banks and the exporters in the respective states and export promotion organisations should take initiative in coordinating the meetings.

RBI ACTION ON THE RECOMMENDATIONS OF THE WORKING GROUP ON EXPORT CREDIT

As part of the on-going efforts to address various issues relating to customer service to exporters, the Reserve Bank of India constituted a Working Group in May 2005, consisting of select banks and exporters' organisations to review export credit. The Group came out with a comprehensive set of recommendations, most of which have been accepted and communicated to banks. The Reserve Bank of India issued a Master Circular DBOD. DIR (Exp.) No.03/04.02.02/2005–06 dated 1 July, 2005 on the recommendations of the Working Group on Export Finance. It contained the following points:

1. Customer service and simplification of procedures

i. Banks may provide timely and adequate credit and also render essential customer services/guidance in regard to procedural formalities and export opportunities to their exporter clients.

ii. Banks should open Export Counsel Offices to guide exporters, particularly the small ones and those taking up non-traditional exports.

2. *Gold card scheme for exporters* The Government (Ministry of Commerce and Industry), in consultation with the RBI had indicated in the EXIM Policy 2003–04 that a Gold Card Scheme would be worked out by it for creditworthy exporters with good track record for easy availability of export credit on best terms. Accordingly, in consultation with select banks and exporters, a Gold Card Scheme was drawn up. The Scheme envisages certain additional benefits based on the performance record of the exporters. The Gold Card holder would enjoy simpler and more efficient credit delivery mechanism in recognition of his good track record. The salient features of the scheme are:

i. All creditworthy exporters, including those in small and medium sectors with good track record would be eligible for issue of Gold Card by individual banks as per the criteria to be laid down by the latter.

ii. Gold Card under the Scheme may be issued to all eligible exporters including those in the small and medium sectors who satisfy the laid down conditions.

iii. Gold Card holder exporters, depending on their track record and creditworthiness, will be granted better terms of credit including rates of interest than those extended to other exporters by the banks.

iv. Applications for credit will be processed at simpler norms and under a process faster than for other exporters.

v. The banks would clearly specify the benefits they would be offering to Gold Card holders.

vi. The charges schedule and fee-structure in respect of services provided by the banks to the exporters under the Scheme will be relatively lower than those provided to other exporters.

vii. The sanction and renewal of the limits under the Scheme will be based on a simplified procedure to be decided by the banks. Taking into account the anticipated export turnover and track record of the exporter, the banks may determine need-based finance with a liberal approach.

viii. "In-principle" limits will be sanctioned for a period of 3 years with a provision for automatic renewal subject to fulfilment of the terms and conditions of sanction.

ix. A stand-by limit of not less than 20% of the assessed limit may be additionally made available to facilitate urgent credit needs for executing sudden orders. In the case of exporters of seasonal commodities, the peak and off-peak levels may be appropriately specified.

x. In the case of unanticipated export orders, norms for inventory may be relaxed, taking into account the size and nature of the export order.

xi. Requests from card holders would be processed quickly by banks within 25 days/ 15 days and 7 days for fresh applications/renewal of limits and ad hoc limits, respectively.

xii. Gold card holders would be given preference in the matter of granting of packing credit in foreign currency.

xiii. Banks would consider waiver of collaterals and exemption from the ECGC guarantee schemes on the basis of card holder's creditworthiness and track record.

xiv. The facility of further value addition to their cards through supplementary services like ATM, Internet banking, International debit/credit cards may be decided by the issuing banks.

3. *Delay in crediting the proceeds of export bills drawn in foreign currency* Delays are observed in passing on the credit of export bills drawn in foreign currency to the exporters after the foreign currency amounts are credited to the "Nostro" accounts of the banks. Although there are instructions that the concessional post-shipment interest rate will cease from the date of credit to the "Nostro" account, the credit limits enjoyed by the exporters remain frozen till the actual date of credit of rupee equivalent to the account of the customer. There is, therefore,

the need to promptly restore the limit of the exporters on realisation of bills and pass on the rupee credit to the customer.

i. In respect of the delay in affording credit in respect of credit advices complete in all respects, the compensation stipulated by the Foreign Exchange Dealers Association of India (FEDAI) should be paid to the exporter client, without waiting for a demand from the exporter.

ii. The banks should devise a system to monitor timely credit of the export proceeds to the exporter's account and payment of compensation as per the FEDAI rules.

iii. The internal audit and inspection teams of the banks should specifically comment on these aspects in the reports.

4. Sanction of export credit proposals The sanction of fresh/enhanced export credit limits should be made within 45 days from the date of receipt of credit limit application with the required details/information supported by requisite financial/operating statements. In the case of renewal of limits and sanction of ad hoc credit facilities, the time taken by banks should not exceed 30 days and 15 days respectively, other than for Gold Card holders.

i. At times, the exporters require ad hoc limits to take care of large export orders which were not foreseen earlier. The banks should respond to such situations promptly. Apart from this, they should adopt a flexible approach in respect of exporters, who for genuine reasons are unable to bring in corresponding additional contribution in respect of higher credit limits sought for specific orders. No additional interest is to be charged in respect of ad hoc limits granted by way of pre-shipment/post-shipment export credit.

ii. In cases where the export credit limits are utilised fully, the banks may adopt a flexible approach in negotiating the bills drawn against L/Cs and consider in such cases delegating discretionary/higher sanctioning powers to branch managers to meet the credit requirements of the exporters. Similarly the branches may also be authorised to disburse a certain percentage of the enhanced/ad hoc limits, pending sanction by the higher authorities/board/committee who had originally accorded sanctions to enable the exporters to execute urgent export orders in time.

5. Other requirements

i. All rejections of export credit proposals should be brought to the notice of the Chief Executive of the bank explaining the reasons for rejection.

ii. The internal audit and inspection teams of the banks should comment specifically on the timely sanction of export credit limits within the time schedule prescribed by the RBI.

iii. The export credit limits should be excluded for bifurcation of the working capital limit into loan and cash credit components.

iv. The banks should nominate suitable officers as compliance officers in their foreign departments/specialised branches to ensure prompt and timely disposal of cases pertaining to exporters.

v. It is necessary to submit a review note at quarterly intervals to the Board on the position of sanction of credit limits to exporters. The note may cover, among other things, the number of applications (with quantum of credit) sanctioned within the prescribed timeframe, number of cases sanctioned with delay and pending sanction explaining reasons therefor.

6. *Simplification of procedures*   With a view to ensuring timely delivery of credit to exporters and removing procedural hassles, the following guidelines may be brought into effect. These guidelines are applicable to rupee export credit as well as export credit in foreign currency.

i. **Guidelines for simplification of procedures**

- The banks should simplify the application form and reduce data requirements from the exporters for assessment of their credit needs, so that they do not have to seek outside professional help to fill in the application form or to furnish data required by the banks.

- They should adopt any of the methods, namely, projected balance sheet method, turnover method, or cash budget method, for assessment of working capital requirements of their exporter-customers, whichever is most suitable and appropriate to their business operations.

- In the case of consortium finance, once the consortium has approved the assessment, the member banks should simultaneously initiate their respective sanction processes.

ii. **Guidelines for sanctioning line of credit to exporters**

- The banks provide "Line of Credit" normally for one year which is reviewed annually. In the case of delay in renewal, the sanctioned limits should be allowed to continue uninterrupted and urgent requirements of exporters should be met on ad hoc basis.

- In the case of established exporters having satisfactory track record, banks should consider sanctioning a "Line of Credit" for a longer period, say, 3 years, with in-built flexibility to step-up/step-down the quantum of limits within the overall outer limits assessed. The step-up limits will become operative on attainment of pre-determined performance parameters by the exporters. The banks should obtain security documents covering the outer limit sanctioned to the exporters for such longer period.

- In the case of export of seasonal commodities like agro-based products, they should sanction peak/non-peak credit facilities to exporters.

- They should permit interchangeability of pre-shipment and post-shipment credit limits.

- ✷ Term loan requirements for expansion of capacity, modernisation of machinery and upgradation of technology should also be met by banks at their normal rate of interest.

- ✷ Assessment of the export credit limits should be "need based" and not directly linked to the availability of collateral security. As long as the requirement of credit limit is justified on the basis of the exporter's performance and track record, the credit should not be denied merely on the grounds of non-availability of collateral security.

iii. **Guidelines for waiver of submission of orders or L/Cs for availing pre-shipment credit**

- ✷ The banks should not insist on submission of export order or L/C for every disbursement of pre-shipment credit, from exporters with consistently good track-record. Instead, a system of periodical submission of a Statement of L/Cs or export orders in hand, should be introduced.

- ✷ They may waive, ab initio, submission of order/LC in respect of exporters with good track record and put in place the system of obtaining periodical statement of outstanding orders/LCs on hand. The same may be incorporated in the sanction proposals as well as in the sanction letters issued to exporters and appropriately brought to the notice of the ECGC. Further, if such waivers are permitted at a time subsequent to sanction of export credit limits with the approval of the appropriate authority, the same may be incorporated in the terms of sanction by way of amendments and communicated to the ECGC.

iv. **Guidelines for handling of export documents**   The banks are required to obtain, among others, original sale contract/confirmed order/proforma invoice countersigned by overseas buyer/indent from authorised agent of overseas buyer for handling the export documents as per Exchange Control regulations. Submission of such documents need not be insisted upon at the time of handling the export documents, since the goods have already been valued and cleared by the Customs authorities, except in the case of transactions with the Letters of Credit (L/Cs) where the terms of the L/C require submission of the sale contract/other alternative documents.

v. **Guidelines for fast track clearance of export credit**

- ✷ At specialised branches and branches having sizeable export business, a facilitation mechanism for assisting exporter-customers should be put in place for quick initial scrutiny of credit application and for discussions for seeking additional information or clarifications.

- ✷ The banks should streamline their internal systems and procedures to comply with the stipulated time limits for disposal of export credit proposals and also endeavour to dispose of export credit proposals ahead of the prescribed time schedule. A flow chart indicating chronological movement of credit application from the date of receipt till the date of sanction, should also accompany credit proposals.

- ✷ They should delegate higher sanctioning powers to their branches for export credit.

- They should consider reducing at least some of the intervening layers in the sanctioning process. It would be desirable to ensure that the total number of layers involved in decision-making in regard to export finance does not exceed three.

- They should introduce a system of "Joint Appraisal" by officials at branches and administrative offices, to facilitate quicker processing of export credit proposals.

- Where feasible, they should set up a "Credit Committee" at specialised branches and at administrative offices, for sanctioning working capital facilities to exporters. The "Credit Committee" should have sufficiently higher sanctioning powers.

vi. *Guidelines for publicity and training*

- Generally, export credit at internationally competitive rates is made available in foreign currency at select branches of banks. In order to make the scheme more popular and considering the competitive interest rate on foreign currency loans and to mitigate any possible exchange risk, exporters need to be encouraged to make maximum use of export credit in foreign currency. Banks located in areas with concentration of exporters should, therefore, give wide publicity to this important facility and make it easily accessible to all exporters including small exporters and ensure that more number of branches are designated for making available export credit in foreign currency.

- The banks may also arrange to publicise widely the concessions available in the interest rates for deemed exports and ensure that operating staff are adequately sensitised in this regard.

- Officers at the operating level should be provided with adequate training. In the matter of transfer of officials from critical branches dealing in export credit, banks should ensure that the new incumbents posted possess adequate knowledge/exposure in the areas of forex as well as export credit to avoid delays in processing/sanctioning of export credit limits and thereby subjecting exporters to the risk of cancellation of export orders.

vii. *Guidelines for customer education*

- The banks should bring out a Hand Book containing salient features of the simplified procedures for sanction of Export Credit in Foreign Currency at internationally competitive rates as well as in rupees for the benefit of their exporter-clients.

- To facilitate interaction between banks and exporters, they should periodically organise Exporters' Meet at centres with concentration of exporters.

7. *Monitoring implementation of guidelines*

i. They should ensure that exporters' credit requirements are met in full and promptly at competitive rates. The above referred guidelines must be implemented, both in letter and spirit, so as to bring about a perceptible improvement in credit delivery and related banking services to export sector. They should also address the deficiencies, if any, in the mechanism of deployment of staff in their organisations to eliminate the bottlenecks in the flow of credit to the export sector.

ii.   They should set up an internal team to visit branches periodically, say, once in two months to gauge the extent of implementation of the Guidelines.

8. *Constitution of a separate sub-committee under state level bankers' committee* Consequent upon the winding up of the State Level Export Promotion Committee (SLEPC), issues relating to export finance and other bank related issues at the state level will be taken up, henceforth, by a Sub-Committee of the State Level Bankers' Committee (SLBC). This Sub-Committee, known as "Sub-Committee of SLBC for Export Promotion", would include local exporters' associations, the State Bank of India, two/three leading banks handling sizeable export business, Directorate General of Foreign Trade, Customs, State Government (Department of Commerce and Industry and Department of Finance), the Export–Import Bank, Export Credit and Guarantee Corporation, Foreign Exchange Dealers' Association of India besides the Reserve Bank (Foreign Exchange Department and Department of Banking Supervision) at the regional level, as members.

The Sub-Committee is expected to meet at half-yearly intervals, or earlier, if considered necessary. The convener bank of the SLBC would be the Convener of the Sub-Committee in the respective states and the meetings would be chaired by the Executive Director of the convener bank.

9. *Export credit performance indicator for banks*   As a result of the recommendations of the Working Group on Export Finance, the banks are required to reach a level of outstanding export credit equivalent of 12% of each bank's net bank credit. Accordingly, the performance of banks is being reviewed by the RBI, DBOD (Directives Division) at quarterly intervals. The performance of the banks in extending export credit will be assessed on the basis of the average export credit outstanding reported in the fortnightly statement of Export Credit Refinance Limits submitted on reporting Fridays, to Reserve Bank of India, Monetary Policy Department, Central Office, Mumbai.

The banks should endeavour to reach a level of export credit equivalent to 12% of the bank's net credit. Where they have already provided export credit to the extent of 12%, endeavour should be made to increase the same to a higher level and ensure that there is no fall in the ratio. No worthwhile export order should be denied export credit from the banks. Failure to achieve the stipulated level of export credit and or failure to show a distinct improvement in export credit performance could invite bank-specific policy responses which could include raising of reserve requirements and withdrawal of refinance facilities. The Directives Division, DBOD, of the Reserve Bank of India would closely monitor the export credit performance of the banks.

THE RBI AND GLOBAL ECONOMIC SLOW-DOWN

The Reserve Bank has painted a grim picture of the Indian economy in the last quarter of 2008 and early 2009. A day after scaling down the economic growth to 7.5–8% in the credit policy, the RBI Governor Duvvuri Subbarao said that if the global recession continued, growth would fall further in the financial year 2009–2010. However, he also said India was not in a recessionary mode, and the steps taken by the RBI to boost liquidity were adequate.

In view of the difficulties being faced by exporters on account of the weakening of external demand, the RBI has decided to extend the period of entitlement of the first slab of pre-shipment rupee export credit, currently available at a concessional interest rate ceiling of the benchmark prime lending rate minus 2.5% points from 180 days to 270 days with immediate effect.

The banks will get an additional liquidity support to the tune of about ₹22,000 crore as the eligible limits of scheduled banks (excluding RRBs) under the export credit refinance (ECR) facility has been enhanced to 50% of the outstanding export credit eligible for refinance. The rate of interest charged on the ECR facility will continue to be the prevailing repo rate.

Taking into account the need to ensure the growth momentum in the employment-intensive sectors of micro and small enterprises and housing, the RBI has decided to immediately allocate amounts, in advance, from scheduled commercial banks for contribution to the Small Industries Development Bank of India (SIDBI) and the National Housing Bank (NHB) to the extent of ₹2,000 crore and ₹1,000 crore, respectively, against banks' estimated shortfall in priority sector lending in March 2009.

The allocation now made in respect of SIDBI and NHB will be adjusted against the banks' actual achievement of the target/sub targets for priority sector lending as at the end of March 2009. The bank-wise allocations would be notified separately.

The Reserve Bank will continue to closely monitor the developments in the global and domestic financial markets and will take swift and effective action as appropriate.

THE EXIM BANK OF INDIA

The Export–Import Bank (EXIM Bank) of India was established by an Act of Parliament. It is a wholly government owned financial institution, set up for the purpose of financing, facilitating and promoting India's foreign trade. It commenced operations on March 1, 1982. Its mission is to facilitate globalisation of Indian business. The Bank's mission statement: to develop commercially viable relationships with externally oriented companies by supporting their internationalisation efforts, through a diverse range of products and services. The EXIM Bank is managed by a Board of Directors, which has representatives from the Government, Reserve Bank of India, Export Credit Guarantee Corporation of India, a financial institution, public sector banks and the business community. Headquartered in Mumbai, the Bank has nine offices in India and six overseas offices.

As on 31 March 2010, the EXIM Bank had an authorised capital of ₹2000 crore and a paid-up capital of ₹1700 crore. The bank also raises funds from domestic and international markets. It has a global and national network of institutional and professional linkages. It has six global offices at Washington D.C., Singapore, London, Durban, Dubai, and Dakar. The bank has strategic institutional linkages with

- Multilateral agencies such as the World Bank, and Asian Development Bank
- Export Credit Agencies
- Trade and Investment Promotion Agencies abroad
- Trade and Industry Associations in India

The Bank's seven offices in India help the Bank respond to regional developmental activities in the export sector. They identify special needs of the export business through close interaction with existing and prospective clients and suggest innovative instruments appropriate to the region's potential. They also regularly interact with commercial/developmental/government agencies and strengthen the Bank's policy mechanism with their critical inputs on market perceptions and the export environment.

OBJECTIVES

The objectives of the EXIM Bank are to

1. Translate national foreign trade policies into concrete action points.
2. Provide alternate financing solutions to the Indian exporter.
3. Develop mutually beneficial relationships with the international financial community.
4. Initiate and participate in debates on issues central to India's international trade to forge close working relationships with other export development and financing agencies, multilateral funding agencies and national trade and investment promotion agencies.
5. Anticipate and absorb new developments in banking, export financing and information technology.
6. Be responsive to export problems of Indian exporters and pursue policy resolutions.

FUNCTIONS

The Bank's functions are segmented into three major operating groups

1. **Overseas Investment Finance** which handles a variety of financing programmes for Export Oriented Units (EOUs), importers and overseas investment by Indian companies.
2. **Project Finance/Trade Finance** which handles the entire range of export credit services such as supplier's credit, pre-shipment credit, lines of credit, buyer's credit, finance for export of projects and consultancy services, guarantees, forfeiting etc.

3. **Export Services Group** which offers a variety of advisory and value-added information services aimed at investment promotion. Apart from these, there are the Support Services groups, which include Planning and Research, Accounts, Funds Management, Merchant Banking, Management Information Services, Information Technology, Legal, Human Resources Development and Coordination.

Role of the EXIM Bank

The EXIM Bank plays a four-pronged role with regard to India's foreign trade: those of a coordinator, a source of finance, consultant and promoter.

- It is the coordinator of the Working Group Mechanism for clearance of Project and Services Exports and Deferred Payment Exports (for amounts above a certain value—currently ₹200 crore). The Working Group comprises the EXIM Bank, the Government of India representatives (Ministries of Finance, Commerce), the Reserve Bank of India, and the Export Credit Guarantee Corporation of India Limited. Some of the commercial banks have been designated as authorised group for according clearance to contracts (at the post-award stage) sponsored by other commercial banks and the EXIM Bank. This Group operates as a one-window mechanism for clearance of term export proposals. On its own, the Bank can now accord clearance to project export proposals up to ₹200 crore in value.

- The Bank offers a diverse range of financing services for the Indian exporter, including a variety of export credit facilities and finance for export oriented companies.

Export Credits

The Bank offers the following export credit facilities, which can be availed of by Indian companies, commercial banks and overseas entities.

1. *For Indian companies executing contracts overseas pre-shipment credit* Where the manufacturing cycle of the export contract exceeds six months, the Bank's pre-shipment credit facility provides access to finance at the manufacturing stage—enabling exporters to purchase raw materials and other inputs. Exporters can also avail of foreign currency pre-shipment credit facility to import raw materials and other inputs required for export production.

2. *Supplier's credit* At the post-shipment stage, this facility enables Indian exporters to extend term credit to importers (overseas) of eligible goods.

3. *For project exporters* Indian project exporters incur rupee expenditure while executing overseas project export contracts. The Bank's facility helps them meet these expenses. These would generally include costs of mobilisation/acquisition of materials, personnel

and equipment, payments to be made in India to staff, sub-contractors and consultants and project-related overheads in Indian rupees.

4. *For Exporters of Consultancy and Technological Services*   The Bank offers a special credit facility to Indian exporters of consultancy and technology services, so that they can, in turn, extend term credit to overseas importers. The services covered include providing personnel for rendering technical services, transfer of technology, knowhow, preparation of project feasibility reports, maintenance and management contracts etc.

5. *Forfeiting*   Forfeiting is a financing mechanism that enables a company to convert credit sale to cash sale. The Bank acts as a facilitator for the Indian exporter, enabling him to access the services of an overseas forfeiting agency. It offers rediscounting facility to commercial banks, enabling them to rediscount export bills of their SSI customers, with usance not exceeding 90 days. It also offers Refinance of Supplier's Credit, enabling the commercial banks to offer credit to Indian exporters of eligible goods, who in turn extend them credit over 180 days to importers overseas.

6. *Other facilities for Indian companies*   Indian companies executing contracts within India, but which are financed by multilateral funding agencies, can avail of credit under Finance for Deemed Exports facility, aimed at helping them meet cash flow deficits.

7. *For overseas entities*   Overseas buyers can avail of buyer's credit from the Bank, for import of eligible goods from India on deferred payment terms. Besides, the Bank extends lines of credit to overseas financial institutions, foreign governments and their agencies, enabling them to lend term loans to finance import of eligible goods from India.

8. *Finance for export-oriented Units (EOUs)*   For the purpose of the Bank financing, an export-oriented company is defined as any company with a minimum export orientation of 10% of net sales, or annual export sales of ₹5 crore, whichever is lower. Finance for setting up EOUs for textile and jute Industries, software industry and those Indian companies involved in port development and related activities is also provided by the Bank. Equipment finance is also provided for vendors of EOUs. Finance for R and D and export product development, underwriting, export marketing finance, and import loans are also provided. Guarantee facility, and finance for joint ventures between Indian and East Asian companies are also available.

9. *Finance for ventures overseas*   The Bank offers term loans to Indian companies, both for equity investment in their ventures overseas as well as for on lending purposes. It also undertakes direct equity stake in Indian ventures abroad, to enable Indian companies to supplement their equity with the Bank's equity contribution.

10. *Export services*   It offers a diverse range of information, advisory and support services, which enable exporters to evaluate international risks, exploit export opportunities and improve competitiveness.

   i. For Multilateral Agencies Funded Project Overseas (MFPO)

     (a) Commercial services

     (b) Country profiles

   ii. Financing Counselling

   iii. Internalisation

   iv. Support Information Access

   v. Building Export Capability

11. *International merchant banking services* It also provides advisory services to Indian exporters to enable them to offer competitive financial packages when they bid for exports.

12. *Promotional programmes* The following promotional programmes are undertaken by the EXIM Bank of India.

- Grants to Indian firms for the MFPO bids.

- Under the Strategic Market Entry Support Programme, the Bank reimburses the cost of tendering for Indian firms who have bid successfully for the MFPO contracts.

- Grants to Indian firms for obtaining product/process certification.

- The Bank provides grant support of up to 50% of the costs incurred by the company in obtaining certification. The product/process certifications covered under the programme include ISO 9000 and CE/GS certifications.

- Grants to Indian consultants for undertaking services abroad. Under the Project Preparatory Services Overseas (PPSO) Programme, the Bank provides loan/grant finance to enable Indian consultancy firms to take up project preparatory studies in developing countries.

- In an arrangement with International Finance Corporation (IFC), Washington, the Bank is a participant in the trust funds set up by the IFC in different parts of the world. As a result of this arrangement, Indian consultants can avail of grant finance for undertaking specific assignments in select countries in Africa, Eastern Europe and the Mekong delta region.

THE EXPORT CREDIT GUARANTEE CORPORATION OF INDIA (ECGC)

The Export Credit Guarantee Corporation of India Limited (ECGC) was established in the year 1957 by the Government of India to strengthen the export promotion drive by covering the risk of exporting on credit. Being essentially an export promotion organisation, it functions under the administrative control of the Ministry of Commerce and Industry, Department of Commerce, Government of India. It is managed by a Board of Directors comprising representatives of the Government, Reserve Bank of India, banking, insurance, and exporting community. The ECGC of India is the fifth largest credit insurer of the world in terms of coverage of national exports. As on 31 March, 2010, paid-up capital of the company is ₹900 crore and authorised capital ₹1000 crore.

On 21 January, 2009, the ECGC, Kolkata, paid two large value policy claims totaling ₹23.50 crore to two exporters from Kolkata under the policies held by the respective exporters on account of failure in realisation of their export proceeds against shipments of polished gems effected by them to a buyer in Hong Kong. This claim was the highest ever claim paid by the ECGC under policies in the entire Eastern Region. Releasing the claim cheques at a meeting organised at Hotel Taj Bengal, Kolkata, Shri S.Prabhakaran, Executive Director of the Corporation, stated that it was the endeavour of the Corporation to support exporters and banks at all times with cost effective credit insurance products and efficient service delivery including prompt claim payment.

FUNCTIONS OF THE ECGC

The ECGC performs the following functions:

1. Provides a range of credit risk insurance covers to exporters against loss in export of goods and services;

2. Offers guarantees to banks and financial institutions to enable exporters to obtain better facilities from them;

3. Provides Overseas Investment Insurance to Indian companies investing in joint ventures abroad in the form of equity or loan

HOW DOES THE ECGC HELP EXPORTERS?

The ECGC helps the exporters in the following ways:

1. Offers insurance protection to exporters against payment risks

2. Provides guidance in export-related activities

3. Makes available information on different countries with its own credit ratings

4. Makes it easy to obtain export finance from banks/financial institutions

5. Assists exporters in recovering bad debts

6. Provides information on credit-worthiness of overseas buyers

NEED FOR EXPORT CREDIT INSURANCE

Payments for exports are open to risks even at the best of times. The risks have assumed large proportions today due to the far-reaching political and economic changes that are sweeping the world. An outbreak of a war or even a civil war may block or delay payment for goods exported. A coup or an insurrection may also bring about the same result. Economic difficulties or balance of payment problems may lead a country to impose restrictions on either import of certain goods or on transfer of payments for goods imported. In addition, the exporters have to face commercial risks of insolvency or protracted default of buyers. The commercial risks of a foreign buyer going bankrupt or losing his capacity to pay are aggravated due to the political and economic uncertainties. Export credit insurance is designed to protect exporters from the consequences of the payment risks, both political and commercial, and to enable them to expand their overseas business without fear of loss.

POLICIES, GUARANTEES AND COVERS PROVIDED BY THE ECGC

The ECGC issues the following types of policies, guarantees, and covers to the exporters.

1. Shipments (Comprehensive Risks) Policy or Standard Policy
2. Packing Credit Guarantee
3. Exchange Fluctuation Risk Cover
4. Policies for Small and Medium exporters
5. Export Production Finance Gurantee
6. Post-Shipment Credit Guarantee
7. Export Finance Guarantee
8. Export performance Guarantee
9. Specific Policy for Supply Contracts
10. Services Policy
11. Software Project Policy
12. Construction Works Policy
13. Specific Policy for Supply Contract
14. Insurance Cover for Buyer's Credit and Line of Credit

In view of its importance and unique role played by the ECGC in the promotion of exports in India, a detailed discussion on it will be taken up in a separate chapter titled "Export Credit Insurance" in this book.

COMMERCIAL BANKS

Commercial banks have Gold Card Scheme for creditworthy exporters. Simplified access to export credit on very good terms is available. Gold card holders enjoy better terms of credit including rates of interest than those extended to other exporters by the Bank. They enjoy the following advantages over others:

1. Processing of applications for credit is faster than for other exporters.

2. Simpler norms, subject to specific requirements in each case, if any.

3. "In-principle", the credit is limited for a period of 3 years with a provision for automatic renewal, subject to fulfilment of the terms and conditions of sanction.

4. They enjoy preference for grant of packing credit in foreign currency (PCFC), subject to availability of foreign currency funds.

5. They also enjoy lower charges schedule and fee-structure than those provided to other exporters.

6. Relaxation in the norms is given in respect of security and collaterals, wherever feasible.

7. Other facilities/benefits are available to the exporters, subject to the fulfilment of extant rules and regulations applicable to export finance.

TYPES OF FACILITIES FOR EXPORTS

Let us now study the facilities available for exporters in our country.

Rupee Export Credit (Pre-shipment and Post-shipment)

A commercial bank provides both pre- and post-shipment credit to the Indian exporters through Rupee Denominated Loans as well as foreign currency loans in India. Credit facilities are sanctioned to exporters who satisfy credit exposure norms of the banks. Those exporters having firm export orders or confirmed L/C from a bank are eligible to avail the export credit facilities. Rupee export credit is available generally for a period of 180 days from the date of first disbursement. In deserving cases extension may be permitted within the guidelines of the RBI. The corporates may also book forward contracts with the banks in respect of future export credit drawals, if required, as per the guidelines/directives provided by the RBI.

Pre-shipment Credit in Foreign Currency (PCFC)

Commercial banks offer PCFC in the foreign currency to the exporters enabling them to fund their procurement, manufacturing/processing and packing requirements. These loans are available at very competitive international interest rates covering the cost of both domestic as well as import content of the exports. The corporates/exporters with a good track record can avail a running account facility for the PCFC. The PCFC is generally available for a period of 180 days from the date of first disbursement. In deserving cases, extension may be permitted within the guidelines of the RBI.

Features Under the PCFC, withdrawals are permitted in a foreign currency other than the currency of export. The exporter bears the risk in currency fluctuations. The foreign currency withdrawals are restricted to major currencies at present. In case, the export order is in a non-designated currency, the PCFC is given in US$. For orders in Euro, Pound Sterling and JPY, the PCFC can be availed in the respective currencies or US$ at the choice of the exporter. Multi-currency withdrawals against the same order are not permitted at present due to operational inconvenience.

Repayment The PCFC is to be repaid with the proceeds of the export bill submitted after shipment. In case of cancellation of export order, the PCFC can be closed by selling equivalent amount of foreign exchange at TT selling rate prevalent on the date of liquidation. The PCFC in foreign currency are granted at various branches through Integrated Treasury Branches.

Negotiation of bills under L/C

The Authorised Forex Branches are active in negotiation/discounting of sight/usance international export bills under L/Cs opened by foreign banks as well as branches of Indian banks abroad. Normally, a commercial bank offers the most competitive rates. These transactions are undertaken by branches within the Bank/Country Exposure ceilings prescribed by the concerned bank.

Export Bill Rediscounting

A commercial bank provides financing of export by way of discounting of export bills, as a post shipment finance to the exporters at competitive international rate of interest. This facility is available in four currencies that is, US$, Pound Sterling, Euro and JPY. The export bills (both Sight and Usance) drawn in compliance of the FEMA can be purchased/ discounted. Exporters can avail this facility from the banks to cover the bills drawn under L/C as well as other export bills.

Bank guarantees

A commercial bank, on behalf of exporter constituents, issues guarantees in favour of beneficiaries abroad. The guarantees may be Performance and Financial. For Indian exporters, guarantees are issued in compliance to RBI guidelines.

SUMMARY

❈ The RBI introduced the Export Financing Scheme in 1968. The policy behind the Scheme was to make short-term export finance available to exporters at internationally competitive interest rates while at the same time ensuring that the rates are well above the financing banks' cost of finance for short-term loans of the same duration in the relevant currency. The mid-term Review of the Monetary and Credit Policy for the year 2002–03 had proposed deregulation of interest rate on rupee export credit in phases.

❈ The RBI desired that a Working Group may be set up to quickly review the scheme of export credit and that the report of the Group should be placed in public domain for feedback. The Group reviewed the existing procedures for export credit and made several recommendations.

❈ The Reserve Bank of India had issued a Master Circular DBOD. DIR (Exp.) 03/04.02.02/2005–06 dated 1 July, 2005 on the recommendations of the Working Group on Export Finance. The circular contained several provisions including directives to the commercial banks regarding export credit.

❈ The Export–Import Bank (EXIM Bank) of India was established by an Act of Parliament. It is a wholly government owned financial institution, set up for the purpose of financing, facilitating and promoting India's foreign trade. The Bank's functions are segmented into three major operating groups:

1. Overseas Investment Finance,

2. Project Finance/Trade Finance, and

3. Export Services Group.

❈ The commercial banks have Gold Card Scheme for creditworthy exporters. Simplified access to export credit on very good terms is available. Gold card holders enjoy better terms of credit including rates of interest than those extended to other exporters by the Banks.

❈ The commercial banks also offer the following services to the exporters:

i. Rupee Export Credit,

ii. Pre-shipment foreign credit in foreign currency,

iii. Negotiation of Bills under L/C,

iv. Export Bill Rediscounting, and

v. Offering of bank guarantees.

REVIEW QUESTIONS (SHORT)

1. Explain briefly the recommendations of the Working Group of the RBI.
2. Explain briefly the Gold Card Scheme for exporters.
3. Explain fast track credit clearance for exporters.
4. State the objectives of the EXIM Bank of India.
5. What is forfeiting?
6. What are the functions of the ECGC?
7. How does ECGC help exporters?
8. What are the risks covered under the Standard Policy of the ECGC?
9. What is packing credit guarantee?
10. What is exchange fluctuation cover?
11. What is Specific Shipment Policy—Short-term?
12. What is a buyer exposure policy?
13. What is a Consignment Exports Policy?
14. What is a service policy?
15. Explain the features of construction works policy.

REVIEW QUESTIONS (DETAILED)

1. Discuss the role of the Reseve Bank of India in promoting foreign trade.
2. Explain the contributions of the RBI's Working Group in streamlining the bank credit for exporters.
3. Explain in detail the action taken by the RBI on the recommendations of the Working Group.
4. Discuss the role of the ECGC in promoting foreign trade in India.
5. Discuss the role of the EXIM Bank in promoting foreign trade in India.
6. Explain the different policies issued by the ECGC.
7. Discuss the role of the commercial banks in promoting foreign trade.

REFERENCES

1. Reserve Bank of India FERA Guidelines.

2. Sujata Srinivasan, eHow contributor, *Foreign Exchange Regulations Act.*

3. Foreign Exchange Management Act 1993.

12

EXPORT PAYMENTS AND FINANCE

LEARNING OBJECTIVES

After reading this chapter, you will be able to

* recognise the significance of export finance

* know about the methods of payments by the importer, and

* know the details about pre-shipment finance and post-shipment finance.

INTRODUCTION

Export credit plays a very important role in the international trade system. In developed and developing countries, it has been a tool for pushing exports of manufactured and capital goods, as well as some specific services, such as big-ticket items that have high price and long pay-back period. Whatever one's level of experience as an exporter, he needs to be aware of the issues, complexities and options in export finance at a very early stage in his development of an export strategy or of a specific export marketing plan. The trade of manufactured goods has been increasing both in amount and in importance all over the world. Having a greater aggregate value, manufactured goods are sold easier in a foreign market with an appropriate financing mechanism. In effect, payment facilities may soften some aspects concerning price and sometimes they are considered as a component of their prices.

For instance, if a company decides to buy a new machine to produce better merchandise, it will take time to get profit from this acquisition "in cash". In general, the company has to pay a partial amount in advance (down payment) to assure its order. Simultaneously, it has to arrange for local people in addition to people coming for installation of the new machine. Installation of a big machine itself would cost more money. Thus, favourable conditions to make this kind of investment are fundamental; otherwise the companies would face cash-flow problems or fail to improve their production factors, losing competitiveness and consequently market share.

As trade in manufactured goods and services speeds up the transmission of knowledge and technology, many countries have established specific financing programmes to foster the development of their strategic industries. In this context, the banking system's financing programmes have been a very useful tool to increase the country's exports, as well as to restore, update and expand the existing plants, strengthening industrial competitiveness. Thus, this financial support has been one of the prerequisites for the creation of productive capacity in the economy. Since trade is a two-way street, inasmuch as a country can profit from its own export credit policy, it can also profit by others' export credit policies by importing capital goods under more favourable conditions.

The export credit has helped the construction of many big-ticket projects, power stations, water sanitation, transportation systems, telecommunications networks, and the growth of Indian companies on a large scale. The requirements of business in seeking export finance will depend on some of the following questions:

1. Do you require financing before being able to refine or adapt your product or service for export?

2. Do you have a production and distribution process in place domestically, but require funds for market or feasibility analysis, fact-finding trips, international marketing or other pre-shipment activities?

3. Have you opted to do business in a part of the world that is subject to political and economic uncertainty, and are you now in need of services that will help you optimise/mitigate risk?

4. Have you shipped the goods, granting extended payment terms to your buyer, and now require short-term financing until payment is received?

Each of these situations requires a corresponding set of financing requirements, and will suggest a series of public and private sector financing options and sources. In this chapter, we will study finance for exporting in two broad categories:

1. Pre-Shipment Finance

2. Post-Shipment Finance

Pre-shipment finance refers to a broad category, including the financing of new export ventures, as well as specific, transaction-level export finance.

THE CHALLENGE OF EXPORT FINANCE

Export finance includes all the challenges and risks of domestic business finance, familiar to any entrepreneurial venture, plus a series of extra challenges. These extra challenges include:

1. Longer delivery and payment time frames

2. Exchange rate risks and exchange controls

3. Limited and costly dispute settlement and legal recourse options

Financing international trade, specifically exports, can be accomplished in a variety of ways, using a broad range of public and private sector sources, in addition to any funds provided through internal financing, using the company's own resources. Certain export finance solutions can address or mitigate many of the risks noted above.

UNDERSTANDING RISKS

An overriding aspect of international trade, as well as financing related to trade, is the significantly higher risk of pursuing business overseas. An awareness and understanding of export risk, coupled with the appropriate risk strategy, will determine the success or failure of the venture, and will largely shape the financing options. Export-related risk is similar to domestic risk, but vastly different in scope. The many additional factors, the exporter/importer needs to account for in international commerce and the techniques used to manage those risks, should be at the forefront of any well-considered export strategy and export finance approach the exporter chooses.

As a manufacturer, one may have a successful domestic business operation, and exporting an existing product (with the necessary modifications) may be a growth strategy. Or he may be in start-up mode, having identified a product or service that he believes will be attractive to international markets.

MANAGING RISKS

At its core, the main risk related to export finance is the risk of non-payment or of incurring some transaction-related financial loss. Risk management or risk optimisation strategies focus on ensuring timely and secure payment as well as a reasonably predictable flow of funds over the course of an export transaction. Assessing export finance risk typically involves a risk assessment of the trading partner, that is, exporter/importer. The key factors to consider include:

1. Credit-worthiness of the business

2. Commercial character

3. Financial strength of the enterprise

4. Business and political climate in which the buyer/seller operates.

Such assessments ultimately boil down to a judgment call based on a combination of factors. But with the availability of comprehensive information, including extensive historical data, and the development of sophisticated analytical tools, one can use credit scoring and develop fairly thorough risk assessment checklists.

FINANCING EXPORT TRANSACTIONS

Export financing is often a key factor in a successful sale. Contract negotiation and closure are important, but at the end of the day, the company must get paid. The exporters naturally want to get paid as quickly as possible, while importers usually prefer to delay payment until they have received or resold the goods because of the intense competition for export markets. Being able to offer attractive payment terms customary in the trade is often necessary to make sale. The exporters should be aware of the many financing options open to them so that they choose the most acceptable one, to both the buyer and the seller. In many cases, government assistance in export financing for small and medium-sized businesses can increase a firm's options. The following factors are important to consider in making decisions about financing.

1. *The need for financing to make the sale*   In some cases, favourable payment terms make a product more competitive. If the competition offers better terms and has a similar product, a sale can be lost. In other cases, the buyer may have preference for buying from a particular exporter, but might buy the product because of shorter or more secure credit terms.

2. *The length of time the product is being financed*   This determines how long the exporter will have to wait before payment is received and influences the choice of how the transaction is financed.

3. *The cost of different methods of financing* Interest rates and fees vary. Where an exporter can expect to assume some or all of the financing costs, their effect on price and profit should be well understood before a pro forma invoice is submitted to the buyer.

4. *The risks for pre-shipment finance and for post-shipment working capital* Production for an unusually large order, or for a surge of orders, may present unexpected and severe strains on the exporter's working capital. Even during normal periods, inadequate working capital may curb an exporter's growth. However, assistance is available through public and private sector sources discussed in this chapter.

For help in determining which financing options may be available to the exporting endeavours, the following sources may be consulted:

- The banker
- The local Department of Commerce Export Assistance Centre
- The Export–Import Bank of India.

METHODS OF PAYMENTS BY IMPORTERS

Let us now study the different methods of payments followed by the importers.

1. ADVANCE PAYMENTS

This method of payment favours the exporter, as the goods are only shipped (or in some cases manufactured) once payment has been received from the buyer (importer). Under this method, the buyer pays the seller before the goods have been shipped, or in some cases before the goods have been manufactured. Payment can be effected by bank draft or electronically. On conclusion of the contract of sale, the buyer sends the exporter an advance payment. The exporter's bank will receive an inward transfer in his favour. He will need to supply his bank with the appropriate settlement instructions, as well as conversion instructions if the transfer is in foreign currency. The exporter ships the goods and forwards the documents to the buyer. Securing an export transaction that includes payment in advance by the importer is the ideal scenario for the manufacturer engaged in exports.

Characteristics of advance payments

- *Complexity* Minimal
- *Risk* Low to exporter
- *Trade Relationship* Higher-risk relationships on export markets
- *Features* Various options as to timing and proportion of prepayment
- *Cost* Low

A deal may be to ensure partial or full payment in advance. There are several ways in which advance payments can be structured. In any of them, the exporter avoids credit risk, since payment is usually received prior to the transfer of ownership of the goods. While advance payments are generally to the advantage of the exporter, there are several situations where such arrangements add value to both trading partners. Advance payment arrangements provide the greatest value from the financing and risk mitigation perspectives.

Payment facilitation   Payment in advance is an export payment approach which focuses more on the timing of remittances, rather than the actual payment process. Once the terms of payment are agreed to, it is likely that the actual payment will be made through a bank, financial institution or government agency.

Financing   Advance payments can become a source of financing for an exporter if the payment is made far enough in advance. The exporter may then use such payments to source materials for production or to fund the export venture in another way. Payment in advance may be defined with a variety of specific terms, including "cash with order" or "cash before shipment".

Advance payment terms may also apply in transactions involving the provision of specialised equipment.   Such transactions may involve arrangements referred to as progress payments, and may extend throughout the period of construction of the equipment. Progress payments involve remittances at specified milestones in the trade transaction. In addition, payments in advance may be used between affiliated companies to finance overseas procurement.

From an overall transaction cost perspective, advance payments can help trading partners conclude deals in the most cost-effective way. If financing costs are lower in the country of the importer, it may be advantageous to conclude business though advance payment.

Risk mitigation   Advance payments tend to involve minimal risk for the exporter. Irrespective of the timing of the payment, the exporter avoids credit risk and may benefit from a financing advantage. Advance payments may also provide an opportunity for the importer to avoid exposure to unfavourable foreign exchange fluctuations.

Although the advance-payments approach typically shifts the burden of risk nearly completely onto the importer, it is possible that an importer will agree to this option if the exporter provides a bank guarantee to protect against non-performance or the production of poor quality goods.   Alternatively, some form of performance guarantee may be requested. A guarantee will allow the importer to recuperate funds paid by drawing on the guarantee, and provides motivation to the exporter to ensure that the goods shipped are consistent with the sales contract.

2. Letter of Credit (L/C)

A documentary credit—also referred to as a Letter of Credit or L/C—is a payment promise or undertaking made by the Issuing Bank, which assures the exporter that payment will be made under the L/C, provided all the terms and conditions of the credit have been met. L/Cs have been used for hundreds of years and have a wide range of features, benefiting the importers and the exporters alike. These instruments are among the most secure available to international traders and offer a variety of options for trade financing. An L/C is intended to offer a fairly secure means for transacting trade. But remember, these kinds of instruments assume that there is a shared desire and the goodwill necessary to pursue and complete a trade transaction. While banks are required to carefully verify shipping documents against an L/C to ensure compliance, they do not become involved in underlying sales contracts. It is important to note that L/Cs do not necessarily protect against fraud.

Characteristics of a letter of credit   The characteristics of an L/C are discussed briefly here.

- ✪ *Complexity*   High
- ✪ *Risk*   Low and secure for both importer and exporter provided all terms and conditions adhered to.
- ✪ *Trade relationship*   Applicable to all levels and types of relationships; may be a necessity in certain markets irrespective of the trade relationship.
- ✪ *Features*   Wide range of payment, financing and risk mitigation options.
- ✪ *Cost*   Relatively expensive in terms of transaction costs; labour intensive.

L/Cs are arrangements whereby a bank, (the issuing bank) acting on behalf of the applicant, usually an importer or buyer, makes payment or authorises payment to be made to the beneficiary or exporter against the receipt of stipulated documents, provided all the terms and conditions of the L/C have been complied with.

Documentary credits provide three critical functions in an international trade transaction.

Payment facilitation   L/Cs offer an efficient and trusted means for importers and exporters to assure a timely transfer of monies in most currencies, in exchange for compliant shipping documents. Traders can use the bank's extensive international communication and authentication facilities to help complete a transaction, and can link an L/C payment to other bank services such as, cash management and foreign currency conversions.

Under an L/C, the importer is assured that no payment will be made against non-compliant documents without the importer's consent. Similarly, an exporter has the security of knowing that payment is guaranteed once the compliant documents are tendered.

Financing (acceptance financing)   Letters of credit can be structured with a variety of terms and conditions, including a number of options for the payment timeframe. This allows financing to be extended to several of the parties in a trade transaction. A documentary credit which is available on a "term" basis may be payable, for example, 60 days after receipt of the shipping documents at the bank specified in the L/C, or it might be payable 30 days after the shipping date of the goods.

As with domestic transactions, conditions that extend the payment timeline increase the likelihood that financing will be required. Term L/Cs (or the bank drafts which often accompany them) can be discounted for immediate payment to the exporter. The rate of discount will vary with the term of the discount, and its proportion to the risk associated with the transaction. These types of arrangements, where a draft has been accepted for payment, and then discounted, are referred to as "Acceptance Financing".

Term L/Cs allow the importer or buyer to delay payment, favourably affecting cash flow and payables management. A well considered export pricing formula may account for discount charges, if the exporter is aware that these will likely be incurred at some stage of the transaction. Alternatively, discount charges may be specified to be the buyer's responsibility.

Term L/Cs also offer the opportunity for importers to avail themselves of financing, by having the issuing bank effect payment under the L/C and delaying the reimbursement by the importer to some agreed future date. The bank's party to the transaction may also seek to delay their remittance obligations due to exchange controls or lack of foreign currency, and would seek financing from the other participating bank.

Risk mitigation   Letters of credit are a means of replacing the payment promise of a trading partner with that of a credible international bank. In effect, an L/C-based transaction offers credit enhancement, since the issuing bank's payment promise is independent of its relationship with the applicant or importer, and therefore, based upon the creditworthiness of the bank, rather than that of the importer.

L/Cs are among the most secure of the traditional international trade payment and financing vehicles. They protect both trading parties to a significant degree. One of the fundamental, yet overlooked, benefits of an L/C relates to fraud prevention, in that letters of credit are "advised" (that is, transmitted or provided) to exporters only after the advising bank has verified that the L/C originates from the issuing bank, and has been issued in a form that will allow the trade transaction to be completed. Besides the general characteristics of an L/C which can help mitigate risk, the terms and conditions of the credit may also contribute significantly to reducing risk in the trade transaction. Requirements to insure the shipment or to provide third-party inspection certificates are typical examples.

L/Cs usually include specific instructions through the Incoterms used in international trade, which define the transport responsibilities, insurance requirements, and the transfer of ownership of the shipment between buyer and seller. The Incoterms specified in an L/C indicate where an exporter must deliver the shipment, what insurance cover is required, and at which point in the transport, title to the goods (and hence risk) shifts to the buyer. Perhaps less intuitively, the payment terms of an L/C can provide critical security to an exporter.

L/Cs, negotiable or payable at the counters of an Indian or US bank, for instance, assure the exporter that payment decisions will be made according to familiar criteria and standards, and that funds will be available for payment of the export. Legal jurisdiction in the event of dispute could also be defined by the payment terms and might prove helpful to remedy the underlying disagreement.

It is possible to substantially mitigate the risk associated with the L/Cs, by accessing third-party products or services designed for this purpose.

Types of letters of credit   Letters of credit can be structured using a variety of characteristics and conditions. The following features or types of the L/Cs are particularly notable.

Revocable vs irrevocable L/C   Letters of Credit can be issued as "Revocable", or "Irrevocable". A Revocable L/C may be amended or cancelled by the applicant or importer at any time, without prior notice or consent. Revocable L/Cs are rarely, if ever, used in trade between arm's-length organisations. They are occasionally used between parent companies and their subsidiaries conducting business across borders.

As an Indian exporter trading with foreign firms, any L/C received from overseas in his favour should be irrevocable, assuring that any changes to the terms of the L/C are done via formal amendment, subject to his agreement. Equally important, the credit cannot be arbitrarily cancelled once it has been issued.

Confirmed L/C   An L/C that explicitly includes the option of adding a "Confirmation" is particularly important and useful to exporters pursuing business in higher-risk markets. Generally, the ultimate payment undertaking in an L/C rests with the issuing bank, which, from the point of view of the exporter, is a foreign bank.

When an exporter is operating in a high-risk market, where political upheaval, economic collapse, devaluation or exchange controls could put the payment at risk, the exporter will value the opportunity to shift the payment promise to a safer environment.

Adding a confirmation to an L/C occurs when a bank (usually, but not necessarily the advising bank) adds its own, distinct and separate payment undertaking to a documentary L/C, in exchange for a confirmation fee. An exporter will pay for the added security of Confirmation, when the market risk is high enough, or when the exporter lacks confidence in the payment promise of the issuing bank.

Generally, L/Cs may be confirmed only if the terms of the credit allow for this option. In some markets, it is possible for an exporter to request a "silent" or "blind" confirmation— one that is added without the knowledge of the other trading parties or banks involved in the transaction. Silent confirmations are rare in the Indian market. But they do occasionally take place. A bank offering a silent confirmation is arguably exposing itself to additional risk by operating outside the intended boundaries and therefore will likely charge a premium for this service.

Transferable and "back-to-back" L/Cs   Transferable and "Back-to-Back" credits are typically used when an exporter is actually an intermediary, sourcing goods (in whole or in part) from a third party, and wishes to effect payment in a manner that is linked to the eventual sale of the goods.

When an L/C is issued as Transferable, the beneficiary or exporter may "transfer" the payment obligation under the credit to one or more "second beneficiaries" who will supply the goods under the same terms and conditions stipulated under the original L/C. Certain conditions under the original credit, such as shipping dates and unit prices, may be changed to permit the shipment to be received by the first beneficiary with ample time for delivery in the timeframes defined under the original credit. Under a transfer, the transaction is closely linked. Failure to comply with the terms of the transferred portion will usually result in the non-compliance under the primary L/C. Therefore, the exporter must make sure that the terms of the original credit will ensure a workable transfer.

Assignment of proceeds   The proceeds (or funds paid) under an L/C may be assigned by the exporter to a supplier. An assignment of proceeds may be used in lieu of a transfer under an L/C, if the applicant refuses to allow the L/C to be transferable. In the case of an assignment, only the proceeds are assigned. The performance obligation and the right to payment under the L/C remain with the exporter. Assignments of proceeds can be used by suppliers as security. They offer a useful option for exporters seeking to provide a payment promise to suppliers, in order to secure goods or help fund production.

Revolving letters of credit   Revolving L/Cs are used when an exporter has numerous shipments of the same merchandise over a specified period. Revolving L/Cs may be revocable or irrevocable. They are typically issued with specific terms, such as "₹1,00,000 per month for 6 months" which means the credit is, in effect, for ₹6,00,000.

Revolving L/Cs may be issued as cumulative, meaning that funds not drawn down in one period can be carried over to the next period for subsequent drawdown. Non-cumulative credits are L/Cs where funds are available "per period" and monies not drawn down are no longer available.

The following is the format of a Letter of Credit:

FORMAT FOR LETTER OF CREDIT (FOB)

From: (Name and Address of the opening bank)

To: (Name and Address of the advising bank)

(FOR Haldia Shipments) State Bank of India Overseas Branch Kolkata; Swift Code: SBININBB106; (FOR Vizag Shipments) State Bank of India Overseas Branch Vizag; Swift Code: SBININBB123.

A)   **Type of L/C**: Irrevocable

B)   **L/C Number:**

C)   **Date of Issue:**

D)   **Date and Place of Expiry:** ______________________________in India

E)   **Name and Address of the Applicant:**

F)   **Name and Address of the Beneficiary:** Steel Authority of India Limited, Central Marketing Organisation, J.N.Road, Calcutta-700001, India

G)   **Amount of Credit in US Dollars/Euro/Any other Freely Exchangeable Currency (In Figures and Words):**

H)   **Percentage Credit Amount Tolerance:** As per contract

I)   **Credit Available with:** State Bank of India, Kolkata/Vizag

J)   **Credit Available by:** Payment

K)   **Usance of the Drafts**; At Sight

L)   **Drafts to be Drawn on:**

M)   **Partial Shipment**: As per contract

N)   **Transhipment:** As per contract

O)   **Shipment From:**

P)   **Shipment To:**

Q)   **Latest Shipment Date:**

R)   **Description of Goods:**

    (a) Description of Materials

    (b) Size (in mm) (except for Pig Iron) and Quantity (in MT)

    (c) Specification

    (d) Tolerance (except for Pig Iron)

(e) Quantity

(f) Quantity Tolerance

(g) Price per MT (in USD/Euro/any other freely exchangeable currency)

S) **Documents Required**:

1. Beneficiary's Commercial Invoice—one original plus two signed copies covering materials shipped. Invoices will be raised on the basis of (THEORETICAL/ACTUAL/DRAFT SURVEY) WEIGHT.

2. Full set 3/3 original on board ocean or charter party Bills of Lading (CONGEN) issued to the order of the Shipper and blank endorsed marked "Stowed under deck" further more marked "freight prepaid/freight payable as per charter party/ freight to pay" evidencing shipment from __________ Port, India to ________ Port in ________. Bills of Lading (CONGEN) with remarks "Materials partly rust stained/ rusty edges/ wet before shipment/ rust stained/ some rusty edges" and/or "unprotected cargo" and/or "said to be" and/or "said to weigh" and/or "stored in open area prior to loading" are acceptable.

3. Works Test Certificate in duplicate issued by the Steel Plant (s) of the beneficiary and confirming that the materials are as per contracted specification.

4. Pre- shipment Inspection certificate issued by M/s ., (herein after referred to as) certifying the following: (a) The materials were inspected prior to loading at the load port and that the markings were as per General Terms and Conditions for Export(FOB) between beneficiary and the opener. (b) Quantity loaded on board the vessel. (c) The materials were loaded on board the vessel without apparent damage and were found to be in good order and condition. That the loading was done under their supervision, and were properly lashed and secured (except for pig iron) inside the hatches/ holds of the vessel.

   Remarks such as "materials partly rust stained/ rusty edges/ wet before shipment/ rust stained/ some rusty edges" and/or "stored in open area prior to loading" and/or "unprotected cargo" appearing on pre-shipment inspection certificate are acceptable.

5. Beneficiary's packing list indicating details of the materials shipped (as mentioned under Clause 5 of the said Contract)-3 copies.

6. Certificate of origin.

7. Copy of cable or Telex/e-mail or Fax from Steel Authority of India Limited, ________/Kolkata/NEW DELHI addressed to the opener's Telex No. ________ or FAX No.________ within FIVE working days. After the on board Bill of Lading (CONGEN) date advising the name of the vessel, Bill of Lading (CONGEN) number and date, materials and quantity, destination ports in ________ (Country), covering shipment of ________ METRIC TONNES.

T) Additional Conditions

1. Marine Insurance to be covered by the opener.

2. Any amendment to the letter of credit without the prior written consent of the beneficiary shall not be taken cognizance of under this letter of credit.

U) Charges

All Bank charges incurred outside India shall be borne and paid for by the opener. All Bank charges incurred in India shall be borne and paid for by the beneficiary.

V) Period for Presentation within 15 days from the date of B/L.

W) Confirmation Instructions:

Paying Bank may add their confirmation to this Letter of Credit at the request and expense of the beneficiary and such confirmation shall also apply to any amendment (s) to this credit.

X) Reimbursement Instructions:

Upon presentation to you of documents complying in all respects to Letter of Credit terms, you are authorised to claim on us by tested telex certifying that all terms and conditions have been complied with and that the relative documents have been forwarded to us by Registered Airmail Courier. We undertake to remit within two working days after receipt by us of your tested telex/swift claim in US Dollars/Euro/any other freely exchangeable currency, in accordance with your instructions. This Letter of Credit is subject to the Uniform Customs and Practice for Documentary Credits (2007 Revision) International Chamber of Commerce Brochure No. 600. This telex/swift may be treated as the operative instrument. All apparent spelling mistake/mistakes in LC documents, which do not alter meaning/specification/description/ quantity/value of goods are acceptable and will not count as a discrepancy.

Issuing Bank's Seal   Signature of the Banker

3. Collections through Banks

Using a documentary collection process requires that a seller ships the product and creates a negotiable document, usually a draft or bill of exchange. The draft and shipping documents are then processed either through a buyer's bank (the collecting bank) or through the seller's and buyer's banks. Upon arrival at the buyer's bank, the buyer is notified to make payment; then the documents are released and used to clear the shipment through customs upon arrival.

The primary advantage of documentary collections is that a seller who extends credit terms to a buyer under a D/A collection obtains an enforceable debt instrument in the form of a trade acceptance. The seller's rights to payment are protected under the negotiable instruments law of the buyer's country. In the event, this buyer defaults or delays payment at maturity, the possession of the trade acceptance may put the seller in a stronger position before the court than if he had sold under open account, in which evidence of indebtedness is provided by the unpaid commercial invoice alone. In addition, a bank presenting a collection on behalf of a seller may obtain prompt payment from a buyer who might be inclined to delay payment if the seller were invoicing under an open account.

A documentary collection is best used for ocean shipments where original bills of lading are required. An original bill of lading is a document of title which enables a buyer to gain possession of the goods. When all the originals of a bill of lading are sent to the collecting bank, it is in the interest of the buyer to effect payment in order to obtain title to the goods. Documentary collections may be more competitive than the L/C terms because they are less costly, and do not require the buyer to tie up his local bank credit lines.

A documentary collection is a transaction, whereby the exporter or the "principal" entrusts the collection of a payment to the remitting bank, usually the exporter's bank. The remitting bank sends documents to a collecting bank (usually the importer's bank), along with instructions for payment. Funds are received from the importer and sent to the exporter through the banks involved in the collection.

Characteristics of collections   The following are the characteristics of collections.

- ✪ *Complexity*   Medium
- ✪ *Risk*   Medium—risk to the trading parties is higher than under L/Cs, given that there is no verification process and limited recourse in the event of non-payment.
- ✪ *Trade relationship*   Recommended for use in established and secure trade relationships and stable export markets.
- ✪ *Features*   Limited flexibility and features; opportunity for financing.
- ✪ *Cost*   Moderate

Collections may be "documentary", where commercial/shipping documents accompany the request for payment and are sent to the importer via the banks, or "clean", where the exporter sends only a draft, promissory note or other financial document representing the underlying amount due. Commercial or shipping documents do not accompany a clean collection.

Collections have been in use for many years. They should be used between trading partners who have an established and trusted business relationship. Documentary collections are somewhat more secure (overall) than open account or advance payment transactions, but considerably less secure than letters of credit. Although the banks do act as facilitators for their clients under collections, the banks' role is very specific and provides limited security to either the importer or the exporter.

The banks involved in a collections transaction verify that the required documents have been provided by the exporter and that funds are remitted to the exporter in exchange for those documents. It is not certain that the documents will be verified. Collections are arrangements whereby a bank (the remitting bank), acting on behalf of the exporter, secures payment from the importer through a collecting bank, in exchange for documents presented by the exporter under the collection.

Collections provide three critical functions in an international trade transaction.

Payment facilitation   Collections, whether documentary or clean, offer an efficient and trusted means for importers and exporters to assure a timely transfer of funds in most currencies, in exchange for documents or promissory notes/bills of exchange. Traders can use the banks' extensive international communication and authentication facilities to help complete a transaction, and can link the payment of collections to other bank services such as cash management and foreign currency conversions. Under a collection procedure, the importer is assured that payment will be made only upon receipt of the stipulated documents. The exporter is assured that funds will be remitted as agreed upon on the presentation of the necessary documents.

Financing (acceptance financing)   Collections can be payable on receipt of the required documents (documents against payment, or D/P) or on acceptance (documents on acceptance or D/A) of a bill of exchange for payment on an agreed future date. If the collection provides for acceptance of a draft or payment on some future date, there is an option to discount the related draft and offer immediate payment to the exporter. This is referred to as acceptance financing. The rate of discount will vary with the term of the discount and in proportion to the risk associated with the transaction.

Collections involving an acceptance allow the importer or buyer to delay payment favourably affecting cash flow and payables management. A well considered export-pricing formula may account for discount charge, if the exporter is aware that these will likely be incurred at some stage of the transaction. Alternatively, discount charges may be the responsibility of the buyer.

Collections also offer the opportunity for importers to avail themselves of financing, by securing agreement from their bankers to pay the collection and obtain reimbursement from the importer on an agreed future date.

Risk mitigation   Collections provide some basic risk mitigation for traders. The primary mitigation relates to the security for both the trading parties of knowing that the required documents will be exchanged for the agreed payment or acceptance, through a neutral third party.

In the event of non-payment or non-acceptance, collection instruments offer some structured legal recourse, including a "protest". A collection must include specific instructions for the banks to follow in the event of non-payment or non-acceptance. An exporter must also appoint a representative who is called as a "case-of-need". His authority and powers are to be defined in the collection order. Ultimately, refusal or inability to pay on the part of the importer may require the exporter to warehouse and insure the shipment at the port of destination, which can lead to a substantial expense. It may be necessary to dispose of the shipment through another buyer at substantial discount, or incur the expense of returning the shipment to the point of origin.

4. OPEN ACCOUNT

An open account transaction is a sale where the goods are shipped and delivered before the payment is due, which is usually 30 to 90 days. Obviously, this option is the most advantageous to the importer in terms of cash flow and cost, but it is consequently the highest-risk option for an exporter. Because of intense competition in export markets, foreign buyers often press exporters for open account terms. In addition, the extension of credit by the seller to the buyer has become more common abroad. Therefore, exporters who are reluctant to extend credit may lose a sale to their competitors. However, though open account terms will definitely enhance export competitiveness, the exporters should thoroughly examine the political, economic, and commercial risks as well as cultural influences to ensure that payment will be received in full and on time. It is possible to substantially mitigate the risk of non-payment associated with open account trade by using such trade finance techniques as export credit insurance and factoring. Sometimes the exporters may also seek export working capital financing to ensure that they have access to financing for production and for credit while waiting for payment.

Three aspects of open account transactions to consider are:

Payment facilitation   Open account transactions can involve payments being made in a variety of ways, from cash and cheques, to electronic payments through the banking infrastructure. Facilitating payments is not a major focus of an open account approach.

Financing   Open account terms are often extended to the importer due to competitive pressure in the market and strong desire on the part of the exporter to conclude a given transaction or maintain a profitable and successful trade relationship. Trade on open account often allows for 30 to 90 days or longer before payments is due. The exporter typically finances the entire transaction, over the agreed term, plus any payment delays that might arise.

There is an option for the exporters to enter into arrangements with a bank (or a third party) to secure funds immediately on a discount basis. An exporter may avail himself of invoice discounting services through a financial institution or of factoring through an organisation that specialises in providing financing against such receivables.

Risk mitigation As an exporter trading on open account, an Indian exporter faces significant risk, with little in the way of mitigation options arising directly from the arrangement. In the event of non-payment under an open account transaction, an exporter may have to pursue collections through a local agency or legal action, both of which are expensive propositions in international jurisdictions.

It is strongly advisable under the open account transactions to ensure that a comprehensive paper trial is created, and that the importer explicitly acknowledges the debt associated with each export shipment. Such documentation may prove critical in obtaining remedy in the event of a legal dispute or collection effort.

5. Other Methods: Receivables/Invoice Discounting

The exporters may obtain financing through arrangements that provide for the payment or advance of funds against export receivables. Once an export receivable is created, through the shipment of goods to the overseas buyer and the issuance of an invoice, an exporter may approach a bank or finance company to secure receivable-based funding. The financier may wish to approve the buyer up front, and may opt to set a ceiling on the receivables to be financed from a single buyer. The exporter should consider the following factors.

1. *Ownership of the receivable* Receivable discounting may involve the outright purchase of an invoice (or invoices) by the financier, or merely the use of a receivable as security to fund a credit facility. If the receivable is sold to a third party as a condition of the financing, the exporter is, in effect, free of any subsequent issues related to delayed payment, collection activities, or non-payment by the importer.

2. *Recourse* Receivable financing may be concluded on a recourse basis or on a non-recourse basis. Recourse refers to the right of the financier to seek remedy from the exporter if the importer does not pay. Non-recourse financing indicates that the financier accepts the risk of non-payment, as well as any other costs related to the collection of the debt. Also, non-recourse financing shields the exporter from unfavourable fluctuations in exchange rates and interest rates which might occur over the life of the receivable. In most cases, if the receivable is purchased, financing is on a non-recourse basis.

WHERE TO GO FOR RECEIVABLES FINANCING?

There are a number of options for receivables or invoice financing. Banks are generally cautious about providing receivables finance. But several of them are receptive to providing it for export receivables. They may, however, restrict the amount of financing extended based on the receivables from one foreign buyer. Also, they will often retain recourse to the exporter in the event of non-payment.

Finance companies also offer funding based on export receivables. They may do so on a discount basis or by using export receivables to secure a credit facility. Factoring can be expensive. But it does offer significant risk mitigation and effective financing.

BUYER AND SUPPLIER CREDITS

Supplier credit involves an arrangement, whereby an exporter contracts to sell goods and services to a buyer in another country. Credit terms are included in the supply contract. Supplier credit usually includes export credit insurance for commercial risks, such as default by the buyer, insolvency of the buyer, refusal by the buyer to take delivery of the goods, as well as political risks, such as preventing payment being made, wars, and civil wars. Supplier credit is most commonly used for short-term credit (up to 360 days); but it can be used for the supply of capital goods with longer credit (up to five years).

Buyer credits are arrangements in which an exporter contracts with an overseas buyer to supply capital goods or services. There is a separate and parallel loan arrangement between a lending bank (normally in the exporter's country) and a borrower (often a bank) in the buying country. The exporter is paid by receiving disbursements under the loan. Such disbursements normally need the prior approval of the buyer/borrower or are made according to a pre-agreed drawdown schedule. The loan is repaid over the credit period, normally in half-yearly repayments of principal and interest. Buyer credits are normally used only for medium- and long-term credits.

It is usually a standard feature of a buyer credit arrangement that the borrower has an obligation to repay the loan whatever may have taken place under the supply contract. The buyer must pursue or take legal action against the supplier under the terms of the supply contract.

Arrangements separating the loan repayment obligations and the supply contract non-performance are sometimes referred to as "Isabella clauses". Buyer credits can help minimise the overall cost of a trade transaction, if they can be used to shift the financing to the low-cost market. The buyer should submit his application for a buyer's credit to the exporter's banker along with following documents.

1. *Confirmed export order/contract or L/C in original*　Where the confirmed export order/contract/L/C is not available, an undertaking to the effect that it will be produced to the bank within a reasonable time for verification and endorsement should be given.

2. *An undertaking* An undertaking that the advance will be utilised for the specific purpose of procuring/manufacturing/shipping, and the like of the goods meant for export only, as stated in the relative confirmed export order or the L/C.

3. If the seller is a sub-supplier and wants to supply the goods to the export/trading/star trading house of a merchant exporter, an undertaking from the merchant exporter or export/trading/star trading house stating that they have not/will not avail themselves of packing credit facility against the same transaction for the same purpose till the original packing credit is liquidated.

4. Copies of Income Tax/Wealth Tax Assessment Order for the last 2/3 years in the case of sole proprietary and partnership firm.

5. *Copy of a valid RCMC* (Registration-cum-Membership Certificate) held by the exporter and/or the export/trading/star trading house certificate.

6. *Appropriate policy/guarantee* of the ECGC.

7. *Any other document* required by the Bank.

PRE-SHIPMENT FINANCE (PACKING CREDIT)

The objective of this facility is to provide an exporter with new sources of working capital, at competitive rates, which are tailor made for a client who is in need of working capital to continue or expand production. The facility is secured by the receivables accruing to the producer from the sales of the produced goods/commodities. One of the pre-conditions of the facility is the existence of a document, that is, export contract with acceptable off-takers that can be assigned to the bank as security for the financing. This facility may be revolving as it is tailored to the client's production cycle thus allowing the client to access funding before the production and sale of the commodity. An application for pre-shipment advance should be made by the exporter to his banker along with the following documents.

1. *Confirmed export order/contract or L/C, and the like in original* Where the confirmed export order/contract/L/C is not available, an undertaking to the effect that it will be produced to the bank within a reasonable time for verification and endorsement should be given. Generally, only recognised exporters are provided with this relaxation.

2. *An undertaking* that the advance will be utilised for the specific purpose of procuring/ manufacturing/shipping and the like of the goods meant for export only, as stated in the relative confirmed export order or the L/C, if the seller is a sub-supplier and wants to supply the goods to the export/trading/star trading house stating that they have not/will not avail themselves of packing credit facility against the same transaction for the same purpose till the original packing credit is liquidated.

3. Copies of *Income Tax/Wealth Tax assessment order* for the last 2–3 years in the case of sole proprietary and partnership firm.

4. Copy of *Exporter's Code Number* (CNX) Copy of a valid RCMC (Registration-cum-Membership Certificate) held by the exporter and/or the export/trading/star trading house certificate.

5. *Appropriate policy/guarantee* of the ECGC.

6. *Any other document* required by the Bank.

For encouraging exports, the RBI has instructed the banks to grant pre-shipment advance at a concessional rate of interest. The present rate of interest is 10% p.a. for pre-shipment advance up to an initial period of 180 days. This rate of interest is subject to change and the exporter is advised to contact his banker to ascertain the prevailing rate of interest. Pre-shipment advance for a further period of 90 days is given at the concessional rate of 13% p.a. However, the banks are free to determine the interest rate for advances beyond 270 days and up to 360 days.

The following special schemes are also available in respect of pre-shipment finance.

1. The EXIM Bank's scheme for grant of foreign currency pre-shipment credit to exporters for financing cost of imported inputs for manufacture of export products.

2. Scheme of export packing credit to sub-suppliers from export order.

3. Packing credit for deemed exports.

4. Pre-shipment Credit in Foreign Currency (PCFC).

Enterprises require pre-shipment financing to fulfil export orders. This can come from the exporter's own resources, or the buyer-creditor's short-term credit from financial institutions. In fact, the bulk of pre-shipment financing is provided by financial institutions. However, financial institutions may serve pre-shipment finance needs of large, well-known exporters more easily than emerging and small exporters (ESEs). One reason is that banks in many countries have underinvested in systems and training necessary to adequately appraise non-performance risks, especially for ESEs. Instead, they mainly favour collateralised lines of credit, which firms use at their discretion. As such, large and well-known exporters can generate pre-shipment working capital from bank overdraft facilities backed by the exporters' collateral. ESEs, on the other hand, do not have adequate internal resources and they lack access to short-term bank loans or credit because of their high perceived credit risks. Even if these exporters hold a confirmed L/C, banks may still require a pledge of the exporter's assets before they extend the pre-shipment loan. The reasons behind this market failure are the informational asymmetries on the part of banks about ESEs' ability to execute export orders according to buyers' standards of quality, cost, and delivery (that is, nonperformance). Export credit insurance and guarantees, offered by most export insurance agencies, do not address this market failure. Instead, they protect exporters and banks granting export finance against foreign buyers' nonpayment risks, rather than exporters' nonperformance.

POST-SHIPMENT FINANCE

Post-shipment finance is a kind of loan provided by a financial institution to an exporter or seller against a shipment that has already been made. This type of export finance is granted from the date of extending the credit after shipment of the goods to the realisation date of the export proceeds. The exporters don't wait for the importer to deposit the funds. Post-shipment finance occurs when the exporter asks the bank to advance funds against a shipment that has already been made by him. The funds so obtained are infused into his business to ease his cash flow. He gets paid for the shipment without waiting for the importer to actually deposit the funds.

FEATURES

The features of post-shipment finance are:

1. *Purpose of finance*   Post-shipment finance is meant to finance export-sales receivable after the date of shipment of goods to the date of realisation of export proceeds. In cases of deemed exports, it is extended to finance receivable against supplies made to designated agencies.

2. *Basis of finance*   Post-shipment finance is provided against evidence of shipment of goods or supplies made to the importer or seller or any other designated agency.

3. *Types of finance*   Post-shipment finance can be secured or unsecured. Since the finance is extended against evidence of export shipment, and the bank obtains the documents of title of goods, the finance is normally self-liquidating. In that case it involves advance against undrawn balance, and is usually unsecured in nature. Further, the finance is mostly a funded advance. In few cases, such as financing of project exports, the issue of guarantee (retention money guarantees) is involved and the financing is not funded in nature.

4. *Quantum of finance*   Regarding the quantum of finance, post-shipment finance can be extended up to 100% of the invoice value of goods. In a few special cases, where the domestic value of the goods increases the value of the exporter's order, finance for a price difference can also be extended and the price difference is covered by the government. This type of finance is not extended in case of pre-shipment stage. Banks can also finance undrawn balance. In such cases, banks are free to stipulate margin requirements as per their usual lending norms.

TYPES OF POST-SHIPMENT FINANCE

The post-shipment finance can be classified as follows:

Export bills purchased/discounted (DP and DA Bills)   An export bill (non L/C bill) is used in terms of sale contract/order may be discounted or purchased by the banks. It is used in the case of indisputable international trade transactions and the proper limit has to be sanctioned to the exporter for purchase of export bill facility.

Export bills negotiated (bill under L/C) The risk of payment is less under the L/C, as the issuing bank guarantees the payment. The risk is further reduced, if the bank guarantees the payments after confirming the L/C. Because of the inborn security available in this method, banks often become ready to extend the finance against bills under an L/C. However, there are two major risk factors for the banks:

1. the risk of nonperformance by the exporter, when he is unable to meet his terms and conditions. In this case, the issuing banks do not honour the L/C.

2. the bank also faces the documentary risk where the issuing bank refuses to honour its commitment.

So, it is important for the negotiating bank, and the lending bank to properly check all the necessary documents before submission.

Advance against export bills sent on collection basis Bills can only be sent on collection basis, if the bills drawn under an L/C have some discrepancies. Sometimes, the exporter requests the bill to be sent on the collection basis, anticipating the strengthening of foreign currency. Banks may allow advance against these collection bills to an exporter with a concessional rate of interest depending upon the transit period in case of D/P Bills and transit period plus usance period in case of usance bill. The transit period is from the date of acceptance of the export documents at the bank's branch for collection and not from the date of advance.

Advance against export on consignments basis The bank may choose to finance when the goods are exported on consignment basis at the risk of the exporter for sale and eventual payment of sale proceeds to him by the consignee. However, in this case, the bank instructs its overseas counter part to deliver the document only against trust receipt/undertaking to deliver the sale proceeds by a specified date, which should be within the prescribed date, even if according to the practice in certain trades a bill for part of the estimated value is drawn in advance against the exports. In the case of export through approved Indian owned warehouses abroad, the time limit for realisation is 15 months.

Advance against undrawn balance It is a very common practice in the export trade to leave a small part undrawn for payment after adjustment due to difference in rates, weight, quality, and so on. Banks do finance against the undrawn balance, if this undrawn balance is in conformity with the normal level of balance left undrawn in the particular line of export, subject to a maximum of 10 per cent of the export value. An undertaking is also obtained from the exporter that he will, within 6 months from due date of payment or the date of shipment of the goods, whichever is earlier, surrender the balance proceeds of the shipment.

Advance against claims of duty drawback Duty Drawback is a type of discount given to the exporter in his own country. This discount is given only when the in-house cost of production is higher in relation to international price. This type of financial support helps the exporter to fight successfully in the international markets. In such a situation, banks grant advances to exporters at lower rate of interest for a maximum period of 90 days. These are granted only if other types of export finance are also extended to the exporter by the same bank.

After the shipment, the exporters lodge their claims, supported by the relevant documents to the relevant government authorities. These claims are processed and eligible amounts are disbursed after making sure that the banks are authorised to receive the claim amounts directly from the concerned government authorities.

FORFEITING FINANCE BY AUTHORISED DEALERS

The Reserve Bank of India has permitted the authorised dealers (banks) to arrange forfeiting of medium term export receivables on the same lines as per the scheme of the Export–Import Bank of India and many international forfeiting agencies have now become active in Indian market. Forfeiting may be usefully employed as an additional window of export finance particularly for exports to those countries for which normal export credit is not granted by the commercial banks. It must be noted that the charges of forfeiting are eventually to be passed on to the ultimate buyer and should, therefore, be so declared on relative export declaration forms.

EXTERNAL COMMERCIAL BORROWINGS

Proposals for raising foreign currency loans/credits namely, buyer's credits, supplier's credits or lines of credits by firms/companies/lending institutions, banks, and so on for financing cost of import of goods, technology or for any other purposes, other than short-term loans/credits maturing within one year should first be submitted to Government of India, Ministry of Finance (Department Economic Affairs), ECB Division, New Delhi for necessary clearance. The proposals are considered by the government on the merits of each case and in the light of prevailing government policy.

EXIM BANK OF INDIA FINANCE

Besides commercial banks, export finance is also made available by the EXIM Bank of India. The EXIM Bank provides financial assistance to promote Indian exports through direct financial assistance, overseas investment finance, term finance for export production and export development, pre-shipment credit, lines of credit, re-lending facility, export bills re-discounting, re-finance to commercial banks, finance for computer software exports, finance for export marketing, and bulk import finance to commercial banks. The EXIM Bank also extends non-funded facility to Indian exporters in the form of guarantees. The diversified lending of the

Bank covers various stages of exports, that is, from the development of export markets to expansion of production capacity for exports, production for export and post shipment financing. Its focus is on export of manufactured goods, project exports, exports of technology, services and export of computer software.

Forfeiting Finance from the EXIM Bank

A new financing option for the Indian exporters is available under the forfeiting finance scheme recently introduced by the EXIM Bank. Forfeiting is a form of trade finance involving discounting of medium-term export receivables with or without recourse to the exporter. The arrangement envisages discounting by Indian exporters of bill of exchange/promissory notes relating to export transactions which are guaranteed by the buyer's bankers with overseas forfeiting agencies on "without recourse" basis. The procedure involved in the scheme of finance by the EXIM Bank is discussed here briefly.

The exporter initiates negotiations with the prospective overseas buyer with regard to the basic contract price, period of credit, rate of interest, and the like. After successful negotiations, he furnishes the relevant particulars such as name and country of overseas buyer, contract value, nature of goods, tenure of credit, name and country of guaranteeing bankers to the EXIM Bank and requests for an indicative discounting quote. The EXIM Bank obtains the indicative quote of forfeiting agency.

On receipt of the indicative quote from the EXIM Bank, the exporter finalises the terms of the contract, loading the discount and other charges in the value, and approaches the EXIM Bank for obtaining a firm quote. The EXIM Bank arranges to get it from an appropriate overseas forfeiting agency, and furnishes the quote to the exporter. At this stage, the exporter would be required to confirm acceptance of the arrangement to the Bank within a specific period as stipulated by it.

The export contract clearly indicates that the overseas buyer shall prepare a series of guaranteed promissory notes in favour of the exporter, and hand them over against the shipping documents to his banker. The promissory notes will be endorsed with the words without recourse by the exporter and handed over to his banker in India for onward transmission to the EXIM Bank.

Alternatively, the export contract may provide for the exporter to draw a series of bills of exchange on the overseas buyer which will be sent with the shipping documents though the latter's bank for acceptance by the overseas buyer. The overseas buyer's bank will handover the documents against acceptance of bills of exchange by the buyer, with the signature of the guaranteeing bank. Guaranteed and accepted bills of exchange will be returned to the exporter through his banker. The exporter will endorse these guaranteed bills of exchange with the words "without recourse" and return them to his banker for onward transmission to the EXIM Bank.

The EXIM Bank will forward the bills of exchange/promissory notes after verification to the overseas forfeiting agency for discounting by the latter. The EXIM Bank will arrange to collect the discounted proceeds of promissory notes/bills of exchange from the overseas forfeiting agency and effect payment to the nostro account of the exporter's bank as per the latter's instruction.

SUMMARY

- The exporter needs to be aware of the issues, complexities, and options in export finance at a very early stage in the development of export strategy or of a specific export marketing plan. Export finance includes all the challenges and risks of domestic business finance, familiar to any entrepreneurial venture plus a series of extra challenges.

- An overriding aspect of international trade, as well as the financing related to trade, is the significantly higher risk of pursuing business overseas. An awareness and understanding of export risk coupled with appropriate risk strategy, will determine the success or failure of the business man's venture, and will largely shape his financing options.

- The methods of payments by the importers are: advance payments, letters of credit, collection through banks, open account, and others. A deal may be designed to require partial or full payment in advance. There are several ways in which advance payments can be structured.

- A letter of credit is a payment promise or undertaking made by the issuing banks, which assures the exporter that payment will be made under the L/C provided all the terms and conditions are met.

- Collection through the bank is a transaction whereby the exporter or "principal" entrusts the collection of payment to the remitting bank, usually the exporter's bank. The remitting bank sends documents to the collecting bank (usually the importer's bank), along with instructions for payment.

- Under open account terms, the parties agree that the exporter will ship the goods and transfer the ownership to the importer, prior to payment. Factoring typically involves the outright purchase of export receivables by a factoring house at a discount and most often on a non recourse basis.

- Counter trade is a category of international trade that involves arrangements between buyers and sellers ranging from straight barter, to various arrangements linking the export sale to some type of reciprocal purchase by the exporter.

REVIEW QUESTIONS (SHORT)

1. Discuss briefly the significance of export finance.
2. Explain the challenges of export finance.
3. Explain advance payments by the importer.
4. What is a revocable letter of credit?
5. What is a confirmed letter of credit?
6. What is a revolving letter of credit?
7. What is a open account?
8. What is invoice discounting?
9. What is packing credit?
10. What is post-shipment finance?

REVIEW QUESTIONS (DETAILED)

1. Explain the various methods of payments by the importer.
2. Explain the nature and types of letter of credit.
3. Explain in detail the method of collection through banks.
4. Discuss the forfeiting finance procedure followed by the EXIM Bank.

REFERENCES

1. www.rbidocs.rbi.org.in/rdocs/PublicationReport/Pdfs/63664.pdf
2. www.eximbankindia.com/glo-nepad.pdf
3. www.ecgc.in/portal/aboutus/aboutus.asp
4. www.rbi.org.in/scripts/NotificationUser.aspx?Id=1639&Mode=0
5. www.ucobank.com/international_banking.htm

13

EXPORT CREDIT INSURANCE

INTRODUCTION

Export business has become complex, very competitive and highly risky. Insolvency rate is on the increase. After the great depression of 1930's, the year 1982 saw the highest rate of bankruptcy in the developed countries. The 2007–09 mini-depression of the US defied all the efforts of the US administration for a long period. In 2009, the US government sanctioned a 700 million dollar loan to bail out its financial institutions which were in great trouble and to save the US economy from collapse. Several US banks went bankrupt and filed insolvency petitions. Millions lost their jobs. Lakhs of people filed insolvency petitions in the US courts. Such was the state of affairs in the US and some other European nations. It was feared that this economic downfall of the US might be another Great Depression and also that this might affect the whole world. However, the stringent measures adopted by the Obama administration saved the US economy from a situation very near to collapse.

Economic problems characterised by acute balance of payment difficulties severely affect the capacity of many countries to pay for what they import. Political instability and civil disturbances in many countries have complicated the problems further. In this high-risk situation, export credit insurance can be of immense help to exporters and the banks who finance the export transactions.

Export credit insurance covers foreign receivables against the risk of nonpayment by a foreign buyer and the sea-borne and other risks of cargo during transit. In addition to the protection offered, it can also be a very useful marketing and financing tool. It allows the exporters to offer more favourable credit terms, thereby enhancing their competitiveness. The insurance policies can also be assigned to the EXIM Bank as collateral for the discounting of foreign receivables, or may also be assigned to other financial institutions as part of a collateral package to secure loans.

Export credit insurance provides risk protection to the exporters against payment default by the foreign buyers on goods and services exported on credit terms. With this protection, they are given the confidence to venture into emerging markets thereby expanding the export thrust. Today, overseas buyers are demanding much longer credit terms. Therefore, failure to provide such credit would likely result in a curtailment of export sales. Such market dynamics are characteristic of the new ideology of "Free Trade" where borderless markets now form an important part of the financial landscape.

Increased volatility in the international marketplace, however, requires the exporters to constantly review their exposure to overseas buyers and to even those with whom they continue to enjoy a long and satisfactory trading relationship. With appropriate insurance policies, exporters can obtain protection against political and commercial risks (also called comprehensive risks).

THE EXPORT CREDIT GUARANTEE CORPORATION OF INDIA LIMITED

In India, the export credit insurance is undertaken by the Export Credit Guarantee Corporation of India Limited. The Export Credit Guarantee Corporation of India Limited (ECGC) is a company wholly owned by the Government of India. It provides export credit insurance support to Indian exporters and is controlled by the Ministry of Commerce. Government of India had initially set up Export Risks Insurance Corporation (ERIC) in July 1957. It was transformed into The Export Credit and Guarantee Corporation Limited in 1964 and to The Export Credit Guarantee Corporation of India Limited in 1983.

WHAT IS ECGC?

The Export Credit Guarantee Corporation of India Limited was established in the year 1957 by the Government of India to strengthen the export promotion drive by covering the risk of exporting on credit. Being essentially an export promotion organisation, it functions under the administrative control of the Ministry of Commerce and Industry, Department of Commerce, Government of India. It is managed by a Board of Directors comprising representatives of the government, Reserve Bank of India, banking, insurance, and exporting community. The ECGC is the fifth largest credit insurer of the world in terms of coverage of national exports. As on 31 March, 2010, the paid-up capital of the company was ₹900 crore, and the authorised capital was ₹1000 crore.

ECGC COVERS

The covers issued by the ECGC could be divided broadly into four groups:

1. *Standard policies* These are issued to exporters to protect them against payment risks involved in exports on short-term credit.

2. *Specific policies* These are designed to protect Indian firms against payment risk involved in (a) exports on deferred terms of payment, (b) services rendered to foreign parties, and (c) construction works and turnkey projects undertaken abroad.

3. *Financial guarantees* These guarantees are issued to banks in India to protect them from risk of loss involved in their extending of financial support to exporters at the post-shipment as well as pre-shipment stages.

4. *Transfer guarantee* Transfer Guarantee is meant to protect banks which add confirmation to L/Cs opened by foreign banks, insurance cover for buyers' credit/ lines of credit, overseas investment insurance, exchange fluctuation risk insurance, and export finance (overseas lending) guarantee.

STANDARD POLICIES

The Shipments (Comprehensive Risks) Policy is the one ideally suited to cover risks in respect of goods exported on short-term credit. This policy is known as Standard Policy because this is the policy used commonly by traders. This policy covers both political and commercial risks from the date of shipment. Under this Policy, risk of pre-shipment losses due to frustration of export contract is zero or very low since the goods to be exported on short-term credit are raw materials, primary goods, consumer goods or consumer durables which can be resold easily.

Contract policies are another category of Standard Policy. They cover risks from the date of contract, and are issued only in special cases when goods to be exported are manufactured to non-standard specifications of a buyer.

RISKS COVERED

Let us list out the risks covered by the standard policies.

i. Commercial risks

   ○ Insolvency of the buyer.

   ○ Buyer's protracted default to pay for goods accepted by him.

   ○ Buyer's failure to accept goods.

ii. Political risks

   ○ Imposition of restrictions on remittances by the government of the buyer's country or any government action which may block or delay payment to the exporter.

   ○ War, revolution or civil disturbances in the buyer's country.

   ○ New import incensing restrictions or cancellation of a valid import licence in the buyer's country.

   ○ Cancellation of export licence or imposition of new export licensing restriction in India (under contracts policy).

   ○ Payment of additional handling, transport or insurance charges occasioned by interruption or diversion of voyage which cannot be recovered from the buyer.

   ○ Any other cause of loss occurring outside India, not normally insured by commercial insurers, and beyond the control of the exporter and/or the buyer.

RISKS NOT COVERED

The following risks are not covered by this policy.

i. General or marine insurance risks which will result in loss, theft, pilferage or damage to goods.

ii. Failure of the exporter to fulfil the terms of the export contract or negligence on his part.

iii. Default or insolvency of any agent of the exporter or of the collecting bank.

   iv. Causes inherent in the nature of the goods.

   v. Buyer's failure to obtain import or exchange authorisation from authorities in his country.

   vi. Fluctuation in the exchange rate of the currency of invoice.

   vii. Commercial disputes raised by the buyer, unless the exporter obtains a decree from a competent court of law in the buyer's country in his favour.

POLICY CONDITIONS

With a view to assist the exporters to maintain their policy in good order, this section explains certain important conditions of the policy and major obligations of the policy-holder. These guidelines are not exhaustive, and do not modify or amplify in any way the terms and conditions spelt in the concerned policy documents.

1. WHOLE TURNOVER PRINCIPLE

The ECGC expects a fair spread of risks of the insured. Therefore, an exporter is required to insure all the shipments that may be made by him during the policy period (2 or 4 years) except those made against advance payment or irrevocable letters of credit confirmed by banks in India. Exclusions are, however, possible where items are not of an allied nature. It is customary in credit insurance to make the insured share a small per cent of the risk. The ECGC normally pays 90% of the losses on account of political or commercial risks.

2. MAXIMUM LIABILITY

Maximum liability is the limit fixed by the Corporation up to which claims may be paid for shipments effected in any policy year. It will be advisable for exporters to estimate the maximum outstanding payments due from all overseas buyers at any time during the policy period and to obtain the policy with maximum liability of equal value. The maximum liability fixed under the policy can be enhanced subsequently, if necessary.

3. L/C SHIPMENTS

Shipments made against irrevocable L/Cs do not involve commercial risks but the payments may be affected by political risks. Premium rates for such shipments are far lower than those applicable for D/P or D/A shipments. If the exporter has opted to cover such shipments he should check whether the necessary endorsements have been made to the policy. It must be noted that once the endorsement is made, all L/C shipments should be covered under the policy. Only such L/Cs as have been confirmed by a bank in India can be excluded.

4. SHIPMENTS TO ASSOCIATES

Shipments made to an associate, that is, a buyer in whose profits the exporter has an interest or who is, in the understanding of the Corporation, related to the exporter, is covered only for political risks. Exporters wanting political risks cover for shipments to associates must ensure that the policy bears an endorsement to that effect.

5. Consignment Exports

In the case of shipments made on consignment basis, the insurance cover is extended by the Corporation to meet two types of needs.

1. Cover against risks on sales from overseas stocks (ultimate buyers).

2. Cover against risks on sales from overseas stocks (agent/buyer).

In the case of (1) above, the Corporation shall cover risks of insolvency and protracted default by ultimate buyer subject to valid credit limit on him. In the case of (2) above, the Corporation shall cover risks of insolvency and protracted default by the agent subject to valid credit limit on him. The cover is provided against political risks in both types of transactions from the date of shipment. These risks are covered subject to necessary endorsements to the policy.

6. Procedure to Obtain Policy

An exporter intending to have the Policy should fill in a proposal form available with all the ECGC offices and submit it to the nearest office. After examining the proposal, the ECGC would send him an offer letter stating the terms of its cover and premium rates. The Policy will be issued after the exporter gives his consent to the premium rates and pays a non-refundable policy fee of ₹100/- up to ₹5 lakh, ₹200/- between ₹5 lakh and ₹20 lakh, and ₹100/- for each additional ₹10 lakh or part thereof subject to a ceiling of ₹2,500/-

7. Steps to be Taken after Obtaining the Policy

The Policy is only a framework for covering the shipments to be made during the policy period. To get the shipments properly covered under the policy, the exporter has to do the following:

1. *Normal care and prudence* The business should be conducted with due care and prudence. The Policy is intended to cover only such losses as could not be prevented by the exporter.

2. *Good faith* The policy warrants utmost good faith from the exporter. The exporter should always keep good faith with the Corporation and should promptly pass on to the Corporation any event or likelihood of an event which may adversely affect the risks insured.

3. *Monthly declaration and premium* Premium is payable to the Corporation on a monthly basis. For this purpose, a monthly declaration of shipment should be prepared on Form No. 203 for each calendar month and sent to the corporation on or before the 15th of the subsequent month.

If no shipment has been made in a month, a nil declaration should be sent to the Corporation on Form No. 206. In the event of non-availability of the form, a letter to the Corporation, saying that no shipment has been made in the month in question, would be sufficient.

8. Calculation of premium

Form No. 203 provides columns for the premium rate for each shipment (which can be ascertained from the premium schedule attached to the Policy) and for the amount of premium (which can be arrived at by applying the premium rate to the gross invoice value of the shipment). After all the shipments made during the month have been included in the declaration, the "amount of premium" column should be drawn in favour of the Corporation. The cheque should be sent to the Corporation along with the declaration.

Premium has to be paid at the comprehensive rate for all the shipments made on documents against payment (D/P) or documents against acceptance (D/A) terms of payment. As full coverage is not available for shipments made to buyers on whom credit limit is not in force, the following rules should be applied.

i. If no application for credit limit has been made by the exporter, premium should be paid at normal comprehensive rates.

ii. If an application has been made but the limit has not yet been approved, the premium should be paid at normal comprehensive rates, but the portion of the premium relating to commercial risks will be refunded to the exporter if the limit is ultimately refused.

iii. If a credit limit has been refused by the Corporation, the premium is payable at rates as applicable for political risks.

iv. If the credit limit is approved only for cash against delivery (CAD) terms as against the exporter's requirements of D/A terms, the exporter may exercise, in writing, an option of not accepting the CAD terms-approval, in which case he could exclude cover for commercial risks on all shipments made to the buyer and pay the premium applicable for political risks cover only. But, if the exporter avails of the credit limit approved for CAD terms, he has to pay premium for comprehensive risks even on shipments made on D/A terms, as grant of credit excess of the terms permitted by the Corporation aggravates the risk even in respect of the payment terms covered.

v. Premium at normal comprehensive rate is payable on the full value of each shipment even if the credit limit on this buyer is lower than the value of the shipment or the amount outstanding with the buyer.

9. Failure to Declare Shipment

As payment of premium on all the shipments made during the policy period is an essential condition of the policy, it should be ensured that no shipment gets omitted from the monthly declaration.

If shipments are made on open-delivery basis or on any other terms of payment for which premium rate is not given in the policy, the Corporation should be asked to indicate the appropriate rate. If the Corporation has refused to grant a specific approval, the exporter need not pay any premium on the shipment in question.

10. Credit Limit

In terms of the policy, the ECGC requires the exporter to obtain a credit limit on each buyer to whom he makes shipments on D/P, D/A, or open delivery terms. The purpose of approving credit limits is to have another independent check on the credentials of the buyer and to tell the exporter, in clear terms, the extent up to which the ECGC will pay claims on account of the buyer. The credit limits are approved for a specified amount in terms of rupees, stating the terms of payment and the effective date of the limit.

11. First Application

When an application for a limit on a buyer is made for the first time, it should be made on Form No. 144. The application form should be completed properly and legibly. Application should be made in advance to enable the ECGC to get reports (if not already available) on the buyer from the banks or credit information agencies in the buyer's country for taking a decision on the application.

The exporters themselves can also supply status reports on their buyers to the ECGC to help it approve the credit limit quickly. They can get reports through their bankers. If large-value orders are being negotiated with a buyer, the bank reports, which are usually very brief, may not suffice. In such cases, the exporter can directly ask a suitable credit information agency for a detailed report. But these reports are relatively expensive. The ECGC will supply, on request, names and addresses of credit information agencies.

12. Enquiry Fee

The application should be sent to the Corporation together with a fee of ₹50/-. If the limit is needed urgently, that is, within 2 or 3 weeks, a fee of ₹400/- should be remitted to enable the ECGC to get reports by cable. No fee need to be paid on application for a limit of ₹2,00,000/- or less, if a bank report or an agency report in original is furnished to the Corporation. These should not be more than 6 months old.

13. Credit Limit Approval

A limit approved on certain terms of payment will apply to shipments made on terms less favourable to the buyer as well. For instance, a limit approved on D/A 90 days basis will also cover shipments made on D/A 60 days or on D/P terms. The effective date of the limit should be noted because the limit will cover shipments made only from that date.

14. Effective Date of Credit Limit

Normally a credit limit approval will be effective from the date on which the application was received in the office of the Corporation. If the exporter desires the limit to be effective from an earlier date, he should make specific request for that purpose while applying for the credit limit.

15. Validity of Credit Limit

Once approved, a credit limit will be valid as long as the exporter holds the policy without a break but it will become invalid if no shipment is made during a period of 12 months, or if the buyer has defaulted any payment before the receipt of communication approving the limit. If the limit becomes invalid due to non-shipment, the exporter has to make a fresh application if he needs the limit again.

16. If Limit Approved is Inadequate

If the Corporation approves a limit lower than what the exporter has applied for or requires, the exporter can take either of the following two courses of action:

1. If the exporter has no information capable of justifying a higher limit, he can take the limit approved by the Corporation as a true measure of the buyer's credit-worthiness. Shipments may be made within the limits approved or shipments may be made in smaller lots, spacing them in time so that the outstanding payment at any point of time do not exceed the credit limit.

2. If he has information which can justify a higher limit, he should write to the Corporation making out his case clearly.

If the credit limit approved by the Corporation is found later on to be inadequate, the exporter should apply to the Corporation for a suitable enhancement of the limit on Form No.144-A for shipments made on or after the effective date of the enhanced limit.

17. Exports to Restricted Cover Countries

For countries which suffer from serious political or economic problems, approval is given by